You Have Chosen to Remember:

A Journey from Perception to Knowledge, Peace of Mind and Joy

James Blanchard Cisneros

Second Edition

For further information or to purchase additional copies of this book, visit:

www.chosentoremember.com

Library of Congress Control Number 2009926686

ISBN: 0-9728421-3-6

CONTENTS

Chapter One: The Dream

Chapter Two: The Ego-Self

Chapter Three: The Godself

Chapter Four: A Fulfilling Life

Chapter Five: Work on Yourself First

Chapter Six: Trusting God

Chapter Seven: Freedom Through Forgiveness

Chapter Eight: Being in the Now

Chapter Nine: Choosing One's Attitude

Chapter Ten: Taking Responsibility for Our Destiny

Chapter Eleven: Dreams, Prayer, Out-of-Body Experiences, and Meditation

Chapter Twelve: At Peace with the Afterlife

Acknowledgements

I would like to thank my good friend and life coach Olaf Halvorssen. Thank you Olaf, for among many things introducing me to "A Course In Miracles" in 1991.

I would like to thank Renee Rosen and Jennifer Reinfeld (reinfelddesigns.com) for their kindness and the endurance that it took to read and review the first draft of this book. I would also like to thank Jennifer for the design and management of my website, www.chosentoremember.com.

I would like to thank my editor Arlene Allen-Mitchell (prpro174@bellsouth.net) for her discipline, professionalism and patience.

I would like to thank my Godfather Oswaldo Cisneros for his support. It is because of his work ethic that the members of our family have the freedom to follow their personal dreams.

I would like to thank my mother Linda for her continuous love and devotion.

☾ Dedication

To the reader: My friend, it is my honor to share a part of this journey with you. This book is my soul's reflection on paper. If you choose to read this material with an open heart and mind you may very well see your soul's reflection, and it will not surprise you to see and feel deep inner beauty and knowledge being reflected back.

Introduction

"When you eventually see through the veils to how things really are, you will keep saying again and again, this is certainly not like we thought it was."

Rumi

I am a simple man. I am not a so-called "expert" in any one religion or spiritual practice. In this, I believe, lies my greatest strength. It is with the desire for simplicity and the hope for eloquence that I share what offers me peace of mind and joy in the present moment. Ralph Waldo Emerson once wrote that "eloquence is the power to translate a truth into language perfectly intelligible to the person to whom you speak." I trust this book will eloquently touch that part in all of us that is the same.

My friend, there are many paths we may choose to take to achieve peace of mind and joy in the present moment. The journey is as complicated as we choose to make it, or as easy as we allow it to be. You may choose one path now, and select another one later, or you may choose more than one path at any given time. Do not concern yourself with what others say is the right, trendy, truthful or acceptable way to grow. Move toward those paths that offer you peace of mind and joy and are in alignment with your present values. Within your heart, there lies a memory of your trueself. It is this memory you search for, and it is this memory you will one day remember. Once this memory is recalled, you will find a place that you have never left.

I am not looking to "teach," for teaching implies that there is something you lack or still need to learn. Rejoice, for there is nothing you lack. There is nothing more for you to learn because all wisdom already resides within you. My aspiration is simply to assist you in remembering your true nature. Any moment that we are not at peace comes about because we have forgotten our true nature. My hope is that this book will assist you in remembering what you may have forgotten. Yet, even in forgetting there is good news and it is this: You must have known in order to have forgotten. In fact, once you begin to remember you will smile, for you will suddenly recall that, "Yes, I feel as though I have always known this; this is familiar to me. I am at peace with this information." It will feel right, and you will be at peace, for truth brings about a peaceful state. My brother and sister, all truth lies within us. We may have temporarily forgotten this, but we have now chosen to remember.

I feel very blessed to have lived the life I've lived. At the time I began this writing, I was 30 years old. Although I understand that in life I may still be considered a young man, none of the thoughts in this book are new. I have not given origin to the thoughts in this book, for all truth is already available. I have simply reorganized them in an effort to find peace of mind and joy.

I believe that anyone reading this book is reading it for a reason. I hope that there is something in this book that will speak to you, something that will go directly to your heart - the God in you. If this book facilitates your journey in any way, then I am truly honored to have been of service. Service, I once read, is love put into action. I have been reminded of my mission in this life, and it is this: to love and serve. This book is part of that mission.

I will be using the "G" word throughout this book. If you're uncomfortable with this word, please forgive me and substitute it for any idea or word you like. If you think that what I just said is blasphemous, please forgive me and continue reading. Whatever you believe or not about God is fine. It is with an open and honest heart that I respect whatever God means to you. My personal view is simply this: There is nothing in this world more valuable than faith and trust in a loving God.

So with an open heart and mind I share my thoughts. Those thoughts that resonate with you will simply reinforce what you consciously or unconsciously already know. Those thoughts which do not resonate with you - I invite you to question or simply put aside. Regardless of what you choose to do with the thoughts that are presented, I do wish you well on your journey.

Peace, health, happiness, love, laughter and light.

Your brother,

James Blanchard Cisneros

1

THE DREAM

Imagine yourself in God's arms. You have fallen asleep, and you begin to dream. Some dreams take you outside your home, others to different countries, and still others to different worlds. Yet, if you were to awaken, you would still find yourself in God's arms. Regardless of the dreams you created, regardless of what you chose to believe and experience in those dreams, regardless of how scared you were, or the words you chose to use, God watched over you with everlasting love, patience and peace.

Imagine yourself smiling as you watch your children sleep. So too does God watch over you with absolute love. Regardless of what you choose to see as true, regardless of how you view Him or dream of Him, He waits patiently for you to awaken. You might scream or kick Him, but He understands that you dream, and that you are simply reacting to a dream. He embraces you with perfect love and acceptance. He strokes your head, and although you sleep, you feel His love. And deep within, although you sleep, you are grateful for His love. My friend, you will awaken. And when you do, you will awaken to a place you have never left.

Some of you have a difficult time believing that God loves you unconditionally. You may look at your life, having experienced pain, guilt, anger, suffering, envy, lust and jealousy, and ask, "How could God really love me if I am all these things and more? How could God lovingly hold me in his arms while I experience such emotions?" Remember, God is looking at you while you sleep. He also knows what you are like when you are awake. (Yes, we are still talking about God, not Santa Claus.) He created you in His image. If you choose to believe God knows you not, then allow as true that God knows Himself. If He knows Himself, then he knows His image, and if He knows His image, then He at least knows the truth about you.

God knows who you have always been, even if you don't know who you are now. My friend, we dream, and in our dreams we make ourselves into characters who can experience emotions such as pain, guilt, anger, suffering, envy, lust and jealousy. Yet, dreams and illusions are, by their very nature, temporary. In fact, our dreams are but a blink of eternity's eyes.

If you have not yet given birth to a son or a daughter, imagine creating such a being. Imagine the absolute love you would have for him or her. Now, imagine yourself suddenly judging or even hating this perfect creature because he or she chooses to blink. This is what many believe God could and is doing to us. Can you now begin to conceptualize the scale and magnitude of our illusions? God's love for us is changeless and eternal, and this life is a momentary blink in eternity's eyes. Would you judge or hate your child for blinking? Would God?

My friend, if God does not judge His creations, why would we ever want to judge them? God loves His creations, and if we do anything but love His creations, we will have feelings of separation. The opposite of love is fear, and fear is manifested through judgment. Judgment is the basis for separation, which is the ego's goal. When we judge a brother or sister, be it in thought or action, we create a sense of separation, which then results in feelings of guilt. Inwardly, we feel guilty because we judge what God loves and sees as perfect. If we judge God's child, then, by definition, we have judged ourselves. If we judge ourselves without knowing that we are doing so, then we create confusion. Once we experience enough confusion we create a chaotic state.

A life lived in chaos and confusion will not bring about peace of mind and joy. Our tolerance for chaos and confusion may be high, but it is not without limit. There comes a time for all of us when we say to ourselves, "There must be a better way, a better, more productive answer than chaos and confusion." And as we begin to question ourselves, we start to awaken and remember our true-selves. We realize and remember that just as confusion and chaos are the result of meeting our brothers and sisters with judgment, so too are peace of mind and joy the result of meeting our brothers and sisters with acceptance and love.

My friend, allow your brothers and sisters to experience the illusions they perceive as real. Often it is only when our brothers and sisters physically, emotionally and spiritually experience the emptiness of their actions and reactions that they realize the futility of these actions. Please understand that I'm not saying that you should not make an effort to guide your brothers and sisters in a positive direction. But, be very aware of the subtle differences between guidance and control. These differences are more often than not very muddled in the ego's thought system. If asked, we may offer our brothers and sisters guidance, but we need to refrain from attachment to outcomes. Be not attached to your brothers and sisters following your direction. Look within your heart, offer support and love, and trust that His will will be done. If your brothers and sisters insist on falling, let them fall, for sooner or later they will land on their knees, and when they do they will not experience pain but relief. One of the greatest gifts you can offer your brothers and sisters is the loving space they need to fall, land on their knees and experience their perfection.

The Unconscious Habitual Belief System or Ego

Throughout this book, I will be discussing the ego because it is so intricately woven onto the fabric of our being. If we believe in limitations, separations, judgment and fear of any kind, we have bought into the illusion of reality that has been sold to us by the ego. Likewise, if we respond to any person, place or thing with judgment, sadness, negativity, stress, anxiety, annoyance or anger, know that we have bought into the same illusion. These beliefs and responses have been ingrained and reinforced in us in such a way that they have become habitual. These habits, this habitual belief system (simply referred to as the ego-self or ego) is what we use to react to our daily experiences. This habitual belief system is mostly an unconscious belief system that manifests itself as our beliefs and attitudes. These beliefs and attitudes influence our daily reactions, responses and behaviors toward ourselves, our fellow humans and the world in general. Like robots, any time we react with limitation, separation, judgment or fear, we are simply reacting as we have been programmed to. Eventually, we learn that this is not how we want to act, react, be or live. Slowly, we consciously become aware of our unconscious habitual belief system, and we can then begin to de-program ourselves. This is a time of great celebration, for as we become aware of our programming we also begin to understand the possibility of choice. We learn that we indeed have the choice of seeing things as we've been programmed to, or examining what we currently believe to see if it fits with what we truly desire. We can then choose whether we want to continue with that limited belief system or replace it with a more empowering understanding.

If we believe that we are not good enough, that we are not deserving of love, that we have limited possibilities, that we're separate from our brothers and sisters, or that fear is real, then these attitudes and perceptions have become part of our unconscious habitual belief system that we now see as our real selves. In the ego's world there is a mass thought system, a deep-seated belief that we are unworthy, that we are not good enough, that we do not deserve happiness, and that our future and the world's future looks grim. These perceptions have been programmed into us and have often become part of our belief system. We see our belief system as a reflection of our real selves - as our reality.

What we believe about ourselves, we look for and manifest in our daily experiences. This is what we allow as possibilities for ourselves, and in an unconscious way, we prove ourselves right when we experience it. It gives us a certain level of satisfaction to know that we are right, and yet, at the same time we are disturbed by what we are experiencing. This creates a level of confusion that slowly develops into a chaotic state. Most people wait for this chaotic state to manifest before they begin examining and questioning their unconscious habitual belief system. Eventually, as we look into and question our unconscious habitual belief system, we begin to recognize and remember that this is not how we want to react or behave, that this is not who we truly are. We begin to loosen our attachments to our old selves. And as we do, we begin to realize and remember that we have a choice - the choice of seeing and reacting to people and the world as we truly want to. Our old selves believed in limitations, separations, judgment and fear. We have now learned that these thought patterns are not who we are or what we want. We do not want to live in a confused or chaotic state any longer; we want to live in a peaceful and joyful state. New choices, new thought patterns begin to align themselves with our trueselves. Peace is the opposite of chaos, and in order to experience the opposite state, we must believe that its opposite is possible.

Self-Image Transformation

Self-image transformation, becoming aware of our trueselves, begins with the willingness to accept that limitlessness, unity, forgiveness and love are things we truly desire in our lives. Self-image transformation means changing the way we perceive or see ourselves. For this to occur we do not need to change what we do, we simply need to change our perception of who we think we are. We do not need to change the outside environment or how others think, act or react. We simply need to change our minds. Because it is an inner change, we have the final and ultimate decision on whether or not this is something we truly want and desire. A little willingness to obtain this is all we'll ever need.

As we will soon recall, peace is eternally available to us. Our recognition of its availability is all that is needed for us to obtain and experience peace. As peace is eternally available to us, so too are limitlessness, unity, forgiveness and love. They are eternally available to us because these are aspects of our trueselves. Again, it is simply our willingness to obtain and experience them that will allow them to manifest in our lives. The more we believe them to be available to us, the more we will see them being manifested in one way or another in our lives. Slowly, what we once judged, we will now forgive. Who we once feared, we will now love. What once separated us from our brothers will now join us. And what once caused us confusion and chaos will now bring understanding and peace.

To experience self-image transformation, we can simply allow the negative thoughts in our unconscious habitual belief system or ego to surface. For it is in their surfacing that light will shine on them, and we'll be able to finally see and understand what they are truly offering. When we understand that we truly do not want what they offer, we will release these limited beliefs. When we release them, we will let go of all we thought we were. Finding out who we are in truth, many times, begins with the realization of who we are not.

Many people have self-esteem issues, yet even those with high self esteem limit themselves when they use the ego to measure and define their trueselves. The ego-self only allows a limited level of self-esteem. If we consider ourselves to be below this limited level, the ego labels us as shy and timid, causing our fellow humans to look down on us. If we consider ourselves to be above the level it sets for us, it labels us as conceited, causing others to judge and ridicule our beliefs. If we fall within the ego's "safe" level of self-esteem, it still has every brother and sister whose views differ from ours judge and question our beliefs about ourselves and the world. Understand that with the ego, even when we win we lose and any victory is conditional upon our feeling guilty and unworthy of it. This is what has been taught to us. This is what we have likely accepted to be true and to be the way life is. This is what we are now realizing we do not want. The more we realize what it is we do not want, the closer we come to finding out what it is we do want.

How would you like to give up your limited ego-self and replace it with an infinite Godself? How would you like to give up nothing and get everything in return? Would you like to give up judgment and receive forgiveness, give up fear and receive love, give up separation and receive unity, give up confusion and chaos and receive peace of mind and joy? This is God's offer to us but it is our choice through free will whether to accept it or not. God offered this when we were created. It is our inheritance. It is our essence. It is our truth. There is only one thing that we need to do to obtain everything. Offer our brothers and sisters what we want to experience. For we are all one, and what we offer to them we gift ourselves.

Allow what you wish to experience to flow through you. Let forgiveness, love, unity and peace flow through you. Let these thoughts and feelings expand to your brothers and sisters. As you acknowledge that they are worthy of these thoughts, you are also secretly acknowledging that you too are worthy of them. The more these types of unlimited thoughts are allowed in, accepted and expanded, the more they will manifest in your life. The more you offer these thoughts, the more you will want to experience them. The more you experience them, the less you will want their opposites.

Being Born Into a Dream

Imagine being born into a dream - a mass illusion transformed over thousands of years by billions of people into what today we call reality. The billions of people subdivided into territories they called countries, into belief systems they called religions and into groups they called races. Countries subdivided into states, provinces and cities, which were then subdivided into neighborhoods that subdivided into buildings or single-family homes. Religions divided into conservative and liberal sects, which then grew into more conservative and liberal branches. Races divided themselves by all of the above, including color, tone, ethnic makeup and financial status.

Each group then teaches and defends that its way is the way, and its truth is the truth. And each group creates its own reality out of what it believes. Each group then tries to sell us on its current forms and laws, telling us that this is what is "right." Each teaches us that the closer we are to following its form, the happier, more successful and peaceful we will be. And somewhere deep within, we know that it is our right to be happy and to be at peace. So we buy into it, and regardless of how little sense the illusion makes, we keep participating for if we stop we will be judged as outcasts, trouble-makers or bums. We are taught that if we stop participating in the group's way of life, our hopes for happiness, success and peace will also end. The group we are in tells us that if we go against the norm, we will not find happiness, peace or success. So we buy into the illusion the group offers us, believing that there is no other way. We carefully weave and contour the illusion into one we can live with for now. But my friend, regardless of how we choose to weave, contour and experience the illusion, it is still an illusion.

All these divisions, separations and sects continuously punish and judge each other for being different, and punish their own group members for not being the same. This makes little sense to our trueselves so we create a mask, or false self that allows us to live more comfortably in the illusion. I refer to this mask, or false self, as the ego-self. The ego-self or ego is not part of our physical bodies. The ego is a belief system within our minds. And so with our ego-selves, we shape the illusion into one we can live with. We call it reality - not our reality, but reality nonetheless. We defend this reality with all our might, for if it fails, we believe that so too will our chances at happiness, success, peace and joy.

The Dream of Separation

One of the ego's favorite games in this dream is the idea of separation. It teaches that we can find true peace of mind and joy through separation. It wants us to believe in the idea of separation so that it can serve as our only guide. The ego wants us to see it as valuable and useful, for it has trained us to discard the valueless and useless.

The ego wants us to believe in the idea of completion but never actually achieve completion. It doesn't want us to achieve completion because we would no longer need it. So it serves as our guide, offering us one treasure map after another, and we buy into this reality. We cannot yet acknowledge to ourselves that the treasure lies within, and so we look outside for what the ego says will make us happy and whole. We search but we rarely find. The few times we find the treasure chest, we become momentarily satisfied, only to open it and find it empty. We start to question the ego, but as we do, it offers us a new map and promises that this time it will bring us peace of mind, joy and completion.

Every map, every guidance the ego offers tells of an outward journey in a world of scarcity, where in order to succeed we must find a limited number of idols (false Gods) before our brother or sister does. It tells us that we should join those brothers and sisters who think as we do and abandon those who do not. It begins its game by separating its illusion into thousands of different ideas that we make into idols. It whispers that we must obtain these idols, material things and ideas to achieve completion. This way it covers itself by making sure that we will bite at a few of these thousands of idols and spend our time trying to obtain them. For the more time we spend searching for them, the less time we have to question the ego's guidance. Like a wise old fisherman, the ego keeps switching bait until it finds the right one for the fish it is trying to catch. We then decide which idols are most important to our completion, and live our lives trying to acquire them. We look for brothers and sisters who are in search of similar idols in the form of ideas, material things and status. And we abandon and separate from the brothers and sisters who do not share our views.

My friend, it is not the idols we seek, but completion itself. We will not find completion by discarding any brother or sister. We will not find completion by attaching ourselves to an individual brother or sister or to a specific group. We will never find completion by searching for illusions. For only in the illusion can parts of a whole join together at the exclusion of other parts and call themselves complete and whole. And only in a mass illusion can idols offer us something God can not. There is no end to illusions and the only way to find completion is to awaken.

Judging the Dreamer

Every day we help mold and develop people by what we offer them. If we offer people patience, love and forgiveness, they have a greater chance of growing into patient, loving and forgiving people. And we will live in gratitude if these people touch our lives or the lives of our children. These people will in turn be grateful to us and our children, for they will remember that it was our patience, love and forgiveness that allowed them to become who they are today.

My friend, offer what you want to experience. Offer patience, love and forgiveness, and you will manifest them in one way or another in your life. Offer judgment and ridicule, and sooner or later, this is what you will manifest into your life.

Our brothers and sisters' words and actions are gifts. If their words or actions are not understood as gifts, then we are misperceiving reality. We can perceive a person's words or actions as gifts to be grateful for, or as bricks we must defend against. One decision will bring us peace, and the other will bring us judgment and pain. Understand that only in the dream can a gift be turned into a brick that we must defend against.

Dream Offered for Chapter One - The Gift

In every chapter of this book I asked for and received either a dream or an out-of-body experience (OBE) that could be useful in explaining this material. My hope is that each personal experience will be useful to you. I do a lot of lucid and non lucid dream and OBE work. I meditate before going to sleep and invite my spirit guides to offer me a dream that can enhance or clarify the material. This has been and is a very useful growth tool for me. In Chapter 11, I will invite you to try it. You can train yourself to remember the details of your dreams and OBEs. Much knowledge can be extracted from the dream state. Along with the message that is offered through the imagery of the dream, there are also verbal messages that are offered. For me, these messages sometimes sound like a young, yet mature baritone voice within my head, and other times participants in the dream or OBE offer me input. All the messages intertwine and dissolve into one cooking pot that I then serve into my dream and OBE journal.

In the following dream sequence, I participated in a meditation exercise before going to sleep. The meditation question I asked my higher self and guides was: How did I create the current dream/illusion that I am experiencing? The following occurred:

In this dream, a person said a word, and before a single thought entered my mind, there appeared a plain box. I then understood that I had two choices. They were to take this box and see it as a gift that my brother was offering, or see it as a brick that I must defend against. I was also led to understand that every word or action, regardless of tone or manifestation, is the same, and that there are always two choices to deal with as a reaction and response. I understood that one choice would unite me with my brother, and the other choice would separate us. The box itself was physically small, but I understood that the gift that lay within it was as boundless as it was beautiful. Yet, because of fear and judgment, I misperceived my brother's word as an attack, and felt that if I put myself behind this small box, my brother would disappear and I would again be safe. Over and over again, I heard noises I thought were coming from behind this box. My reaction again became fear, and I immediately perceived these noises as an attack against me. Every time I heard a noise, another box appeared, but because of my past experience I chose not to sit for a moment and open the box. Instead, I chose to protect myself by stacking one box on top of another, until I could no longer truly see my brother. Slowly, I surrounded myself with these boxes until no light could seep through. For a while I felt protected, but in the darkness I began to feel isolated, alone and afraid. I believed that isolation and fear were my only two choices. Yet, as I sat quietly in the dark, deep within me a voice for unity whispered. And as it did, I decided to move the boxes apart slightly to see if I could hear or see my brother better. Through the cracks, a little light seeped through, warming my face, and it felt loving and kind. I grabbed at every ray of light, and as I focused on the light I again heard a voice. I heard the voice, but because of past interactions with it, and without paying attention to what it was saying, I immediately closed the cracks until all I could hear were murmurs. These quiet murmurs kept getting louder, for my brother kept trying to reach me. But again I reacted with fear and felt that I needed to reinforce these boxes to keep the voices out. So with judgment and fear, I began cementing these boxes until they took the form of bricks that together took the form of walls. I felt that these walls would protect me from the noises I was hearing and the actions I was seeing. In darkness, I was isolated and alone, but I felt protected by my walls. But once again, I got tired of the darkness and isolation, and once again I began to hear and focus on the voice.

I then began to hear the familiar baritone voice. The best way I can describe it is for you to imagine yourself watching and listening to an instruction video that covers the complete inner vision of your mind. The following message, although very close to the original, is paraphrased. The voice said:

You have chosen to remember. My friend, you now have the opportunity to let light shine through the cracks in your walls. You carry within you the eternal memory of your Godself. As much as you think that you have completely closed yourself, there are cracks in your armor, and cracks in your masks and walls. They may be too small for you to believe that they can change your perceptions, yet within the cracks lie all you truly are. Within, there exists rays of light where you become boundless, and within this boundlessness is all you could ever truly desire. Protection is not needed here, for here there is nothing you need protection from. And if you focus on the light, all your walls will disappear into the nothingness from which they came.

There are places in your life where you have built walls around the truth of who you are. You've built these walls with judgment and cemented them with fear. You strained all your life to build and keep these walls together. These walls that you have built to protect you hold all perceptions, judgments and beliefs about yourself, your brothers and sisters, God and the world. You hide behind and defend these walls with your life; for you believe that if someone were to ever penetrate them, they would recoil in disgust once they saw who was really there. Methodically, on a daily basis, you reinforce these walls, creating emotional, psychological and spiritual barriers. You take secret pride in their structure and strength. Yet with every breeze, you curse the pebbles that bounce off these walls. And you even blame the wind for blowing. You keep telling yourself that you are safe, and yet you fear any breeze that dares caress your walls.

You have been taught to believe that in your walls' changelessness, your strength and safety lies. You are taught to fear change, for it means that your walls would weaken. So you defend these so-called impenetrable walls against anything that challenges their structure. To you, anything and everything that differs from your belief system challenges its structure. You spend your day in defense of pebbles, and curse the wind whenever any of these pebbles are tossed toward your walls. So you end up living your days in defense of these impenetrable walls. The walls that you built to defend you, you end up defending against the outside world, and you judge and curse any attempt to change or weaken them.

You tire of these illusions and try to escape them at night by attempting to sleep. But continuous thoughts of pebbles fill your mind and do not let you. In the darkness, a thousand thoughts flood your mind and so you even fight to fall asleep. Finally once asleep, these pebbles turn into monsters of all shapes and sizes, and you run away from them as they attack your walls. You wake up, afraid of the monsters you have made out of pebbles. You become relieved when you realize it was a dream. Still, you are hesitant to close your eyes and fall back into the dream. You blame the unconscious mind for playing tricks on you. You choose to see the unconscious mind as separate from you and you make yourself believe you have no control over it. You do not realize that it is your conscious belief in illusions that transfers into your unconscious mind - meaning you are the ultimate creator of both your conscious and unconscious thoughts. Finally, you close your eyes and go to bed afraid. In the morning, you awaken as tired as you were when you went to sleep. You receive no rest from your illusions, and wonder why you feel stressed, weak and tired.

My friend, when you awaken, you will understand that the illusions you make out of pebbles in your conscious mind are as unreal as the illusions you allow to become monsters in your unconscious mind. For both the pebbles and the monsters will be seen for what they truly are: illusions and nothing else. Illusions are unreal, thus it is only your recognition of their nothingness that will set you free. You will no longer experience fear once you recognize that all fear, regardless of its manifestation, is based on illusion. Soon you will not need to close your eyes to find rest; soon you will find that true rest does not come from sleeping, but from awakening.

As you live your life in defense of these walls, what you hoped would not happen, happens. Everyone learns who you are by what you defend. You show who you are by what you treasure, and you will defend what you treasure. For you live your life outside yourself, in defense of what you built to conceal and defend yourself. And by defending what you built, all those outside see what you believe yourself to be. You who have made these walls what they are, you who have made these walls out of nothing, have spent your life in defense of that nothingness and wonder why you feel incomplete and unfulfilled.

You thought these so-called impenetrable walls would keep you safe. But these walls have been built on and of sand, and thus by their very nature are unstable and ever changing. Regardless of how slight the wind, it will blow your walls into different forms, upsetting you every time. You live surrounded by an illusion of safety and peace, and then wonder why you feel unsafe and stressed. You live surrounded by walls of your own creation, and wonder why you feel isolated, alone and incomplete. You live day and night in defense of this illusion, and wonder why you feel weakened, stressed and tired.

You have been taught that to defend these walls, that to defend yourself is right and honorable. Yet it is actually not the defending that you fear, but the idea that there is nothing to defend. For if there is nothing worth defending, then you are, by the ego's definition, worthless. My friend, you are not worthless, and within you, you know this to be true. You need not defend, not because there is nothing worth defending, but because there is truly nothing to defend against. Ask yourself, "Would a right-minded person spend his existence defending his walls against pebbles? Would a right-minded person see a pebble and make it into a monster?" There will always be pebbles on this beach. It is up to you to decide if you will make them into monsters, or realize that they are but pebbles. Whenever you feel stressed, tired, alone, incomplete or afraid, it is because you have made pebbles into different-shaped monsters that you believe can attack, and that you must defend against.

My friend, it is not the idea that others will look within you and recoil that frightens you, but that others will look within you and see God's perfect creation. Again, the idea of worth appears. You do not feel that someone who can experience stress, tiredness, loneliness, fear, unhappiness or incompleteness could be God's perfect creation. All of these feelings are thoughts you have made real by your belief in them. These illusions have been shaped by a sense of judgment, fear and separation. The only decision you need to make to feel their opposite is to choose their opposite. A sense of connection and love is their opposite. Every moment you have this choice. One decision will offer you peace, the other decision will not. In the end, this is the choice that is yours to make. The life you create comes from the choices you make, the choices you make come from who you believe yourself to be. Who you believe yourself to be comes from either the perception you have made real, or the knowledge you have accepted.

Acceptance of knowledge is the recognition that your highest will for yourself and God's will are one. The manifestation of this recognition is the state of peace. A little willingness to be open to this possibility is all that you need. If you choose to knock on the door, it will be opened, but you can also choose to recognize that there is no door. There is no door because there are no barriers between you and your creator. The only barriers you will ever encounter are those you believe still exist. Note that you are not judged for any barriers you create. A little willingness and a knock on the door is all it takes to remove any barrier, regardless of its physical, mental or spiritual manifestation.

My friend, I feel deep love for you. You need not take one more step. You need not cry one more tear. You need simply recognize and remember the truth of who you are. That is all you need do. It is much easier than your ego will now let you believe, but as you begin to remove the walls, you will recognize that this is so. As you remove the walls, you will look back and smile at what you had made real, and you too will begin to feel a deeper love for your brothers and sisters. Walls such as color, race, age, belief system, religion, actions, reactions and judgments will begin to crumble, and as they do, you will encounter all your brothers and sisters with open arms. You hold deep love for all your brothers and sisters. You might not yet recognize this, but it is so. For what is true is true, whether you choose to believe in it or not.

The walls that you have built with judgment and cemented with fear will be dismantled by forgiveness. The same individuals you blamed for the walls' existence will themselves assist you in dismantling them. The ones you judged and have forgiven will hold their hands out to you. You will see this for the first time - not because their hands had not been there before, but because you had never chosen to truly open your eyes. Forgiveness is the only requirement for you to truly see. Once you forgive, you will experience gratitude toward your brothers and sisters for their assistance, and you will gladly take their hands and experience the gift. Once you take their hands, you will be elevated into a beautiful world, a world that has, in truth, always been there, simply waiting for you to open your eyes, to awaken and enjoy. All the judgments you ever made, all the brothers and sisters you refused to forgive, and all the anger you chose to hold within, through forgiveness and understanding, will be replaced with love. And you will cry once more, but not from fear, isolation or loneliness, but from your absolute love and respect for God's gift, for your absolute love and respect for your trueself.

The Dreamer and the Dream

How many times in your dreams have you run away from something that frightened you only to awaken thankful that it was not real? How many times in your dreams have feelings of stress, anxiety, anger and judgment come up? Yet, once you awaken, you smile and give thanks that it was only a dream. We run away from monsters in our dreams because we believe the monsters to be real. Equally, feelings of stress, anxiety, anger and judgment feel real because we have made them realities within our minds.

Child of God, learn to trust that your worth is perfect. It is perfect because God gifted it to you. My friend, if it were possible for you to see me as I write this sentence, you would see that I am smiling for I know the beauty of your perfect worth. I know this because I have remembered the beauty of my perfect worth, and you and I are one, no greater and no less. You may have taught yourself to rely on other people's judgments to measure your worth. But what has this thought system ever offered you? It has offered pain, self doubt, a sense of worthlessness. You are as God created you - perfect, awake and whole. You simply haven't let yourself remember this. You can choose to forget it, but you can't change it. Your natural state is to be joyful and at peace. However, most people have learned to accept stress, anxiety, anger and judgment as natural, yet the complete opposite is true. These are unnatural states in which most people choose to live, and there is a place in your heart that knows this to be true. There is a place in your heart that knows that feeling stress, anxiety, anger and judgment are unnatural. These are just the illusions most people have chosen for their dream. We have chosen to fall asleep and dream, and at some point we choose to awaken. My friend, in your heart you know that the alarm clock has sounded and that it is now time to wake up. However, it is up to you to decide how many times you will choose to push the snooze button.

Forgiving the Dreamer

Once you wake up from your dream, you will have no interest in judging those who sleep. And if they curse or kick you while they sleep, you will simply understand that, in truth, all they are doing is dreaming. Every sin, error, accusation and judgment, regardless of form, is forgiven. They are forgiven because you know that they are asleep. That is why once you are healed, once you awaken, the people you meet will be healed. Your healing and awakening is what is required for the world to be healed. Forgive the world, and you will be set free from it.

Our memories need not solely be used to remember the past; they can also be used to remember the eternal truth from which we first originated. Most people are not awake; however, they do not know that they are asleep. What we realize when we awaken is simply this: that which we experience as real is a manifestation of what we believe is real, and what we believe is real resides within our minds. Regardless of the form of attack, the figures in our dreams are made real by us. We are reacting to the figures, and all the pain, suffering, stress and anxiety in our minds is caused not by these figures, but by our reactions to these figures. Once we recognize these figures for what they truly are, all pain, suffering, anxiety and stress will fade away. Once the lesson that we are reacting to figures in our dreams is remembered, we are released from all we thought they did to us. We come to recognize that, because we have done this to ourselves, we also have the power to undo what we have done.

Regardless of the form fear takes, this simple reminder, if taken to heart, will dissipate any fog we might currently be experiencing in our lives. If we forgive the world for what we thought it did to us, we will set ourselves forever free.

Knowing Our Power

If we continue to participate in the illusion, there are rules and laws that we're advised to follow. We are told that those who do not follow these rules and laws are judged and punished. Our parents, our peers and society have rules and laws. If we follow all of their rules and laws, we are then considered good children, friends or members of society. Yet, if we follow the rules and laws of one group, we often break those of another, and thus people who think we are doing the "wrong thing" or "not doing the right thing" are constantly judging us. Individuals in a group may have different views on how the group should be run and behave. They might judge us if we do not follow their steps. Yet even when we follow their every step, we are still not safe from their judgment. Conversely, we, on many occasions, have been the judge, but what has this ever offered us? Pain, sadness, disgust, envy, jealousy, anger and many other negative emotions have resulted from our addiction to judging other people. Judging is not only a bad habit but also an addiction, for what else would we call something that causes us pain over and over again, but we continuously choose to inject into our lives and into the lives of others?

Like a drug dealer, we continue dispersing our judgment with no regard for how our behavior affects those with whom we interact, or how our behavior affects those with whom the people we have judged interact. Imagine being a pebble falling into a pond. The pebble might see and experience the ripples it created by its interaction with the pond. Even as the pebble slowly sinks to the bottom of the pond, it might look back and see the ripples expanding beyond the point of interaction. But soon, as it continues its journey into the pond, it loses contact with the point of interaction. Yet, even though it has lost its view of the surface, the ripples continue to expand, changing the surface and edges of the pond in a way the pebble might never see. Just as the pebble falls into a pond, our judgment of others will be dispersed and shared, and will touch an innumerable number of people that we will never see. Don't believe for a second that what we say or do affects only the person with whom we physically interact. Our judgment or acceptance will be carried from one to many, and they in turn will carry it to many more.

Just as we have the power to judge and spread ourselves like a virus, we also have the power to spread love. This is the one choice we make every time that we interact with a brother or sister. My friends, we touch this world on a much deeper level than we could ever imagine. We will one day see the result of all our words and actions. Know that not only do we have the power to make this world a more ugly or beautiful place, but that we do so every time we choose between judgment and love.

We are powerful beings. How we ultimately choose to use this power is up to us. We might not recognize this power yet, but the day is coming when we will look within and remember. Every person with whom we have ever interacted has acted as a mirror to show us more about ourselves. Every person with whom we interact, now acts as a mirror to show us where we are now within our minds. We are here to learn about our thoughts and emotions, and we will see them reflected not only in the reactions and actions of our brothers and sisters, but also in everything we see around us. There does not exist a person, place or thing in this world that does not reflect who or what we believe about ourselves. When properly perceived, all people, places and things will teach us who we currently believe ourselves to be. All people, places, things and moments reflect what we think and feel about ourselves.

Our reality exists within our minds, and because of this, we can change it if we so desire. Our reality is not as rigid as our egos currently lead us to believe. We can have a world of acceptance, peace, abundance and joy, for these are simply choices we can make. The choices between acceptance and judgment, peace and pain, abundance and scarcity, joy and sadness are simply ours to make. For if we have ever experienced judgment, pain, scarcity and sadness, it is because the reality within our minds made us believe that these were proper, fair, and correct responses to whatever we thought we were experiencing. In the end, these were choices we made. We have been taught by the world, our families, peers and society how to react to circumstances. But look to see where most of the world, our families, peers and society physically, spiritually and emotionally live. They predominantly live in a world of confusion, chaos, anger and judgment, and yet they want us to believe that if we follow their rules and laws, we will find peace of mind and joy.

It is now time for us to recognize that we are powerful beings. It is time to put aside all rules and laws that have resulted in judgment, pain, scarcity and sadness. For deep within, we know this is not what we want. And if we don't want something, does it make sense to pursue it? My friend, there is another way. This other way offers us what we truly desire. This other way has always been available to us, we simply need to recognize its availability.

I know that you are ready to have what you want and I hope through this book you will find one of the many keys that are available to you. My friend, you are a powerful being. Use your creativity and imagination to expand your ideas of what is possible for you to have and achieve. You can and will create a better, more peaceful life for yourself, if that is your desire. The only difference between the people who believe they can have a better and more peaceful life, and those who think they can't, is their belief in the possibilities. If you are not at peace in any of your current circumstances then choose not to accept them as the best you can have. Don't believe people when they tell you that something is impossible for you to achieve or create. Instead of focusing on how your life currently is, picture it how you want it to be. Imagine already having what you want. You can achieve peace in every situation, in all circumstances.

If there is anything in your life that is not bringing you joy or peace, ask yourself why it is that you continue to support that activity. Often you support it because you believe you deserve or need to experience it. You currently have in your life what you consciously or unconsciously want. But I offer you that if you have the power to bring to your life things that do not give you joy and peace, then know that you also have the power to bring to your life things that do offer you joy and peace. You have an active imagination, and you have created what you want and think you need to experience. So if you choose not to experience joy in the moment, then go ahead, play in the mud all you want. This much is true - you do have another choice. You can choose joy and peace in every part of your life. Currently, you may believe that this is not possible, and thus you are not experiencing it.

Friend, have you ever taken five minutes to think about and write on a piece of paper what it is that brings you joy and peace? Do you know? You do have a mission to accomplish in this life, and what you take joy in doing and what brings you peace are both reminders of what that mission is. If you did not have a purpose for being on Earth, then you would not be here. Remind yourself; write down what it is you love and receive joy doing, and there you will find a key to the purpose of your visit.

Invitation #1 - The List

List in your journal or on a piece of paper all the things that you love to do, all the things that bring you joy and peace. On another piece of paper, write down things that you are doing that do not bring you joy and peace in order to bring to the surface these behaviors and patterns.

Keep those papers with you so that you can add and subtract to them as you see fit. Slowly, on a day-to-day basis, work toward obtaining and participating in the things that bring you joy and peace, and work toward letting go of the things that do not bring you joy and peace.

Invitation #2 - Act or Pretend to be Awake

This invitation will help create a new thought pattern, a new way of reacting to your fellow brothers and sisters' actions. Whenever you can, try to replace anxiety with peace, anger with love, and judgmental behavior with understanding. Replacing illusions with truth will assist you in awakening and remembering truth. Approach every situation possible by extending the truth, the love that you are. Make your peace of mind and joy the goal in every situation possible. This is achieved by reacting to your brothers and sisters with forgiveness, love, peace and understanding, regardless of the illusions they might be buying into at the time. When they try to pull you into their illusions, remember that you are awake. Don't judge your brothers and sisters, for they may simply be asleep and dreaming. Would you judge your children for screaming in their sleep, or would you hold and comfort them? Would you scold your children for kicking you while asleep, or would you simply turn them around? Would you laugh at your children if they described the monsters in their dreams, or would you turn the light on and let them see for themselves that there are no such things? Do this, and every time you succeed in remaining awake, congratulate yourself, for you have chosen peace. It is the same situation as before, but instead of buying into the illusion, you have now consciously chosen to see and feel the truth. Look back at how you reacted before, when you were asleep, when you saw the gift as a brick you must defend against. Try to remember what this behavior resulted in: pain, sadness, judgment and regret. Now, experience how it feels to be awake, to react with love, to have true peace of mind, thanks to the recognition and understanding that your brothers and sisters may simply be sleeping.

You need not sleep any longer, and so you now awaken. Your brother and sister may need a little more sleep before they choose to awaken. Let them sleep. Soon they will awaken, and you will be waiting. It will gladden you to see that they have chosen to awaken, for now they can join you on your journey. For where you are going, you cannot go alone and the recognition of your brothers and sisters' perfection is the key that will open your gates. Those who have already awakened wait for you with everlasting patience. They are excited, for they see your shadow gliding through the distant fog. The time has come. Your walls of forgetfulness have now turned to veils, and you simply need to push them aside. Be joyful and remember that your brothers and sisters are simply light posts on your road back home. Be not afraid to take the final steps, for your true home is never dark or empty. Your home is forever lit by love and filled with peace.

2

THE EGO-SELF

The ego is a limited belief system within our minds that we have molded and identified as being who we are. The ego survives by establishing boundaries, borders and limits on everything it sees. The defining of such boundaries, borders and limits gives it the illusion that it can tell us what is right and wrong, all in an effort to control us by instructing us on what we are and are not, how we should act and not act, and why we should judge those who challenge it and the status quo. We are taught the right and wrong way to do things, and the right and wrong way to react. Because we learn from the outside world, we believe that truth lies outside of ourselves.

Judgment and fear feed the ego, generating numerous perceived weaknesses and limitations we believe we must defend as real. The more time we spend in defense of our ego and our limitations, the more we believe that this is who we are. And because we see our ego as real and representing ourselves, we defend our ego against anyone we perceive to be attacking it. In our minds, any view that disagrees with our belief system attacks it.

We perceive the attacks on our ego and its illusions as real, so we become defensive. The more time we spend defending our false or ego-selves, the more we reaffirm the ego's reality. The more we reaffirm the ego's reality, the more willing we are to come to its defense. The more we defend the illusions of the ego-self as real, the more concepts and ideas we will encounter in the world that do not fit into our reality. We perceive different concepts and ideas as assaults to our reality. We defend our ego-selves, through acts of judgment. The exercise of judgment separates us from our fellow brothers and sisters causing stress that may be conscious or unconscious. Stress creates confusion, and a build up of confusion ultimately leads to chaos.

The more time we spend in defense of our ego-selves, the more time we exist in confusion. We might give our state of confusion a hundred different names, such as annoyance, anger, stress, sadness, depression, but they all exist because of our belief in the ego's reality. They all exist within our minds and are fed and kept alive by our belief in our ego-selves.

Our tolerance for pain may be high but our acceptance of our ego-self is not without limit. Many of us ultimately come to a point in our lives where we tell ourselves that there must be a better way, a more fulfilling way of living - that this just can't be what it's all about! These thoughts begin the process of awakening to the knowledge of who we truly are.

The Physical Manifestation of the Ego-Self

The physical manifestation of living through the ego-self results in a feeling of void and a spiritual emptiness because we are living with the sense that something is missing in our lives. On the other hand, love, being the opposite of fear, gives us a sense of fullness and spiritual fulfillment. We have been created in the fullness of God, in the love of God, in His image. Feeling empty or living in fear is by definition an unnatural expression. Feeling empty or living in fear comes from a false belief that we are separated from God. Anytime we allow fear or emptiness to come into our hearts and minds, we have separated ourselves from our trueselves. Our trueselves are literally a part of God, just as our brother or sister is a part of God. God is all, and all is Love. There is nothing else; everything else is simply a contraption of the ego, a manifestation of the illusion of who we believe ourselves to be. It is the ego's best effort to fill us up with itself.

The ego promises us that if we follow its rules and laws, we will obtain peace of mind and joy. But in truth, the ego can only offer what it is. It can offer us what is unreal, temporary and unfulfilling. We have tried to fill ourselves with the gifts the ego offers. At first, the gifts are small but large enough to temporarily satisfy us. Yet, being temporary and unreal, the same gifts that once satisfied us ultimately become small and meaningless. Once our minds have digested the ego's gifts, we again have a sensation of feeling empty. The ego promised us fulfillment. It promised us that its gifts would bring us true joy and peace of mind. But after digesting its gifts, we again feel empty, and we begin to ask why. Then the ego, in order to protect itself from these questions, offers us bigger gifts. It knows it cannot continue to fool us with little illusions for they no longer fill the emptiness within. Thus, it offers us larger illusions, and at first our reaction is, "Wow!" For a short time, we believe that these illusions, that we call real, will satisfy the empty feelings we possess within. Yet, big or small, these are illusions, and illusions, being nothing, can by definition never fill us up.

Again, we ask, "Why? How could this be? I felt satisfied a while back; why am I not satisfied now?" The ego again becomes nervous, for it hates being questioned. It would rather we never ask such questions, or ask no questions at all. It does its best to keep us busy, for it understands that when we're busy we cannot find time to question it. So the ego does its best to fill our time with as many illusions as possible. It understands that its existence is in jeopardy every time we ponder its reality. It understands that it cannot fill us with its lies forever, so it keeps raising the level of illusions in order to temporarily shut us up. And it succeeds every time we buy into it.

Illusions themselves offer their own brand of truth. And if we believe in the illusions we are pursuing, we will also believe in the truth they are offering. Illusions appear to create a truth, which the ego believes is true, and will defend until death. But illusions are nothing, and that which is nothing cannot create truth. Illusions can only create a false truth; this might temporarily satisfy us, but it will never fulfill us.

What is true is eternal, is based in love, and offers us eternal peace of mind and joy. What is false is temporary, and is based on illusions, which can only offer temporary peace of mind and joy, which fades into nothingness, creating a sense of emptiness and a state of confusion. Peace of mind and joy are eternal, and what is eternal cannot be temporary. Temporary peace of mind and joy therefore do not exist. They are illusions created by the ego to keep us from understanding and experiencing real eternal peace of mind and joy.

The ego, once more in defense of its existence, will offer bigger illusions, and bigger lies. Once again we have a choice: we can choose to buy into these greater illusions and lies, or we can choose to question them. By questioning illusions, we take the first step in undoing them.

Freedom of choice is one of our greatest gifts. Let's not judge ourselves for having chosen such illusions in the past, for it is those illusions and their lack of fulfillment that have brought us to this point in our lives. Now we are truly allowing ourselves time to reflect, and to ask if any of the ego's illusions and lies have brought us true happiness. True happiness brings with it peace of mind and joy. Has the ego offered us true peace of mind and true joy? Are we at peace with ourselves, our families, friends, neighbors and with the world in general?

We already know the answers to these questions. We have already experienced enough pain. Eventually, we'll recognize that there must be a better way. To recognize means to "know again," which implies that we knew before. As we begin to recognize our trueselves or our Godselves, we will increasingly be unable to tolerate our beliefs in illusions.

Now that we have chosen to search inside ourselves, understand that the ego will not go quietly into the night. Our search for light and truth is fearful to the ego, for it resides in darkness. It will use its last resources to defend itself. It will make us as uncomfortable as possible. It will tell us that we're being ridiculous, that we should snap out of it. We will hear the ego, but, at the same time, we will remember where it has taken us before. We have heard its defenses before, but now they will no longer work against us. No longer will we choose to blindly follow the ego. Even other people's egos will try to join ours in its defense, for they understand that if one falls, others in the group may follow.

In our everyday lives, we lead by example. Other egos will not be comfortable if we choose to remember our trueselves and decide to change. Once the change toward our Godselves begins, we'll clearly see it in our lives. Those ruled by ego will begin to slowly fade away, spending less time with us. They may attack us for not being our "old selves." Yet, we now understand that we cannot live the way we used to. Even if we start spending less time around certain individuals, our love and respect for them will actually increase. As we increase the love and respect we have for ourselves, so too will we increase the love and respect we have for all our brothers and sisters. Even some of the places we used to go will now seem different, for there are places where the ego feels at ease, and there are places where it doesn't.

We'll go to new places - perhaps places we thought we would never go - and we'll meet new people. These people and places will serve us in our search for remembrance. Throughout the remembrance process, others who are ruled by their ego-selves will attack us, even and especially family members or those closest to us. They will feel their own egos, their way of life under attack. We need only be ourselves during these encounters. We should speak our truth and stay true to ourselves, never attacking others for their beliefs, respecting their processes even though we might perceive them as not respecting ours.

My friend, I am here to remind you that peace of mind, love and joy are our inheritance. Peace of mind, love and joy are the main attributes of the Godself. We all have a Godself, because we are simply our Godselves and nothing else. Everything else, including our ego-selves is an illusion we have created to help us live in the illusionary world. The ego is a speck of dust that we have made into a mountain. Yet still, what is even the highest mountain compared to the universe, to All That Is? As the illusion that is the ego slowly dissolves in the light, so too will the mountain, in time, return to dust.

The Ego's Advice

To summarize how the ego operates in us, remember the following points, which are further explained in the section that follows:

The ego:

• Advises us to judge that which is different from our belief systems.

- Advises us to blame something or someone outside of ourselves for the way we feel.

- Advises us to separate from the one or ones who we perceived made us feel this way.

- Convinces us to judge ourselves for the way we reacted; its goal is for us to feel disheartened by the way we reacted to our brother or sister.

- Advises us to carry this judgment within ourselves for as long as possible.

- Advises that we keep our power by not forgiving our brother or sister.

- Gives us false power if we, against its advice, forgive a brother or sister. It congratulates us and tries to convince us that we are being the "bigger" and "better" person by forgiving. Again, even in forgiveness the ego tries to separate us from our brother or sister.

The Ego and Blame

The ego perpetuates separation from our brothers and sisters by convincing us to blame them for something they did to us. The ego will first have us blame our brothers and sisters for how we feel. It does this because of its belief that our brothers and sisters are easier targets. As a last resort, it will tell us that God is to blame for how we feel. This is a last resort for the ego, for if it fears one thing: the love that God has for each of us. In between blaming other people and God, it will advise us that everything else is to blame for how we feel. Its goal is to separate us from everything and everyone including our own trueselves. The ego does this to have us all to itself. It is trying to convince us that it's just us and our egos against the world. If the ego can have us to itself, it can then become our one guide, our god, the only one we can truly trust.

The ego is happy when we suffer, for when we suffer it knows that we will react by questioning and blaming the outside world, our brother, sister, or even God. The ego knows this because this is how it has trained us to react. The ego will find it safe to project this because its primary lesson teaches us that not only are we totally separate from our brothers and sisters, but we are also totally separate from God. Thus, by blaming others and separating them from us, we are safe to judge and blame them without hurting ourselves.

The ego blames because it wants us to believe that we don't have the power to control our lives. By blaming everything outside of ourselves, it is training us to believe that everything outside of us has power over us, and over how we feel every moment of our lives.

But the ego's victories are always temporary. They are temporary because they are unnatural, and all that is unnatural by definition is temporary. Belief in the unnatural and temporary brings a lack of peace. Because it is unnatural for us to blame others for how we feel, and because it is unnatural to separate from others, we never truly find peace by reacting in this manner, regardless of how right we think we are. Even the ego in victory cannot bring us lasting peace of mind and joy.

The Ego and Separation

The ego wants us to believe that we are separate from our brothers and sisters. It wants us to think this way, because when we do, we also believe that if we attack them, the attack has no effect on us. Not only does the ego want us to believe this, but it also wants us to think that when we attack our brothers and sisters, this action somehow weakens them and strengthens us. In reality, any and all attacks weaken us.

The ego understands that there is a direct correlation between how badly we feel and how willing we are to attack our brother or sister. The worse we feel about ourselves, the quicker we are to anger, and the more willing we are to attack our brother or sister. It wants us to slide on this never-ending, downward spiral of continuing attacks because we become weaker, and as we do we continue to look to the ego for guidance because it has taught us that it is the only one we can trust.

My friend, the ego would like us to believe that we are disconnected and or separated from our brothers and sisters and from God. As much as the ego would like us to believe this, we have never been disconnected from our source. Our source is God. Our brothers and sisters' source is God. We have never been disconnected from God, thus we have never been disconnected from our brothers and sisters. Therefore, what we do to our brothers and sisters, we do to ourselves.

The Ego and Judgment

Because the ego has taught us that we are separate from our brothers and sisters, we believe it is safe for us to judge them. So we judge our brothers and sisters for how we feel, because we believe they are the ones who caused us pain. But because judging a brother or sister is an unnatural act, it simply feels wrong. Regardless of how much the ego promised us that we would be safe, sooner or later we realize that the judgment of our brother or sister has also hurt us, for we have now lost our peace of mind and joy. Still, the ego continues to advise us to carry this judgment within ourselves for as long as possible. It advises us that this is making us stronger, and making our brother or sister weaker. But somewhere within, we begin to realize that what the ego said was true and safe - is not.

The ego has us see ourselves as a drop of water on its rowboat. We are in the middle of the ocean and the ego continually tells us that we do not belong in the ocean. We can see and feel the ocean and something within tells us that it is there we belong. But the ego tells us that if we jump into the ocean we will drown. It tells us that as long as we are with the ego we will be safe. So day by day, we move back and forth on the ego's rowboat. We feel a small sense of safety but also of limitation, separation and loneliness and the ego has us blame the ocean for this. It tells us that it is because of the ocean that we feel limited, separate and alone and we buy into it because we believe that we are literally in the same boat as our ego.

My friend, there is a natural pull we feel toward this ocean, but we can reject its pull if that is our choice. Yet our rejection of it does not stop it from calling us home.

The ego wants us to suffer as much as possible without getting to the point where we question its advice or existence. It does not want us to question why we think and act the way we do. Questioning makes the ego nervous. This is when it begins to plan its defense. If we choose to look at ourselves, it might tell us that we're being absurd and unreasonable, that we're going through a phase. People and the world around us that are run by egos will never offer us support in our attempts at growth. The ego sees these attempts at growth as dangerous to its survival. Yet, somehow we know all this, and that's the reason many people try to keep what they are doing to support their own spiritual growth to themselves.

The ego believes there is power in judgment. It would have us believe that the more we judge another, the more power we have over that person. The ego equates power and judgment with strength and control. Those ruled by the ego believe that strength and power are obtained and maintained by their ability to control others.

The ego wants us to think of it in negative terms, it wants us to judge it. It controls us, and maintains and obtains power through our judgment of it. This gives it more power than if we were to simply ignore or forgive it. Its plan is this - the more we judge it, the more attention we give it. The more attention we give it, the greater part of our lives it becomes. Thus, its relationship with us is strengthened. It wants us to become angry, judge it, and see it as evil, for it understands that if we see it as evil, we will unconsciously perceive a part of our own selves as evil. The ego lives for the day when we will consider the possibility that the capacity for evil lives within us, and that it is a natural part of who we are. If we see the ego as evil and we believe that evil is a natural part of who we are, then we and the ego must be the same. It would serve us well to understand that the ego is not an evil aspect of ourselves; it is simply a misperception that we hold about ourselves, and nothing else.

The ego also wants us to operate according to its perception of the world and wishes for us to operate based on its belief system. The ego's many wishes for us are as follows:

- It wants us to live in the world, but not feel part of it.
- It wants us to know we are suffering, and think we can do nothing about it.
- It wants us to be surrounded by others, but feel lonely and alone.
- It wants us to fear our brothers and sisters, and God.
- It wants us to live our lives in search of love, but never find it.
- It wants us to know that there is something missing in our lives, but never understand what it is.
- It wants us to communicate, as long as that communication separates us from our brothers and sisters.

Invitation #3 - The Ego's Gifts

Can the blind lead the blind? Shall they not both fall into the ditch?

Luke 6:39

My friend, you have chosen the ego as your guide. You have chosen the blind to lead you. You have chosen the king of loneliness, separation and regret to rule over you. You have chosen the father of fear, judgment and darkness to light your path.

For a moment, sit by yourself in quiet remembrance of where your ego has taken you. Sit with the feelings it has offered you. Sit with the gifts judgment has furnished you. Remember the times you blamed your brother or sister, the times you judged your brother or sister, the times you feared your brother or sister. These are the times the ego offered its gifts and you accepted. Sit alone and ask yourself this simple question: What has the ego ever truly offered me?

Gift yourself some time alone to finally question the ego. Questioning illusions and the ego is the first step in undoing them.

Remember the strangers the ego assisted you in condemning. Remember the relationships it assisted you in breaking, the friends it assisted you in hurting, and the family members it told you weren't worth your forgiveness. Sit with at least one of these events or feelings in your mind. Question the ego and your actions, and feel what it has brought and offered you.

The ego has led you into the darkness long enough. Your tolerance for pain has been high, but it is not without limit. There is a time for all of us when we must ask ourselves if there is a better way. My friend, I am here to remind you that there is. Know that there is always hope, for darkness is simply a lack of light, and whenever light enters, darkness dissipates. This light has always been within you and waits with everlasting patience to once again shine through you, illuminating all you see. It is a journey without distance; it simply waits for your willingness to see it, to appear.

A moment of true forgiveness will end a lifetime of pain. Now ask God for assistance in dealing with your past actions and reactions, and it shall be given. Ask God to hold your heart in His hand, and He shall do so. Ask angels to surround you, and know that they will. And with all their assistance and support, take an honest look at how you have reacted to your brothers and sisters. Ask God for forgiveness, ask your brothers and sisters for forgiveness, ask yourself for forgiveness, and forgiveness will surround you in its light.

With your permission, the ego has built walls around your heart, walls between you and your brothers and sisters, walls between you and God. Be with that light and feel it permeating the walls of your ego. It has taken a lifetime for these walls to be built. All you need is a little willingness, a holy instant, to allow God's love to shine through. In that holy instant, you will recognize what has always been true, that you have never been disconnected from your loving source, that you have never been disconnected from your brothers and sisters.

When brothers or sisters attack you they are subconsciously asking for love. They might not ever believe this, but I know in your heart you understand what it is I am sharing with you. This is one of the reasons that you and those living in the light should try to be more patient with angry brothers and sisters. These angry brothers and sisters are lost. They are feeling bad about themselves and taking it out on you. They take it out on you because they believe that you are the easier target. They could not take it out on God because lost brothers and sisters usually have a fear of God.

The next time a brother or sister who is ruled by the ego attacks you, consider that he or she is simply asking for love. He or she is a lost soul asking you for direction. Would you lead him or her toward more darkness or toward the light? This is the choice you make every time you react to a lost brother or sister.

Understand that the choice you make will bring you closer to the place you send him or her. Lead him or her toward darkness, and you too shall feel and experience the darkness. Lead him or her toward light, and you too shall feel and experience the light.

Take this opportunity to choose peace. Deep peace comes from meeting your brother or sister without judgment. In choosing peace, you will understand that your brothers and sisters are fighting their own difficult battles with their egos. Ask your heart, ask your spirit for guidance on the right thing to do, and you'll know what is right, for what is right will bring you peace. It is truly that simple; the right thing to do will bring you peace. Understand that the world you see is the world that exists for you. As you change the way you perceive the world, the world that exists also seems to change. But understand that the world never really changes, it is only how you see it that changes. The world is simply the effect, the cause is how you think, who you believe yourself to be. How you think comes from where you are in your mind. The more peaceful you are within your mind, the more peaceful the world will appear.

Think back to a time when you shared an experience with friends or family members. Even though the experience was the same, you and the others around you may not have reacted the same way. Some may have been more at peace with the experience than others, some may have been more distressed, but it was still the same experience. The way you react is colored by your past experiences that are similar in nature. You might believe that someone overreacted to a situation. Once that situation is discussed, the person who you thought overreacted, might change his or her mind about the reaction, and thus receive peace from changing his or her mind. You can receive peace, not from changing the situation, for that cannot be changed, but from changing your thoughts about the situation. The power lies within you, not outside of you.

Peace is a choice you are able to make in every situation. You can make the choice for peace immediately, or you can take as much time as you want to find peace about the situation. But understand that the amount of time you take to accept peace in any situation is purely up to you. You contain within yourself this ability to choose peace. Yet, judgment is always the ego's answer, and its result is pain, stress and resentment. In every situation the ego offers this gift to you, and it is mighty proud when you accept it.

Dream Given for Chapter Two - A Child's Game

While writing this chapter, I asked my higher self and spirit guides to explain to me how I created my ego-self, so that I could better communicate it to you. The dream that follows is the response I received.

I'm sitting in a rail car (like those that are used in coal mines). A female guide smiles and gives me the thumbs up. I smile back and return the thumbs up. With that, she pushes the rail car and it begins moving on the tracks toward a door. Two angels open the door. The tracks end and I begin to fall. I do not experience fear, but I do experience a falling sensation. The two angels are with me throughout the experience and I feel comforted by their presence. My spiritual body, which has the form of a human body, begins to shrink into a ball of light. The shrinking in no way causes discomfort, but I do see my spiritual body becoming a ball of light. The angels disappear, yet I know they will always be with me. I continue to fall. I enter my mother's stomach.

I then begin to hear a familiar young baritone voice. An instruction video begins within my mother's stomach. This video covers the complete inner vision of my mind. The message I received, although very close to the original, is paraphrased:

You have chosen to remember. Imagine, if you will, perfect love once again choosing the human experience. A baby is born. As this baby grows into a young child, he never thinks to question what truth is. He might sometimes disagree with what he is being told to do, and when he does, he is punished. The punishment can take many forms. The young child soon learns that there are ways to do things, and ways not to do things. If the child does what his family wants, he will be safe. If the child challenges them, he will not be safe. Like children, we are rewarded for doing things one way, and not the other. Our parents' belief systems, the armor parents wear to defend themselves in this world, slowly becomes our armor. We learn that as long as we don't rock the boat we will be safe. Slowly we take on the belief systems of our parents, and this becomes our armor, our truth.

As the child continues to grow into a teenager, his peers become more important to him and again he is rewarded for doing things a certain way and for acting a certain way. Slowly the child learns he can be rewarded or punished by his peers. His peers, who have come with their different sets of armor, reward him for being like them. And so he picks up more armor. The child's peers and his family's armor become his armor and their truths becomes his truth. All along, he watches and listens to different messages society offers, and picks and chooses the beliefs that are acceptable to his family, friends and society. Many times, the belief systems of the child's family and friends differ and clash with his. This creates confusion and sometimes chaos, but the child is told that "this is just the way life is." As a result, this mixture of beliefs becomes the armor that he uses to defend himself against the world and against all those who attack "his beliefs." The child does not yet realize that his beliefs are not really his own, but a compilation of ideas that were offered and he accepted.

The child makes "his belief" into "the truth." He declares the world and people who disagree with this belief system insane for challenging "the truth." For to him, his truth is "the truth." He judges the world as confusing and chaotic, and he judges those who do not share in his beliefs as unsafe and dangerous. He views people shielded in armor similar to his with a feeling of camaraderie and safety. Yet, many times, he is judged and attacked by his own group. Many times, he judges and attacks the group. All this creates confusion and sometimes chaos, but he is again made to understand that this is just the way life is. So regardless of the judgment, confusion and chaos, he decides that, "Yes. This is just the way life is." He looks through his armor and sees the group behaving a certain way, and this becomes his way. He follows the rules and laws and becomes part of the group, and those in the group reinforce in him that by behaving this way he will be accepted and safe.

He sees others walking in circles, protecting their belief systems. He figures that if most are acting this way, it must be the right thing to do. Other shielded ones tell him that indeed, this is the right thing to do, the right way to act, and an honorable way to live. He imagines how important it must be to guard these ideas. These ideas, rules and laws become so important to the group that they create different structures to house and protect them. They call such structures countless numbers of names such as churches, synagogues, banks, government building, courts. These structures and ideals are represented by a foggy image of what first appears as a castle in the dream.

The child in the dream now appears as a young man in his 20's. The young man joins a group of shielded ones and begins to walk in a circle, taking pride in guarding the castle. The shielded ones congratulate and welcome him to "their way." They reward him with more armor and tell him how well he is doing. The shielded ones continue to walk in circles, not quite sure why they are doing what they are doing, but they continue. He sees peers and mentors doing this, and thinks "this must be the way things are." Yet, every now and then when he is quiet, he begins to feel a slight tug within his armor. And every time he focuses on these feelings, there appears in the distance a small group of children laughing and playing on a hill. But he figures that they are but children and have no idea of the importance of guarding the castle, and so again he continues to circle.

The shielded ones spend their time walking around the castle, and encouraging others to continue their task of guarding the castle. They do not take time to either look at or question the castle or the children. In fact, if they are caught looking at or questioning the castle or the children, they are teased and called slackers, dreamers, troublemakers or bums. They have seen how others who looked at the children or at the castle were treated for their nonconformist behaviors. And they promise themselves that they will not be called such names, or ridiculed in front of their peers. They were even shocked and frightened when they saw how a few of their peers simply disappeared after looking at the children or the castle. And they believed the stories the old shielded ones told them about what would happen if they looked at the children or the castle for too long. This thought made them afraid, so they chose not to look or to question.

The child in the dream now appears as a young man in his 30's. The young man continues to wear the armor proudly and work hard. As time passes, he continues the hard work and receives more pieces of armor for good behavior to decorate his body. At first, he wears the armor proudly, but by its nature, it is heavy and difficult to carry. It tires him to carry it everywhere. He even wears it to bed. As he grows, he becomes less comfortable in the armor, and as he does, others become less comfortable around him. As the days fuse into weeks, and weeks draw out into years, the weight begins to tire him. The weight increases with every judgment he makes against a brother or sister. With every judgment he receives a new piece of armor. His shoulders begin to slump, and his legs begin to buckle. He sees this occurring but doesn't understand why, other than "this is just the way life is." They sold him on the idea that if he played by their rules, he would feel successful, rich and fulfilled. He cannot understand why he feels tired, sad, dissatisfied and empty, for he has done all that the old shielded ones and their peers told him to do. Yet now, only the opposite seems to be true.

The child in the dream now appears as a mature adult in his 40's. One day, when he cannot take another step because the weight is too much to bear, he tells himself that there must be a better way, and decides to look toward the children's laughter. His peers immediately notice this and begin to ridicule his efforts. They question his work ethic and sanity and begin to separate themselves from him. They call him a troublemaker, a person without goals. They tell him that he has changed, that he's different. One by one, his peers begin to distance themselves. At first, he is confused because, on one hand, he feels safe in the company of peers, but on the other hand, listening to the laughter on the hill seems to fill him with an understanding, a joy and peace he thought was not possible. When the shielded ones see that they cannot get him back in line, the remaining peers seek assistance from his mentors in order to "save him" from disaster, before "making a big mistake."

The mentors, together with a few remaining peers, try to convince him that he is throwing his life away, that he has worked too hard to be where he is. They congratulate him on all the armor he has collected through the years. They tell him how well he is doing, how well they have done. They show him how hard the shielded ones before him worked and how much armor they accumulated. He tries to share with them the weight of the armor, the laughter he is hearing, the understanding, and peace of mind and joy he is receiving. But the shielded ones are too stuck in their ways, and so they part ways. He leaves and they continue walking their circles as if he had never been there. He then begins to move toward the laughter.

On the way out, he begins to meet new people who have also come from the circle, people who have walked where he walked. Some still wear pieces of armor, but not as much as him or his peers. They appear to be more at peace. At first, this confuses him, for how could having less give you more? But he chooses not to judge his brothers and sisters, for in their stories, he remembers his own. As he shares and joins with his fellow travelers, he notices that because of the joining, sharing and nonjudgmental behavior, he begins to release his own armor. As he begins to do so, parts of the armor just seem to disappear. He becomes lighter, and it becomes easier to breathe and laugh.

He continues the journey toward the laughter. As he reaches the hill, he finds that, indeed, it was the laughter of children he remembered and had heard so long ago. He glances into the children's radiant eyes and remembers his own radiance. As he does, the last piece of armor disappears from his covered heart. In the smiles of the children, he, for the first time, sees his own real reflection, and it is also that of a child. He then realizes that he has always been like a child - innocent, free, with the wisdom of the ages at his command.

For a moment, he reflects on the past and sees where he has been. He looks into the distance and sees the shielded ones still walking in circles. In each circle, he hears them shouting commands and demands at each other. For the first time, he notices that it is not a castle they are all protecting, but piles of dirt that their own steps have created and formed. But he does not judge them, for he now understands that this is the road they have chosen, and he rejoices in their choosing. He knows that it's simply a matter of time before the shielded ones allow themselves to hear the laughter. He sees those who are trying to escape the circle, and those who are trying to convince them to stay. He blesses them both the same. He smiles, realizing that the shielded ones are also children, simply playing a different game. And he now smiles at the game, for could anyone sanely react any other way to children playing games?

A Word of Encouragement to Anyone Experiencing a Crisis or Burnout

Going to a junkyard is a sobering experience. There you can see the ultimate destination of almost everything we desired.

[1]Roger Von Oech, *"A Whack on the Side of the Head"*

I don't read books, meditate or travel to become awake, I am awake. I am just as awake as you are. The only difference is that I

[1]See Notes, page xv.

recognize it and you may not have remembered it yet. Choosing to remember your true state, that of being awake, may be the only decision that separates you from those who already see themselves as awake. Once we choose to awaken, we find that peace and joy become the motivation for more and more of our activities.

The world's material gifts, regardless of their size and outward beauty, are valueless. They are all illusions. Please understand that I'm in no way saying that the material world is bad. What I am saying is that it holds no true value. As mentioned before, the only value that an illusion has is for us to recognize that it is but an illusion. Do you truly believe that filling your life and time with nothing will bring you peace and joy? Has it brought you true peace and joy yet?

Everything that the ego's world offers us as a belief system is, in the end, really just junk. We have placed different values on illusions, and thus, some junk, material things and ideas seem more valuable to us than other junk. Being just illusions, junk's value is ever changing and never lasting. But everlasting peace and joy cannot be found in the never lasting.

Those who choose to fill their lives and time with junk, those who kneel down and worship at the altar of junk will never find lasting peace of mind and joy. This is not because God loves them any less, or because they don't deserve it, but simply because they are looking outside for that which lives within.

There comes a time in the lives of all worshippers of junk when they must ask themselves why, after following all the rules the ego's world asks for, they are still not happy, and why they are not at peace with themselves and their world. In this society, such a time is usually referred to by the ego as a mental breakdown, depression, a mid-life crisis or burnout. These phrases are used by the ego to put down and sedate those individuals who dare to question this world's reality. For in this world, the ego knows when it is losing control of its slaves, and it will not stand idly by. The world is ruled by the ego. The ego has invested a lot of time in these people, and it does not want them to go free. But the worshippers of junk, the slaves of the ego, can only live in an unnatural state for so long before they begin to question how they feel. Soon they begin to wonder if this is what it's all about. When they finally realize that they are measuring their worth by how much junk they have acquired, sadness, lack of peace, a mental breakdown, a mid-life crisis, burnout or depression may set in.

My friend, do not buy into the world's fantasies and negative connotations. If this is what you are experiencing, this moment should become a time of great joy and celebration, for you have, in some manner, finally realized that junk has truly nothing to offer. You now have the opportunity to realize what the worship of junk and illusions has truly offered you, and how its worship has made you feel. For a moment, thank yourself for the worshiping of junk, for it has brought you to the recognition of what it has to offer. It has offered you a sense of separation from your trueself. It has offered you sadness. It has offered you pain. It has offered you stress, confusion, depression, doubt, emptiness, fear and regret. It has offered you nothing you ever truly desired.

Be thankful for your experience at the altar of junk and illusion, for it has allowed you the opportunity to discover that it has nothing to offer. All the money and time you have spent at its feet, the hours awake at night with a thousand heavy thoughts crossing your mind, and the arguments with your family and friends, has taught you one important lesson - that junk is not what you want. Be grateful for this lesson, for it is the beginning of the realization of what you really desire.

My friend, rejoice for you can choose once again. You know which road you have taken, and you know where it has gotten you. It was the road you needed to take to get to where you are now. Be thankful, but understand that it is all in the past. It is now but a memory, and nothing else. It is now time to let go. You have tried it your ego-self's way, now it's time to try it your Godself's way.

Rejoice my friend, for a new day is at hand. You do not need to accomplish anything. You need only remember your trueself by allowing the recognition of peace to come into your awareness. You no longer need to jump through rings of fire or over barrels to earn your peace of mind. Peace of mind is your inheritance. You simply need to remember that peace is your natural state.

The path to enlightenment can be as elaborate or as effortless as you wish it to be. This path ends with the recognition that you are awake. It is a state of mind that recognizes what already is. You do not need to change who you are. You do not need to better who you think you are. You simply need to remember who you have always been. You simply need to extend what exists within.

So rejoice when you hear that someone - maybe even you - is going through a mental breakdown, depression, a mid-life crisis or burnout, for these people are our guides out of the tunnel of darkness that the ego sold to us as being our home. My friend, I am here to remind you, as well as myself, that there is a light at the end of this tunnel.

These people, who will no longer be slaves, are our heroes. They will no longer be slaves to the ego's lies and the world's deceptions. These are the people who will not settle for the status quo any longer. They now realize that it is an illusion they are standing on, and that there is no bridge they have to build or cross to find happiness or peace. They have now realized that the bridge they had been building all alone, a bridge that the world told them they must build to find happiness and peace, is not real. As a result, they fall. Yes, our guides and heroes are falling, but they are falling not from grace but to grace. Fear not for them, for there are other heroes and guides to soften their fall. And from the world's point of view, although it might seem like a long and difficult fall, it is simply a wink of eternity's eye.

Eternity smiles and embraces her heroes and guides as they return home. The journey has been long, but without distance. It has simply been a journey from forgetfulness to remembrance, from fear to love, from pain to peace, and from perception to knowledge. These heroes have traveled, experiencing all the illusions the world had to offer, and all the lies the ego said were true. And so they will look back at the fear, pain, illusions and lies, and smile in remembrance; for now through forgiveness they hold all such memories in light, and by holding their memories in light they receive understanding. The understanding is this: Every moment in their adventures, every moment in their lives, was chosen by them in order to remember who they and their brothers and sisters truly are - the perfect expression of the mind of God physically manifested here on Earth.

3

THE GODSELF

The Godself is the essence of God within us. We are the essence of God physically expressing Himself on Earth. The essence of God is love. Love is all we are; it is our true state, our real self. Love is our base, our foundation. People are taught and have the perception that they must build on their foundation. How we choose to build on our foundation is up to us. However, if we simply extend what we are, we will create more beauty than anything that has ever been built. My brother and sister, our base - our Godself - is perfect, and we need not add or subtract anything from perfection.

Regardless of what perception we have of ourselves and others, it does not change our foundation or our brother or sister's foundation. But we have been offered free will, and with that we may choose to see ourselves and our brothers and sisters as we wish.

There is nothing that any great teacher or guru has obtained that is not obtainable to us. In fact, the Godself is not something that is obtained, the Godself is simply something that is realized and remembered. Nothing that is given to one is withheld from another. God does not play favorites. God's love for us is in no way diminished by our belief that we are less than what we truly are. God loves all, equally, and always.

Our understanding of truth is in direct relation to our ability to love. When we speak of love it is not about "special love" where one individual or individuals are loved more than or over others. When we speak of love, it is an all-encompassing, all-inclusive, non-divisible love. Erich Fromm, in his book, "The Art of Loving," put it this way:

> [2]*Love is not primarily a relationship to a specific person; it is an attitude, an orientation of character that determines the relatedness of a person to the world as a whole, not toward one "object" of love. If a person loves only one other person and is indifferent to the rest of his fellow men, his love is not love but a symbiotic attachment, or an enlarged egotism. Yet, most people believe that love is constituted by the object, not by the faculty.*

[2]See Notes, page xv.

50

In fact, they even believe that it is proof of the intensity of their love when they do not love anybody except the "loved" person. This is the same fallacy, which we have already mentioned above. Because one does not see that love is an activity, a power of the soul, one believes that all that is necessary to find is the right object - and that everything goes by itself afterward. This attitude can be compared to that of a man who wants to paint but who, instead of learning the art, claims that he has just to wait for the right object, and that he will paint beautifully when he finds it. If I can say to somebody else, "I love you," I must be able to say, "I love in you everybody, I love through you the world, I love in you also myself."

As we allow love to fill more aspects of our lives, the truth of who we are becomes clearer. The more we are able to share and extend love, the more we are able to see and experience truth. Both love and truth are boundless. To try and use words to define such energies would be to try and establish boundaries around All That Is.

One who is aware of his Godself or trueself recognizes it in all. Regardless of his position in the world, he will see us as equals, a brother or sister in the remembering process. He will look at us as equals because he recognizes our divinity. His knowledge of himself will strengthen ours. We are here in part to remember our Godselves, our divinity. Our Godself is the truth of who we are. The more time we spend during the day in recognition of our divinity, our Godselves, the more we'll become aware of it in our brother, sister, and in the world. So how do we recognize our divinity? If we feel anything that does not reflect peace, love or joy, then we are not in recognition of our Godselves, our divinity. When we are experiencing or expressing any type of negativity, we are not in recognition of our divinity. Peace, love and joy reflect the presence of God. Peace, love and joy are natural extensions and expressions of someone who has allowed himself or herself the recognition of his or her Godself. Please note that someone extending and expressing his or her Godself will never judge us for how we choose to feel or behave.

Living a Spiritually Fulfilling Life

For some people, the recognition of their divinity begins their pursuit of a more spiritually fulfilling life. Some people fear that if they begin pursuing a more spiritually fulfilling life, they will somehow separate themselves from their current reality. If you have these concerns, do not fear becoming disconnected from family and friends, your workplace and peers. Fear is an illusion and, as such, it is not real. It is a false belief. Understand that even today, you are in a state of constant communication with individuals who have totally different perceptions than you. It is by recognizing this never-ending connection that your fear of disconnection begins to dissolve.

Once we begin living a more spiritually fulfilling life, our sense of connection actually increases. Regardless of how others live their lives, our inner sense of connection and love for those with whom we interact increases. As we recognize the truth in us, so too will we begin to recognize that the same truth exists in all of our brothers and sisters. Others around us might still choose to experience fear and pain which they demonstrate through expressions such as stress, anxiety, judgment and anger. We will have compassion for them, because we will understand where they think they are coming from. But we will not share in their thoughts about themselves, or be involved in their pain and suffering, for we will quickly recognize that it is an illusion they are experiencing.

The ego, like a hurricane, creates and supports a confusing and chaotic world, yet if we stay focused on our Godselves, we will forever live in its eye. By living in our Godself state, we will be at peace wherever we go. We will offer rest to all who come near us, and they will find comfort and peace in our presence. Those bashed around and worn out by the storm, though not understanding why, will find refuge in us. For there are many who know only of the storm. It is their only reality. They will be drawn to us, and question us about our peaceful state. We will provide a temporary shelter, and serve as a gentle reminder that there is another way. They may not yet be ready to leave the storm, but the next time they remember us they will see a break in the clouds and a glimmer of light shining through. If only for a moment, they will experience warmth and reassurance. They will be surprised but not shocked by the experience, for the memory of this light also lives within them. That memory has now been reawakened, and it will offer them peace any time they choose to focus on it.

There will be times when we will forget that we are the perfect expression of the mind of God. During these times when we are off-center, we will feel the winds, the power of the storm. We will feel unbalanced. Our ego will have us curse the wind for blowing, but we will not share in its thought system. We will quickly remember that the winds are a helpful reminder of the truth of who we are. We will thank the storm for its reminder, and soon we'll regain our center. As we come back to our truth, we will again experience peace of mind and joy. We will offer it to others because it is simply the natural extension and expression of who we are.

Those who have lived their lives in the storm of their own making will find comfort in us, because we will see in them what they have yet to recognize in themselves. In these moments of comfort, they will recognize that there is another way of living. They might even recognize that they too have the ability to choose peace. We will be the reminder of the truth in them. They will find great comfort in this memory. In their own ways, they will thank us and we will smile and thank them, for we know that every brother or sister allows us the opportunity to remember our own perfection by recognizing it in them. Through this recognition, we will obtain and retain peace of mind and joy. Joy and peace are manifestations of the presence of God, and our brother and sister are His perfect expression. We now understand that there is no need to alter perfection.

Experiencing Our Godselves in the Moment

We might not understand the value that our current situation or circumstance holds. We might even perceive that it has no value at all. Maybe we perceive our current reality as boring, useless or not worthy of us. Maybe we see our current situation as valueless, insignificant or pointless, and are wondering how this really fits into our lives. Right now, we might not understand what part of our puzzle we are now working on. Yet, my friend, I offer this one piece to your puzzle: there is not one moment in your life, not one thought in your mind, and not one action in your day that is valueless, insignificant or pointless. This is what is meant by "experiencing your Godself in the moment." If we would allow this one thought to enter the realm of possibilities, it would forever change the way we see our lives. In the book "Spiritual Growth, Being Your Higher Self," author Sanaya Roman put it this way:

> [3]*Imagine you are working on a jigsaw puzzle. You put pieces together in one corner and you can see a small house. You may work on a completely different area next, and a tree might appear. They don't seem to be connected until later, when you work on another part and a country scene unfolds. The tree and the house are complete within themselves, but they are also parts of the bigger picture. You may have already discovered that seemingly unimportant things you learned, jobs you took and experiences you had all fit together in a way you couldn't have anticipated at the time. It was only later, when you saw the bigger picture, that you realized the importance of certain things. Your higher self has a larger plan for your life, and every experience you have will fit together and give you value in some way, even if you don't yet know.*

Why is it that we have more faith that the pieces of a puzzle made by a company in Taiwan will all fit together than we have that the pieces of our life that are presented to us by God will fit together? One person chooses to put like pieces together first, while another chooses to put the edges of the puzzle together first, but

[3]See Notes, page xv.

neither individual ever really doubts that the puzzle will somehow fit perfectly. The edges in and of themselves probably have little to do with the main image or idea of the puzzle, yet without it, the puzzle is incomplete. In fact, although these pieces appear to have little to do with the main idea or image, they are nonetheless as important to the puzzle's completion. In the beginning some pieces, even when they fit perfectly together, might not help you to understand what the puzzle is about; only in its completion can you appreciate the parts that at first seemed insignificant and pointless.

There was a moment in existence where God thought, and from this thought we were created. We are the physical manifestation of God's thought. If we truly acknowledge what this means, be it for an instant in time, we would fall to our knees in appreciation. My friend, we are our brother and sister's salvation and they are our salvation. For within our memories lies the truth of who we are. These memories are available to us for recollection any time we want, and can occur with everyone and everything we see. If we have not yet found this piece, we soon will. Yes, my friend, the day is coming when we will accomplish what it is we believe we need to accomplish. When we do, we will look back and understand the importance of every piece of the puzzle.

We need not wait until the end of our journey to enjoy and be thankful for every experience during the journey. Equally so, we need not wait for our accomplishments to appreciate all the pieces of the puzzle. We need simply remember that in order to complete the puzzle, all pieces were of use. In this simple memory and under-standing lies our appreciation of not only the puzzle, but of all its pieces. And in the acceptance of the necessity and usefulness of its pieces lies our peace about the pieces we have already put together and the pieces we will deal with in the future. And of equal impor-tance, we will be at peace with, and have appreciation for, all the pieces we currently are working on.

The ego's world will try to tell us that we're wasting our time, and that we could be doing something else, something the ego perceives to be more important or productive. We might hear all this and more. We might even begin to buy into what it says. I'm not here to tell you that the world is wrong and you are right, or that the world is right and you are wrong. What I'm here to do is to simply remind you that whatever you choose to do in the end, be at peace with your decision. Not because you are doing the right or wrong thing, but because you are completing the puzzle in the best way you currently know how.

My friend, regardless of what the world tells you, or how you perceive your current situation, I offer you this: the road you have taken is the road that you needed to take. You are exactly where you need to be. Do whatever offers you peace now. Make peace with your past, for without it you would not be at this point in your life. The pieces you have chosen to put together are complete. You might not yet know how they fit into the puzzle, but friend, they do and will fit. You are now working on the pieces you believe you need to work on to get you to the next step. Be at peace with the knowledge that they too will fit. You have the choice to be at peace with this knowledge or to judge, criticize and be disappointed with your current decisions and situation. Those are the only two choices you truly have. They are, simply put, the choice between sanity and insanity.

The ego's world, in and of itself, is an insane world, which is the main reason it applauds us for making the insane choice. And so, over and over, we make the insane choice and judge, criticize and feel disappointed with ourselves, our brothers and sisters, and the world. My friend, once we can acknowledge that insanity is but a choice, we find its power over us diminishing. Then, one day, instead of acting insanely, we act with sanity and gratitude, for we understand that one more piece of the puzzle is now in place.

We may have chosen to judge the past, and blame ourselves and many others for where we are today. That is fine. Do that if you choose to, but at least for sanity's sake, ask yourself what this behavior has and is truly offering you? Where has this behavior taken you? At the very least, ask yourself if you are at peace with how you feel about this way of thinking.

My friend, we cannot carry the past with us without feeling weighed down by it. We might not understand that what we are currently feeling is being weighed down. We might define it as being tired, stressed, depressed, but in the end, it is our choice to carry the judgments of the past with us that have made us feel this way. It may be our tendency to believe that some pieces of our past were never meant to fit, and will never fit into our puzzle, which frustrates us. Many of us may not yet understand that these pieces will fit, and that with their contribution we come closer to the puzzle's completion. Yet again, I mention that we do not need to wait for the puzzle's completion in order to be at peace and to be grateful for every one of its pieces now.

We will one day find peace and gratitude in the puzzle's completion. We will one day acknowledge all the pieces for their contribution to the whole. And we will one day give thanks to each of the pieces for their participation. We will look back at those pieces we judged and criticized, and apologize for our interpretation of their value. We will look back, forgive and set free all the pieces we once convicted as guilty. We will kneel down in front of those we punished and sentenced to life without us, and we will ask for their forgiveness. They will in turn kneel in front of us, and ask for ours, and with one embrace all will be forgiven.

When insanity turns to sanity, all judgments will turn into forgiveness, all difficulties into gratitude, all pain into peace, all sadness into joy, and all hate into love. All this comes from the simple recognition that every moment, piece and step of our journey assisted us in getting where we wanted to go. Love and gratitude can be offered now for whatever pieces we are working on. If they are offered now, we find peace now; if they are offered later, we will find peace later. But my friend, we will some day offer love and gratitude, for they are who we are - and it is only who we are – that we can offer others.

In Search of My Godself: My First Spiritual Experience

In the next few sections of this chapter, I'll take you on a "Cliff Notes" journey through events in my life that assisted me in remembering who I truly am.

I have very few early childhood memories, but my first "spiritual" experience was one that I will never forget. It was 1972; I was about five years old and living in Venezuela. Back then people believed that children should have their tonsils removed in order to prevent certain complications later in life. My mother and grandmother had been at odds about whether or not my brother and I should have such an operation. My grandmother believed it had to be done and my mother believed that the procedure was too dangerous. So one day, without my mother's permission, my grandmother took my brother Roberto and me to the hospital.

In Venezuela, even today, anyone who has the resources prefers to leave the country for operations and medical procedures. Imagine what it must have been like in 1972. The doctors told my grandmother that they would have to be careful with Roberto because they believed him to be a bleeder. They said that I should be fine, that they expected no complications. So they operated on my brother first.

For Roberto, it was also a memorable experience. As he recalls even today, he woke up in the middle of the operation. All he could feel was absolute pain, and all he could see was adults dressed in white around the table. He could tell he had something in his mouth so he tried to take it out. As he tried to do this, the doctors went for his arms to hold them down. Somehow he got one of his arms loose (remember, this is happening in the middle of his operation) and he punched one of the doctors in the head. He was a pretty tough cookie for a four-year-old child. The doctors finally got a hold of him and again put him under. This time I'm sure they administered a little more anesthesia than before.

When it was my turn, I was put under. All I remember was looking in, as one does when looking into a store window, and seeing adults dressed in white standing around a single table. I remember it being very peaceful, no panic at all. I could see doctors working on someone. I was standing at the level of a child looking at the operation in progress. At this point, I could not see my face, nor did I feel that the body on the table was mine. Even today, I can easily visualize the image as if it happened yesterday. I don't remember hearing anything, but that scene is still very real. So I'm standing outside my body without knowing it was my body, when one of the men put something over my chest, and suddenly, I see my body jumping inches off the table. Immediately, I was sucked right back into my body. I saw my body going up but as soon as it did, I was back in.

After returning home from the hospital, I remember seeing lights and colors on top of the heads and shoulders of people. Although it did not really concern or scare me, I told my mother what I was seeing. And as any concerned mother would do, she gently smiled, put me in her car, and immediately took me to the eye doctor. Of course, the eye doctor found nothing wrong with me, so off we went to see another eye doctor. After a second trip to an eye doctor, I decided that seeing these lights and colors wasn't such a good idea. Little by little, I started seeing fewer colors and less light around people, until one day my eyesight returned to "normal." At nights, I could remember walking around the house; yet, upon returning to bed, I could see that my body was still in bed. Let's just say that after two very unpleasant visits to the eye doctors and one operation, I decided to keep these travels through my house without my physical body to myself. Eventually, these conscious recollections of my travels also stopped.

Today I know that the colors and lights around people are simply their auras - something all humans have, yet only a very small percentage of the population see. I also understand that the travels around the house without my physical body were simply OBEs (out-of-body experiences). Although today I can see people's auras on a very limited basis, I have not had the need to work on improving that aspect of my vision. Nevertheless, I enjoy conscious or lucid OBEs very much and have learned much through the use of them. In Chapter 11, I discuss the usefulness OBEs have had in my remembering process and how you too can use these experiences to assist you in your growth.

I now see these experiences as the beginning of remembering my Godself. The separation from my physical body during the operation and the separation of my physical and spiritual body that occurred at my childhood home allowed me to understand that I was more than my physical body. Seeing people's auras allowed me to understand that there was something more going on, and that adults weren't "all-knowing."

Realizing My Mind's Influence

I was in high school in the early to mid eighties. The Tylenol scare was in the news. Some lost individual was putting cyanide in Tylenol pills, and two people in the United States died as a result. Everyone seemed pretty spooked. One day I was shopping with my mother and grandmother. I won't make any comments about shopping with them, but on this particular day, let's just say I got a headache. I told my mother about the headache, and she asked a waiter at a restaurant in the mall if he had any aspirin. The waiter gave me an aspirin and I took it. About a minute later, I recalled the whole Tylenol scare and I had my first panic attack. In truth, there was nothing wrong with the aspirin, but somewhere in my mind when I made the connection, I got scared and panicked.

In the next month, I had many more panic attacks. My mother took me to a hospital. They did all kinds of tests and found nothing. Nobody ever mentioned the phrase "panic attack" to me. It wasn't until years later that I found out there was a name for what I went through. Little by little, I could tell that I was making myself sick. Something - anything would set off the attacks, and I could feel my blood pressure rising, my heart pumping. I would become hot and dizzy. After about a month of these attacks, a month of feeling like crap, in and out of bed, I decided that enough was enough, and that if I was doing this to myself then I could also undo it.

I started working to understand the thoughts that were coming into my mind that were resulting in such a negative and fearful reaction. After working on my mind for the next couple of months, the attacks became less frequent and less severe. I was able to get to a point where I understood where my mind was headed, and I stopped the attacks from debilitating me. The more I watched over my mind, the more I was able to understand that the thoughts that were coming in - I was allowing in. Not only was I allowing the thoughts to come into my mind, but I was also putting a personal value on each one. The more I valued a thought, the more I focused on it, and the more I focused on it, the more it affected my mental, emotional and physical state. About a year after they began, the panic attacks completely stopped. My mind had made me sick and my mind had healed me. I was now in full control of my mind. I became truly in awe of the power of the mind. Yet, somehow I understood that I was more than my mind, but that I could still use it as a tool and have it work for or against me. I believe that my interest in psychology and philosophy began about that time. I just knew that there was a lot more to the mind than we were being taught or told.

Dream Given for Chapter Three - Who Am I?

In college, I remember asking myself, "What is truth? Why are we here? What's the whole point of life?" When I received no satisfactory answers, I decided that the only people who had answers to these questions, who understood what truth was, probably lived somewhere in caves in the Himalayan Mountains. Consequently, I chose to put those questions aside, and picked up the nice, cold beer in front of me. Then one day, those belief systems were erased, and the sage in the cave theory was replaced.

The dream that follows was brought about by a sincere, direct, heart-centered prayer over an incident that caused me great distress. This was the first dream that taught me that guidance is available to all of us if we truly desire it.

I was in my second year at Boston University, and I was dating a girl named Susan, whom I truly loved, or at least I thought I did. She caught me with another girl and broke up with me, rightfully so, I might add. This hurt me tremendously and I had a very rough night. I prayed that she would forgive me and asked God whether I would ever fall in love again. I finally fell asleep. Before I woke up, I had a dream that I was sitting at what seemed to be a party. In the dream, I was eating and drinking, with food in one hand, and a drink in the other. I looked around at the people at the party and decided to take a seat and finish my food. There were no chairs available, so I sat on the floor against a wall and began to observe the people at the party. They seemed to be having a good time, eating and drinking; some were standing, others sitting. I looked to the right of the room, then to the center, then turned my head to the left of the room. To my surprise, there was a girl from school whom I admired, and had always wanted to meet, sitting next to me on my left. As I saw her face, I became surprised and woke up. When I woke up, it seemed like a silly dream to remember. I was upset because I could not understand why I couldn't remember a cool dream when I wanted to. And now I could not get this silly dream out of my mind. Soon, I would learn that this dream was not as silly as I first thought.

Later that day, I went to the center of Boston to the public library to do research with a friend. After completing the work, we began walking to the T (the subway system in Boston). I noticed there was a movie playing that I had wanted to see, so I invited my friend to come along. He said he had to get back to campus, so I debated with myself about whether I should go back to school or to the movie. Finally, I decided to see the movie by myself and waved my friend goodbye. In the lobby of the movie theatre, I bought a small bag of popcorn and a soda. As I started to walk into the theatre, I was stopped and told that they hadn't finished cleaning the theatre, and was asked to wait in the lobby. I stood waiting for a little while before deciding to sit down. Since the lobby seats were all taken, I sat on the floor. As I ate my popcorn and drank my soda, I looked around the room. The lobby was becoming full with people eating and drinking as they waited for the theatre to be cleaned. I looked to the right of the room, then to the center, then turned my head to the left of the room. To my great surprise, there was the girl from school whom I had admired and had always wanted to meet, sitting next to me on my left. This was the same girl from the dream earlier that morning. I was shocked, to say the least. The expression on my face must have shocked her as well. I was in such shock that I got up and left the movie theatre. She must have thought that either I had gone nuts or that she was having a really bad hair day!

I saw that girl around campus a few more times, but I never mustered enough courage to introduce myself. At first I thought, "What a tremendous loss of opportunity. I really blew it this time." But then, after a few months of thinking about it, I thought that maybe there was a greater lesson here. Maybe I wasn't supposed to have talked to her and maybe the lesson was that there was something more happening than I could see. Maybe I didn't have to be a sage living in a cave in the Himalayas to get some understanding of what truth is. I mean, who was I to be told the future, to know the future? Why would God, if it was God, answer me with regard to ever finding another girl again? Who was I to be answered in such a quick and precise manner? I mean - God has got to have more important things to do than worry about my love life! Who am I to see what I saw, to have such an experience, such a gift?

This dream taught me that I did not have to be a guru in the Himalayan Mountains to get answers about my life and life in general. I understood that this experience was not something I needed to earn. God's knowledge of my behavior toward my girlfriend prior to the dream did not "earn" me the experience. I understood that I received the experience and guidance simply because I asked for it. I asked for assistance with an open and honest heart and received it. I realized that all answers were available to anyone who truly desired to ask the questions.

Turning Up the Volume in Life

Life is patient and kind. We offer ourselves as many opportunities as we can handle to learn our life lessons. If we choose not to learn the lessons, we will be given more opportunities. Yet each time we decide not to learn our lessons, the circumstances surrounding such opportunities will become more pronounced. This we do for our own good. This we do in order to listen and pay attention. Ultimately, we will pay attention and we will learn what we are trying to teach ourselves; it is simply up to us to decide how and when. It is up to us to decide when to start listening to what's going on in our lives. The longer we decide not to listen, the louder we will turn up the volume. We can choose to pay attention and listen before or after our ears start to hurt. It is our choice. We control the volume, and we control our attention and the station. Our Godselves will turn up the volume until we choose to listen. We have turned to the station we want to hear. Once we hear what it is we are trying to tell ourselves, and learn what we are trying to teach ourselves, we no longer need to increase the volume or repeat the lesson.

I began drinking during my freshman year of college. When it was time to party, my friends and I drank a lot. I remember my friends bringing an industrial size garbage can into our dorm room, and the whole goal for the night was to fill it up with empty beer cans before we went out clubbing. During my sophomore year, I remember having eight of my friends in my small four-seater car and driving onto a sidewalk because I drank too much. I literally could not keep my car on the road. My friends thought I was joking around, but looking back it was definitely no joke. Nothing happened that night, but looking back, it was pretty scary.

In my junior year, I remember being pulled over by a police officer. I was totally drunk. Thankfully, he let me go even though I failed the "follow the flashlight with your eyes only" test. For those who don't know the test, it goes like this: you must follow the cop's flashlight with your eyes only, and not move your head. Sounds simple enough, but it took me four tries to get it right. The bottom line was that the cop did not want to do the paperwork, so he asked me if I was going home. I said "Yes officer, going right home." He let me go and off I went to the next bar. I was awakened the next morning by a jogger's dog. I was in someone's garden in the middle of Denver. I had to call my brother to pick me up. He asked me where my car was and I couldn't tell him. Finally, after an hour of looking for my car, we found it.

During my senior year, I was pulled over again for drinking and driving. That night, I had only had a few beers, so the officer was very unhappy when he could only cite me for DWAI (driving while ability impaired), a charge below DUI. With a good lawyer, I had the charge reduced to driving a defective vehicle. But that did little to stop my drinking and driving.

A year after graduating, I was drinking and driving around 130 miles an hour on a highway. I had just left the highway, took a turn, and seconds later, found my car with its front end climbing a tree trunk. The tree was on the grounds of a synagogue. How much of a clearer message could God send? I couldn't get the car to start, so I left the scene. Thankfully, it was around 3 a.m. and the accident only involved the synagogue's tree and me. Not giving all the facts away, I was able to pay the synagogue for the tree, pay for the repairs to my car and did not get in any trouble with the police.

Two years after graduating, I experienced my first blackout. This happened five or six times. I would wake up in the morning, not remembering how I had driven home. Thankfully, I never found any damage to my car; obviously I made it home without incident. If you have ever experienced a blackout, you will understand that it's a scary experience not knowing what happened toward the end of the night, or how you got home.

A little while after my blackouts, I became allergic to wine and champagne. I literally choked if I drank it. Fearing the possibility of liver damage, I decided that it was time to make a change. My problem was not one of drinking regularly. It was that when I drank, I drank a lot. And although I believed I could control it, I chose to give it up completely. So on my twenty-fourth birthday, I had my last drink, and haven't had alcohol since then. My abstinence is now going on sixteen years.

I share this example simply to illustrate that little by little I kept experiencing more repercussions from my drinking problem. I knew that drinking and driving was not good for me, but I kept doing it. I knew that when I drank, I drank too much, but I kept doing it. I kept turning the volume higher and higher, until I had to listen. Life was kind and I was kind. I gave myself opportunities to learn my lesson the best way I knew how. As I was unwilling to learn this lesson, I gave myself more pronounced opportunities in order to finally learn what I was trying to teach myself. And just when my ears started to hurt enough, I decided to learn my lesson. All these opportunities were, in actuality, gifts to myself. Gifts of growth, the DWAI, the blackouts, the crash, the allergic reactions, all helped me learn my lesson. Most people would perceive the DWAI as bad luck, others would perceive the crash as an accident. But to me, all those situations were, in the end, gifts I offered myself. The police officer was kind enough to give of his time to assist me in my growth, and I now smile every time I carefully and respectfully pass the tree outside the synagogue.

To illustrate the seriousness of drinking, we now know that Jellinek's disease (alcoholism) is responsible for:

[4]50 percent of all auto fatalities

80 percent of all domestic violence/abuse

30 percent of all suicides

60 percent of all child abuse

65 percent of all drownings

It is estimated that when a woman contracts the disease, her husband leaves her in nine out of ten cases. When a man contracts it, his wife leaves in one out of ten cases.

Kathleen W. Fitzgerald

Real Life

About a month after graduating from college, I decided to go to Europe for a few months before starting my "real life." While in Europe, I went to Paris and spent a few weekends at an apartment owned by my uncle. During one of those weekends, my uncle's friend from Miami, Olaf Halvorssen, came to Paris and stayed in the apartment. He was celebrating a second honeymoon with his wife Mirianne. One night, he invited me to dinner.

Before I continue with my story, let me say that this experience instilled in me the lesson that when the teacher is ready the student will appear, and when the student is ready the teacher will appear. During the dinner conversation, I heard something different. I listened and understood concepts that until then I believed to be unavailable to mortal man. Olaf spoke of forgiveness, peace,

[4]See Notes, page xv.

love, religion, death and God in such a simple and non-judgmental way that I was truly in awe. Even though I was in awe, somewhere within I understood that everything he said, I already knew! It was more of a sense of a memory reawakening than a lesson being taught. I said to myself, "I don't know what this man is reading or what he is doing, but I am going to find out and copy every single thing he has done and read every single book he has read."

A month later, I headed to Venezuela to begin my working life. Before heading south to Venezuela I stopped by his house in Miami. I had not shared with him how grateful I had been for his presence, so I made an excuse to visit him. We talked in the living room for a while, and I noticed that he had been reading a big blue book; I figured it was the Bible. I remember being surprised, because my previous encounters with Bible readers felt judgmental; whereas, Olaf just felt, talked and expressed himself in a very non-judgmental manner. Again I did not ask about what he was reading, but as soon as he went to the kitchen, I ran to the couch where he had been seated, picked up the book and read the title - "A Course in Miracles." He had mentioned this book a couple of times.

After leaving his house, I went directly to the bookstore. I picked up the book, put it in my suitcase and headed for the airport. As I began my life in Venezuela, I also began to read the book. It was the first "spiritual" book I had ever read. I could not put it down; with each page I was so thankful to know that I was not alone. Every page seemed to reawaken a memory of who I really was. I realized that I was not crazy for thinking this way. After twenty-three years, I had now found a partner (the material in the book) that agreed with me. This partner did not think I was crazy or strange.

I have since read a great number of beautiful books. But "A Course in Miracles" will always be my first love. And now that I live in Miami, I see Olaf at least twice a month.

The concepts in "A Course in Miracles" and the following poem by Kahlil Gibran point to the truth of who we really are, and how who we are differs from what the world teaches us about who we are. "My Soul Counseled Me" is simply my favorite poem, and I am honored to have it in my book, and grateful that you will take the time to read it. I equate the author's use of the word "soul" to my use of the word "Godself." I also consider it to be very helpful to listen to what someone else's Godself told them.

My Soul Counseled Me

[5]*My soul spoke to me and counseled me to love all that others hate,*

And to befriend those whom others defame.

My soul counseled me and revealed unto me that love dignifies not alone the one who loves, but also the beloved.

Unto that day love was for me a thread of cobweb between two flowers, close to one another;

But now it has become a halo with neither beginning nor end,

Encircling all that has been, and waxing eternally to embrace all that shall be.

My soul counseled me and taught me to see beauty veiled by form and color.

My soul charged me to gaze steadfastly upon all that is deemed ugly until it appears lovely

Before my soul had thus charged and counseled me, I had seemed to see beauty like unto wavering torches between pillars of smoke;

But now the smoke has dispersed and vanished and I see naught but the burning.

My soul counseled me and charged me to listen for voices that rise neither from the tongue nor the throat.

Before that day I heard but dully, and naught save clamor and loud cries came to my ears;

[5]See Notes, page xv.

But now I have learned to listen to silence,

To hear its choirs singing the songs of ages,

Chanting the hymns of space, and disclosing the secrets of eternity.

My soul spoke to me and counseled me to quench my thirst with that wine which may not be poured into cups,

Nor lifted by hands, nor touched by lips.

Unto that day my thirst was like a dim spark laid in ashes

To be put out by a drought from any spring;

But now my strong yearning has become my cup,

Love has become my wine, and loneliness my joy.

My soul counseled me and charged me to seek that which is unseen;

And my soul revealed unto me that the thing we grasp is the thing we desire.

In other days I was content with warmth in winter, and with a cooling zephyr in the summer season;

But now my fingers are become as mist,

Letting fall all that they have held, to mingle with the unseen that I now desire.

My soul spoke to me and invited me to breathe the fragrance from a plant

That has neither root nor stalk nor blossom, and that no eye has seen.

Before my soul counseled me thus, I sought perfumes in the gardens,

In jars of sweet-smelling herbs and vessels of incense;

But now I am aware only of an incense that may not be burned,

I breathe an air more fragrant than all earth's gardens and all the winds of space.

My soul counseled me and charged me to answer and say: "I follow," when the unknown and the adventurous call unto me.

Hitherto I had answered naught but the voice of the crier in the market place,

Nor did I pursue aught save roads charted and well trodden;

But now the known has become a steed that I mount to seek the unknown,

And the road has become a ladder by which I may climb to the perilous summit.

My soul counseled me and admonished me to measure time with this saying:

"There was a yesterday and there shall be a tomorrow."

Unto that hour I deemed the past an epoch that is lost and shall be forgotten,

And the future I deemed an era that I may not attain;

But now I have learned this:

That in the brief present all time, with all that is in time,

Is achieved and come true.

My soul spoke and revealed unto me that I am not bound in space by the words:

"Here, there, and over there."

Hitherto I stood upon my hill, and every other hill seemed distant and far away;

But now I know that the hill whereon I dwell is indeed all hills,

And the valley whereunto I descend comprehends all valleys.

My soul counseled me and besought me to watch while others sleep

And to seek my pillow while they are wakeful,

For in all my years I had not perceived their dreams, nor they mine.

But now I am winged by day in my dreaming,

And when they sleep I behold them free upon the night,

And I rejoice in their freedom.

My soul counseled me and charged me lest I be exalted because of over praise

And lest I distressed for fear of blame.

Until that day I doubted the work of my own handiwork;

But now I have learned this:

That the trees blossom in spring, and bear fruit in summer,

And drop their leaves in autumn to become utterly naked in winter

Without exaltation and without fear or shame.

My soul counseled me and assured me

That I am neither higher than the pygmy nor lower than the giant.

Before that day I beheld mankind as two men,

The one a weakling whom I derided or pitied,

And the other a mighty man whom I would either follow, or oppose in rebellion.

But now I know that I was formed even from the same dust of which all men are created,

That my elements are their elements, and my inner self is their inner self.

My struggle is their struggle, and their pilgrimage is mine own.

If they transgress, I am also the transgressor,

And if they do well, then I have a share in their well-doing.

If they arise, I too arise with them; if they stay behind, I also, to company them.

My soul counseled me and instructed me to see that the light which I carry is not my light,

That my song was not created within me;

For though I travel with the light, I am not the light,

And though I am a lute fastened with strings,

I am not the lute-player.

My soul counseled me, my brother, and enlightened me.

And oftentimes has your soul counseled and enlightened you.

For you are like me, and there is no difference between us

Save that I speak of what is within me in words that I have heard in my silence,

And you guard what is within you, and your guardianship is as goodly as my much speaking.

Honoring Different Paths to the Godself

Truth is. Like you, it is changeless and eternal. However, the vehicle that you use to remember it might differ from that of your brother or sister. The words and feelings that will trigger the recognition of your Godself will probably differ from those that will trigger the same recognition in your brothers and sisters.

We honor our brothers and sisters by acknowledging that the choices they make within the illusion will assist them in their removal from the illusion. Trust this one thought, and respond with unconditional and uncompromising love toward your brothers and sisters. Know full well that these choices are bringing them out of their illusions. Belief in this one thought will save us years of judgment, resentment and pain.

Keep in mind that this vehicle, the idea that there is a process that we need to go through to awaken, is in and of itself a creation of the ego, and thus an illusion. Yet, as is the case with all illusions, its only value lies in recognizing that it is an illusion and nothing else. We are already awake. We are already complete and whole. We are truth and love. And we are the perfect expression of the mind of God. The truth of who we are, our Godselves, is already in us, and it is well aware of itself.

But what use does a vehicle have once we realize that we are on a journey without distance to a place we have never left? Love is who we are, have always been and will always be. Peace of mind and joy are natural expressions of love. When we extend our natural selves, peace of mind and joy are manifested, experienced, shared and enjoyed.

There is a sameness in all of us; this sameness is the expression of God. When truth is expressed through this vehicle, we cannot not be heard. When truth is expressed through love, the sameness in all of us awakens, the fog of forgetfulness is lifted and the spirit shines. When we extend our natural selves, the rebirth of light illuminates all it comes upon; joy and peace are once again reflected, manifested and experienced.

This book, that you have chosen to pick up, will trigger some of these moments of recognition. I say this with confidence, because it is my belief that it is not by chance that you are reading this sentence. It is my honor that you have chosen to experience this book, and it is in gratitude, humility and love that I offer it. To be a small part in your remembering process fills me with great joy.

Invitation #4 - Experiencing Peace

If you honestly desire peace of mind and joy, vow to yourself to do nothing that does not bring you peace of mind and joy.

Yes, that's it. This exercise, as simple as it seems, is the beginning of clarity, the beginning of understanding your Godself. What you might find difficult is the execution of this exercise. It might be difficult for you because this is something that, until now, you have refused to do. To do this exercise, simply recognize the choices you make that do not bring you peace of mind and joy. True self-love begins with the understanding of what does and does not bring you peace of mind and joy. Once you have made a commitment not to do anything that does not bring you peace of mind and joy, you will find peace of mind and joy in all that you do.

My friend, the Godself is within you now. It is that whisper within your heart that is asking to be remembered and expressed. It is the voice that calls for forgiveness when you have judged a brother or sister. It is the memory that recalls the possibility of healing when you feel hurt. It is the opportunity to choose calmness when you are stressed and unity when you have chosen separation. The Godself demonstrates that light is available even when you perceive it too dark to see. It is the invitation to love those others perceive as unlovable, to pray for those you once perceived as not worth your time. My friend, the Godself is the recollection that all you ever wish to be, you already are.

I chose to end this chapter with a passage from "A Course in Miracles." It describes this memory we are in the process of recalling.

6Listen, and try to think if you remember what we will speak of now.

Listen - perhaps you catch a hint of an ancient state not quite forgotten; dim, perhaps, and yet not all together unfamiliar, like a song whose name is long forgotten, and the circumstances in which you heard completely unremembered. Not the whole song has stayed with you, but just a little wisp of melody, attached not to a person or a place or anything particular. But you remember, from just this little part, how lovely was the song, how wonderful the setting where you heard it, and how you loved those who were there and listened with you.

The notes are nothing. Yet you have kept them with you, not for themselves, but as a soft reminder of what would make you weep if you remembered how dear it was to you. You could remember, yet you are afraid, believing you would lose the world you learned since then. And yet you know that nothing in the world you learned is half so dear as this. Listen, and see if you remember an ancient song you knew so long ago and held more dear than any melody you taught yourself to cherish since.

4

A Fulfilling Life

Do you currently believe that you lack certain personality traits that allow you to have a more fulfilling life? You might think of yourself as not having some of these qualities, but my friend, I offer you this reminder: It is not that you don't have these traits; it is simply that you are looking for a greater expression of them in your life. You have everything you need to be who you want to be. It is simply the recognition and expression of this that will awaken your memory.

The more time we spend convincing ourselves that we do not have the traits we need for a more fulfilling life, the more we will increase the power of those thoughts over us. The more we increase their power, the more we will see them as real and true. The more we see them as real and true, the more we will defend them against other thoughts that question their reality. The more we see them as worth defending, the more we will defend them against the world and the more we will believe that they are worth defending. The more we buy into their reality, the harder it is for us to understand that we have done this to ourselves. My friend, we are simply covering the treasure that lies within with dirt. Yet, however many feet of dirt we cover our treasure with, it does not eliminate the fact that the treasure still lies within.

Conversely, the more we analyze, focus on, and implement what we want to become, the closer we will come to its manifestation. Again, the more time we spend remembering that we already have the qualities we want to express, the more power we will give ourselves. As we express these qualities, they will become more real to us. As we continue to increase their expression, they will become more natural to us. Thus, the traits we once felt we did not have will slowly be recognized as natural expressions of our trueselves. We will look back and understand that it was not that we never had these traits, but simply that we had unconsciously chosen not to express them. As we understand this of one trait, we will understand that this is possible with regard to all the traits we believe we need for a fulfilling life. Understand that we already have all the traits that we believe we need for a more fulfilling life. Herein lies the beginning of the recognition of our Godselves.

Once we recognize our Godself, we will begin to recognize it in all others. We will see in others what they themselves cannot yet see. We will begin to have great respect and love for all our brothers and sisters. For we will recognize the beauty and perfection they have yet to recognize in themselves. We will see in every person's eyes the perfect manifestation of God on Earth, and we will be thankful for their presence. Every encounter with a brother or sister will become holy, and we will experience every word and action as gifts. We will create heaven on Earth and an absolutely fulfilling life through our simple recognition of our Godselves.

Our brothers and sisters will experience how we act and treat them, and they will be surprised. They will want to be like us and understand what it is we are doing in our lives to be that way. And we will smile, but not from a sense of superiority, but from the knowledge that what our brothers and sisters are searching for, they already have. They will think of themselves as spiritual children, but we will know them as complete equals and peers. They will ask us questions that they believe they do not know the answers to, and yet when we answer them, a memory will be reawakened, and they will simply recognize that they already know what we are saying. They will understand that the answer has always been within them, simply waiting for the question to be asked. We will remind them that all the questions they could ever ask are exactly like that first question they themselves answered. They will recognize great freedom in this. They will recognize this memory as true. They will thank us for helping them remember their trueselves and we will thank them for not letting us forget ours. We will experience great joy and fulfillment from our interaction with our brothers and sisters. We will live in joy with the knowledge that all our brothers and sisters are either living in joy or searching for it. We will even love and respect those we perceive as not searching for joy, for where they are in their remembering process has nothing to do with their perfection. We recognize and know them all as the perfect expressions of God, and it makes no difference where they believe themselves to be in that recognition.

A fulfilling life is lived by recognizing and expressing our

Godselves. There is nothing that can stop us from experiencing heaven on Earth, other than our belief that it is not possible. Equally so, there is nothing that can stop us from living a fulfilling life, other than our belief that it is not within reach.

Ask, my friend. We ask for so little. The universe waits for us to ask. Ask and be open to the recognition of the gifts that are offered to us every day. The more we focus on what we want, the easier it will be for us to recognize the gifts when they are being offered. The more we recognize the gifts that are being offered to us every day, the more thankful we will become. We will thank ourselves for becoming more aware, and we will thank the universe. We will find ourselves being more appreciative of the little things that life offers. We will acknowledge and be more thankful to our brothers and sisters. In doing this, we will raise our vibration, and it will become easier for us to acknowledge many more of the gifts that we once had not even noticed. We will more clearly see the signs on the road, and this will provide a more comfortable, carefree and joyful ride.

A fulfilling life is not only possible but also immediately accessible. There are no outside traits we must obtain to begin living such a life. If we have the thought of such a trait, it does not come from a sense of lack, but from a memory that is asking to be expressed. Through its expression, we will recognize that we have everything we need. Fulfillment comes as a result of acknowledging that we have everything we need.

Success and the Fulfilling Life

In the world of illusions, success can be measured a hundred different ways, and failure a thousand others. In truth, we achieve success through our simple participation in the life experience. We experience growth, and that is what we have come to do. If we accomplish what we have come to do, then we have succeeded. In that sense, there is no more need to ever talk about being a successful human being. Yet, the ego offers people the opportunity to set different parameters around the idea of success, and they usually bite at those offers. Trying to set parameters around an illusion of success simply leads to confusion and disillusionment. For how could we ever succeed at putting parameters around something that does not exist? So we end up having many different ideas of what having a successful life really means. All these ideas are judged against each other, each chipping away at the other's views. Yet part of what the ego tries to sell us about success is that we cannot really be completely successful unless others also view us as successful. Due to the many individual perceptions of success, this makes the task even more difficult and confusing. To add to the confusion, the ego-self so narrowly defines success that many times there is no place for also achieving happiness. Very often, the ego-self sets success and happiness so far apart that we must sacrifice one to achieve the other. Finally, even if others perceive us as successful, deep within, the ego will try to convince us that we are lying to ourselves and others, that we are really just a fraud who will soon be exposed.

The world would have us believe that success is a far off destination we reach by overcoming adversity, with hard work, and sacrifice. The idea of success is sold to us as difficult to accomplish with only a small percentage of people able to reach this goal. The ego has us see success as a sitting target, reachable only if we follow its directions. Yet once we reach this sitting target, it soon begins to move away from us; for what once seemed to satisfy us, satisfies us no more. The idea of failure is sold to us as a humiliating experience that brings about shame and dishonor. We are taught that there really is little to no middle ground between success and failure, that we are either one or the other. Even when it tells us otherwise, the ego makes sure that we do not rest because if we do - we will also fail. So, with a smirk, the ego sits back watching us sweat it out between a rock and a hard place. As time passes, its smirk widens because it has taught us that we have only a certain amount of time to reach this destination. As time passes, the ego slowly pushes this rock toward us. So we spend most of our "limited" time in an illusionary search for an undefined goal that moves away from us every time we think we have reached it, and we wonder why we feel stressed, unfulfilled and unsuccessful.

The biggest joke the ego plays is allowing us to define, and put parameters around, the illusion of success. And so we proudly and determinedly follow all the rules, laws and regulations that are set by our definitions and parameters. After much work and dedication, the ego may allow us to finally reach our destination, and we feel happiness and satisfaction for a moment in time. But soon, the same thing that we felt fulfilled by, now becomes less meaningful. It turns out not to be the everlasting success we thought it would be. And so the ego convinces us that if we were to set the bar higher, true success would come. But setting the bar higher on something that does not exist will not bring us everlasting success. And it is not until we realize that our definition of success, regardless of our manifestation of it, is a never-ending raising of the bar. When this realization occurs, we achieve freedom from the illusion. It is this realization that enables us to let go of the illusion. For, in this world, success begins with the recognition that we do not need the bar.

So put the bar aside my friend, and remember the true meaning of success. You are a success. Free will allows you the right to hide it, or realize it. You will grow, but it is your choice as to how and how much. You have free will, thus you can decide to grow through pain or through joy. The way you grow is secretly the way you believe you need to grow. As a child of God, you need never grow through pain, but if you believe this is the only way you will listen and succeed, then you will choose this path.

Being On or Off Your Path:
OBE Given for Chapter Four

During the time that I was writing this chapter I had an OBE (out-of-body experience). I was out of my body and looking for a girl named Casey. I'm not sure what brought on this experience, but throughout the night I had a lot of trouble sleeping. I almost never have trouble sleeping, but on this particular night, I woke up almost every hour on the hour.

Finally, I decided that someone was trying to tell me something. I realized that someone wanted me to meditate, to be quiet and listen. So I did. A few minutes later, I found myself out of my body and in search of a girl from my past named Casey, someone I hadn't thought about in a long time.

Casey was the most beautiful young lady I had ever seen. A natural beauty - she never needed makeup. I don't remember angels looking that beautiful, and let me tell you I've seen a few. She literally took my breath away. A simple look at her would make my knees quiver. I can't remember her eyes very well, for getting too near to her would make me nervous. But I believe her eyes were a mixture of light green and blue.

Interestingly enough, the first time I saw her, I had no such reaction. It was my first year at a Colorado university, and I was having lunch by myself in the cafeteria. She was sitting with a friend. I saw them, but really paid no attention to them. After a few minutes passed, she invited me to sit with them. I thought that all people in Colorado were this friendly, so I didn't think too much of it. The year came and went, and I saw her around campus but really did not look at her twice.

Toward the end of my second year, Casey and three students were involved in a car accident in which she was the driver. One of the students died, another was very badly injured and the third recovered after some time. Casey did not receive any serious injuries, at least no physical injuries. Many of us in school were shocked by the news of the accident. Yet, I had no idea that Casey or the others were involved because, at that time, I had forgotten her name and simply did not know the others involved.

A Mass was held for them, and I chose to go simply to offer whatever spiritual help I could give. I cried during the Mass as I prayed for those involved. I was very surprised by my reaction. After the Mass, I found out who the people in the accident were.

Toward the final month of the school year, I noticed that Casey came back to school. I tried to talk to her, but the conversations were simple and I did not feel close enough to her to speak about the accident or anything too heavy. I could see that she simply was not all there.

Then, in my third and last year at the school, I became attracted to her in a way I could not explain. I could not understand what had happened to her or to me during that summer that so changed my attitude toward her. Suddenly, her beauty seemed overwhelming: a living angel, I thought. I had in the past dabbled in poetry, and my feelings for Casey brought back the desire to begin writing poetry again. I wrote a poem about her. I can't recall it now, except maybe the first verse, which went something like this:

God, has an angel fallen from the sky?

If not tell me why,

Twenty times I would die,

For a glance from her eyes.

Although Casey and I talked here and there, I could not muster up the courage to ask her out. I decided that I had to find a civilized way to approach her, so on February 14th, amidst our conversation, I asked her if she had received flowers for Valentine's Day. She responded that for the first time in her life she received no flowers. Well, I thought this was my big chance! The next day, I skipped my first class in order to get her a rose. We had the second class of the day together and after missing the first part of the class, I walked in quite late and received a critical glance from the professor. But nothing mattered now, for I was ready.

After class, I caught up with Casey on the way out. I was quite nervous for I had no idea how she would react. But I went for it. I shared with her that this should not be her first year without flowers, and I presented the rose to her. To my great surprise she seemed really happy to receive it. She even told me that I was now "on her list." I guess that's Colorado talk for being on her good side. Although I failed to ask her out, we talked a little bit, then went our separate ways.

However, I felt that she reacted so favorably to the rose that it would be great to present her with the poem I had written. So the next day I did. She never thanked me, so I felt maybe I had moved too fast, too soon. I was also too shy to ask her how she felt. I soon heard that she began seeing someone else and I decided to simply back off. We talked here and there, but our relationship never went beyond casual conversation.

Until the night of this OBE, I had always asked myself "What if I had tried harder to get to know her, what could have happened?" At least if I had asked her out, the worst that could have happened was that she could have said, "No thanks, psycho!" After graduation, I heard she married the person she was dating and had a child.

So why am I sharing this tale? After a very long time of not thinking about her, I found myself having an out-of-body experience, in search of Casey. I had no clue why I was looking for her and at that point, I did not even ask myself the question. I just knew that I wanted to find Casey.

During the OBE, I saw myself on a hill going downward, and I asked another spirit that was going up the hill where Casey was. She told me that she was at the "halfway house" and pointed in the direction of a yellow house toward the bottom of the hill. I thanked the spirit and went on my way. As I came closer to the house, I knew that I had been there before. It was a very familiar place for me. I walked up a couple of steps and entered through the door. On the other side of the house was a dirt and rock path where spirits were walking up and down the hill. Again I started walking downward looking for Casey. I said to myself, "I don't care if kissing is not allowed in this place. The first time I see her, I am going to give her a big kiss on the lips. Even if they kick me out and send me to hell for rehab, I'm going for the lips!"

Interestingly enough, Casey was hiking up the path with three other people. I saw her and she saw me. She came toward me smiling her perfect smile. I looked at her, walked right up to her and laid a Hollywood movie-type kiss on her lips. "Wow," I told myself, "that was a long time coming!" We both laughed a little and started talking.

We talked about missing our path, although I don't recall if "path" was the actual word mentioned. I told her that it was my fault and that I had been too nervous and shy to ask her out. She kindly told me that she understood that it was my tough childhood that made me react to her the way that I had. She told me not to feel badly because she took another path after we had missed ours. She told me she was with a new "client." I said, "Who do you mean?" wondering about the use of the word client; "Your husband?" She answered, "Yes." I asked her where she was currently on the physical plane, and although she understood my intention, she did not say. She said we might meet again, and that made me happy. She also said something about meeting in a yellow house, and I thought she might have meant the halfway house I had come through to find her. In the end, she said she had to go. I hugged her and she disappeared. As she disappeared, I found myself back in my body.

The reason I bring up this story is because I've often wondered about missing certain "primary paths" while here on Earth due to whatever psychological situation I find myself in. Maybe at that point I was not at the level I needed to be to complete that path so I missed the path with Casey. Casey said I should not worry because she had taken another path. I believe the path she took was another primary path rather than a secondary "just in case" path. I believe that, due to the circumstances involved and where we were in our lives, our getting together would not have been the most opportunistic situation available for our growth at that moment in time.

This brings me to an important point. Some of us have the perception that we have missed our path and, as a result, cannot live a fulfilling life. Most of us have had opportunities, relationships and friendships that we believe never got to "the next level." Somewhere in our hearts, we feel that we blew it! We think that we just didn't make it happen, that the relationship somehow should have been more. Most of us have that feeling, and live with those feelings with a little sadness because of the way certain things, events or relationships turned out. This is a little bit tough, and I know and understand how people feel because, as illustrated, I have felt this way myself.

So what do we do about these feelings? How can we see things differently? Is there another way of looking at this? Again we have to start with remembering who we are and where we come from. We must try to remember our truth, our base for whatever we experience. We are a part of God, and God is only Love. Therefore, we are only love, and to feel anything other than love for ourselves is simply unnatural. We know that peace of mind is our natural state of being. So how do we remember our natural state in such situations?

Right now, we might be feeling a little sadness because we believe that somehow we have missed our mission, that we have lost an opportunity - that we have blown it. Yet, in being silent, we recognize that this feeling is simply unnatural. It is not, in truth, what we are about. We have faith that everything that happens to us happens for a reason, the reason being our own growth and our own good. Because it happens for our own growth and good, it can then be regarded as a gift and not as a lost opportunity or a missed mission. When someone gives us a present, our natural impulse is not to feel sad, but happy and thankful. If we cry at all, it is not because of sadness but because we are grateful. Every experience we have offered ourselves is a wonderful gift, so be grateful for it. Be happy, smile and laugh. Not only have we offered ourselves this wonderful gift, but all those involved have played an important part in our receiving this gift. Be grateful for them, for they have offered us an opportunity for growth, an opportunity to be more at peace with ourselves and to learn.

Today, when I think of Casey, I smile. I thank her in my heart for being a very special person in my life. In her own way, she helped me on my journey toward remembering my Godself. She offered me a wonderful gift; she allowed me to remember that everything that happens, regardless of how I might see it at that moment, is a gift and an opportunity for growth. It is an opportunity to be grateful to my fellow traveler. As she offered me a gift, so too did I assist her on her journey. I allowed her the freedom to pursue what she needed most at that time and in those circumstances. A new and perfect mission was laid for us from which to learn. Although I may never see her again, physically, spiritually in my memories and in my heart, we will always be together. And who knows, maybe we'll meet outside the body again in that yellow house. If we do, I promise you this, I will surely try to steal another kiss.

Success, Our Jobs and Life

Many of us, myself included, were brought up to be like someone in the family. Many of us were brought up without the freedom to be who, in our hearts, we wanted to be. Some of us were told what we would be at an early age, and so we never truly searched our hearts for an answer as to what our highest purpose is in life. Some of us went to college simply because it was the step that society taught us would lead to success. We had no clue why we were going to college other than because it was the thing to do. It was what our parents wanted us to do; it was what our friends were doing. Society and our families told us that if we went to college and worked hard, we would be successful, and if we didn't choose college, we would not. Our families would be proud of us if we went to college; we would disappoint them if we didn't. For many of us, it was implied that we had no chance at happiness if we didn't go to college.

As far back as I can remember, I was told that I would be president of our family's company in Venezuela. My grandfather started the company in 1945. By 1997, it had an 87 percent share of the market. I remember when I was very young, my uncle, who was the president, coming to the house, and my family asking me, on cue, what I wanted to be. Like a great actor, I would say my line: "I am going to be the president of the company." Over and over, I would repeat the line and my family would smile and clap in acceptance. And God forbid, if my mother should ever see me with the competitor's product!

I spent summers working in the company, learning the business and building relationships. After graduating from college, I immediately started working in the finance department. I worked there for more than a year and was then promoted to a charge with more responsibilities in one of its subsidiaries. After having worked for the company full time for three years, I applied and was accepted to the Master of Business Administration (MBA) program at the University of Notre Dame. Everything was going exactly as planned, my family was very pleased and I could foresee achieving the presidency in the not too distant future.

But God works in mysterious and beautiful ways, for in the middle of my MBA program, our company was not only sold, but sold to our archrival, our main competitor. In secret negotiations, my uncle sold our company to our lifelong enemies, and worst of all, I had no idea until a couple days after the deal was completed. My grandmother called and woke me up with the news. So what I had prepared for all my life had, in a moment, disappeared. There I was, in the middle of my MBA program, and for the first time in my life, I had nowhere to go. My lifelong goal had been completely erased from the map.

My younger cousin, who is about seven years my junior, was basically in the same boat except that he was in the middle of his college program at Babson University (the university from which my uncle graduated). Like me, he was also in a state of shock. Yet even more interesting was the exact day his mother called him to tell him the news, during that same phone call, she also wished him a happy birthday! Coincidence? I think not. I could recall his mother teaching him from the time he was born the same family phrase that I had learned. At four years of age, he already knew the answer to the family question: "What are you going to be when you grow up?" He would answer to our family's smiles, "I'm going to be the president of the company." I would smile because I knew that this poor, delusional child was just kidding himself; he could only grow up to be vice-president, for in my mind the president's job was already mine.

I graduated with an MBA from The University of Notre Dame, and asked myself, "What's next?" I had studied enough spiritual material to understand, and more importantly, believe in my heart, that there is no such thing as a coincidence. I knew that a company that had been in my family for over 50 years could not be sold without my knowledge, in the middle of my MBA program, by coincidence. I laughed for a while, and told God that this definitely was one of His best jokes and that He really got me on this one.

In a deeper manner, I understood, and was grateful that He had freed me. He was offering me a respectable way out. He understood that I probably did not have the strength to deny my Latino mother and grandmother the joy of knowing that I was working in the family business. It would have hurt my mother and grandmother deeply if I did not pursue that line of work, and for that reason only, I would have stayed in the business regardless of any real sense of belonging there. God had taken the pressure off me. And for that, I was grateful.

Still, after my MBA, I went back to Venezuela and worked in another family business. However, the family had started this business only seven years prior, thus the responsibility to continue working there was in no way as strong. I worked there as a consultant for nine months, completing a couple of big and interesting projects, but the desire to continue working for the company simply was not there. At the end of the ninth month, I resigned. I then went back to the States, hired my cousin and began a new business. I had my cousin traveling to and from San Paolo, Brazil. There he met the sister of my business partner. This incredible woman became his wife two years later. Coincidence? I think not.

As you can tell, I understand something about the pressures that come with working for a family business and living other people's dreams. As you would not want others telling you what you should do with your life, so too will you save yourself years of questioning, judgments, disappointment, anger and regret if you just allow others the freedom to follow their aspirations and dreams in the best way they know how.

Allow Others to Fulfill Their Dreams

Many people have trouble letting go of the idea that they cannot control the actions of loved ones and, generally speaking, the actions of other people. By letting go, we gift our brothers and sisters with the opportunity to let them experience their journey in the best way they know how. I know that for some people this is a difficult concept to put into practice, so I offer the following five steps to help put into practice the idea of letting go:

- If asked, offer advice but don't be attached to an outcome.
- Respect how a person chooses to live his or her life.
- Never judge yourself or others for the choices you or they make.
- If you so wish, pray or meditate for clarity.
- Trust that God has the perfect scenario in place, so that the individual can learn his or her lesson in the most fruitful way possible.

First, if asked for advice, by all means offer it, but do not be attached to a specific outcome, or to our brother or sister following our advice. My friends, we will save ourselves and others years of stress, anger, disappointment and resentment if we allow our brothers and sisters to follow their own hearts. If our brothers and sisters know that they can come to us for advice without criticism and judgment attached to it, we will forever be their sounding board. They, in turn, will forever respect and most importantly, listen to what we have to say. If we are attached to our brothers and sisters following our advice, we will end up judging and criticizing their efforts and decisions. They, in turn, will put up walls every time we question or try to advise them.

Second, respect an individual's choice and respect how a person chooses to live his or her life. I believe that people, regardless of what they are or aren't doing, are where they need to be at that point in time. We all have lessons to learn in life, and no one other than God knows for sure what those lessons are. Most of the time, we are not consciously aware of what lessons we are in the process of remembering until after the fact. So if we don't know what we are learning at that moment in time, how could any other human know what we are to learn and go through? If we have no clue what a person is in the process of learning, then we should try not to make judgments on how they personally choose to proceed. We will have great difficulty achieving peace of mind and joy unless we respect how others choose to live their lives. That means respecting everyone's choices: the drug dealer on the street, the Pope, a homeless person, the president of the United States. To respect how someone lives his or her life is to be able to look at people without judgment. For example, we can choose to respect a stripper for the human being that he or she is and, at the same time, decide not to support his or her activity financially. To be at a place where we are able to not judge someone's life requires understanding. We need to understand that we don't really know how a person's actions are going to affect him or her or everyone and everything around him or her. We can't judge him or her, because we really don't know for sure what lessons that person needs to learn at that point in time. Thus, because we truly don't understand absolutely everything about the situation, we should not attempt to judge the situation.

The third step toward letting go is to never judge ourselves or others for the choices we or they make. We know when we have made the right choice, because we feel peace in our hearts. If we make a decision and do not have peace about it, we probably did not make the best choices. Choosing with love brings about a peaceful state; a lack of peace is brought about by choosing without love. But again, something very important must be added here: because we have chosen without love does not mean that God judges us for choosing that way, because He knows that, in the end, we will choose with love. Choosing without love simply allows us an opportunity to know how it feels, and offers us the understanding that our choice brought us a lack of peace. We will therefore put ourselves in a similar situation again in order to learn to choose with love. A similar situation will occur and we will have other opportunities to choose with love and receive peace. If we again choose without love, we will experience a little more pain. But this greater pain simply helps us better understand that these are not the kind of choices that are natural to us. The same kind of situation will occur over and over until we learn to choose with love.

The fourth step encourages prayer or meditation in order to receive clarity with regard to our situation. My friend, if you knew how ready the universe is to support us, you would never again question whether our situation is too petty to bring up. We don't ask God for too much, we ask Him for too little. Clarity is eternally available, and our intent to receive it is all that is needed. If our teachers have told us that no question is too stupid to ask, wouldn't we think that the universe is at least as wise? My brother and sister, no question is too petty or small to bring up. Trust me when I tell you that the universe literally smiles when, through our questions, we align with it.

The fifth step is to trust that God has the perfect scenario in place, so that anyone can learn his or her lesson in the most fruitful way possible. How many times have we planned something, but it didn't happen and we became upset? In its place, something else happened, and we enjoyed it more or learned more from it than we would have probably learned from our first choice. Someone once said, "If you want to make God laugh, then tell Him the plan you have for your life." God has the perfect plan for our lives, yet something very important must be added here: God's greatest gift to humans is free will. Free will means that we must make our own choices. My friend, if God offers us free will, don't you think aligning ourselves with God makes sense? God, being all-knowing, already knows how our lives are going to turn out, and the lessons that we will learn. Yet we still make the choice of how and when we will learn our lessons. So we, along with our spiritual guides, set up opportunities and situations that will give us the best chance to learn the lessons we need to learn. God, and only God, already knows what we are going to choose, but it is still our choice to make. Even our spiritual guides don't know what we will choose to do; their job is simply to guide us toward making the most loving choices.

I'm not someone who believes in coincidences or accidents. I believe with all my heart that everything happens for a reason. I believe with all my heart that everything that happens, no matter how we choose to perceive it, happens for our own good, so that we might learn something from it. I believe with all my heart that when we meet someone, be it a homeless person, a person at a party, or an individual through the Internet, there is a reason for our meeting. There is something to be learned through the experience. The relationship could last a minute or a lifetime, but it has been offered to us as a gift to assist us on our journey toward becoming more caring human beings, toward understanding our fellow man or woman better, toward becoming more Godlike.

When I meet another human, I try to see the gift that has been placed before me. I look for the opportunity to remember the perfection in my brother or sister. I know that if I can see it in a so-called stranger, I can see it in myself. For, in my heart, I believe that we are all one, that we are all a perfect part of God. From our homeless brothers on the street to Jesus himself, we are all a perfect part of God, no one is greater or less than the other. And it is in seeing and experiencing this that I remember that I am also a perfect part of God. I forget this sometimes but I know that forgetting is simply a way of remembering better. So when the gift of the presence of other brothers and sisters is offered to me, the gift I receive is the opportunity to remember my perfection by allowing them to choose their own way; and the gift I offer them is to make their time here, be it a moment or a lifetime, a little gentler, kinder and more loving.

Who is the Homeless One?

> [7]*If a man walks in the woods for the love of them half of each day, he is in danger of being regarded as a loafer; but if he spends his whole day as a speculator, shearing off those woods and making Earth bald before her time, he is esteemed an industrious and enterprising citizen.*
>
> Henry Dave Thoreau, *"Life Without Principle"*

As we continue to question ourselves about what a successful or fulfilling life looks and feels like, understand that the ego has already secretly taught us what it looks and feels like. We now think we know how it looks and feels because in one way or another, consciously or not, the ego has already defined it for us, and on some

[7]See Notes, page xv.

level we have already accepted the ego's definition. My friends, continue to question, for if we have not received total peace in regard to this issue in our lives then we have not fully questioned the ego's answer. Consider the following example: There are two men, one who is homeless, and the other driving a Ferrari. Understand that after reading the previous sentence our egos have already stored within our minds what a homeless man and a man driving a Ferrari look like, how successful and fulfilled their lives are, who has followed the rules and who hasn't, and who is the happier being. So what would the ego-self see and what would the Godself see? How would the ego-self feel about both men and how would the Godself feel about them?

The ego-self would see both men as separate; separated by their bodies. It would see one man as being successful and one man as being a failure. The ego is the ruler of the world of illusion and in that world success is mostly defined by material possessions. Those self-enslaved by believing that illusions are real fabricate the idea that happiness is obtained by becoming successful, and that success is mostly measured by material possessions. Put another way, the ego would have us see a homeless man with no possessions as a failure, as an unhappy person, as a lower being to be pitied or feared, or even as someone with whom we should be disgusted. It would also have us see the man in the Ferrari as a happy, successful man and a higher being to be admired and respected.

The ego, the ruler of the world of illusion, would have us believe that the homeless individual is a failure because he has not followed the rules of the ruler. The ego would have us believe that if we were to follow its laws, we would be successful, and if we don't follow its laws, we will fail. The ego is thus saying that this man is homeless because he has failed to follow its rules. The ego would also warn us that if we don't follow its rules, we will also be seen as a failure and made homeless.

The ego rules by fear because that's all it knows. It has invested a lot of time into making us believe its fairy tale is true. It has already instilled in us the belief that we can be a failure. It knows that we fear being a failure and that we fear being homeless, and thus it uses these fears against us in order to control us. But the only reason that we fear being a failure and that we fear being homeless is that we believe that we can be. Fear and failure are used by the ego to chain us to its world. It has also enslaved many others in its name, and has taught them how to judge those who dare not follow its laws. The ego, with its soldiers of judgment, observes our every move. From its ivory tower, it guards our every thought, waiting for us to disagree with its laws, to send its judgment upon us. Those who believe themselves to be enslaved by the ego, those who see the ego as their master, carry out this judgment. They obey the ego because they fear the ego. Because they have bought into the ego's illusionary thought system, they believe that they and their brothers and sisters are separate, and because they are separate, one can be judged without affecting the other.

And so we see the homeless man on the street, and we pity him. Because we believe in separation, we see him as less than us. We tell ourselves that it is because he has not followed the laws of the ego that he is where he is. We might even be disgusted by or afraid of him, for the ego has taught us how to judge those who do not fit its mold. The ego tells us that those who do not follow its rules are dangerous more often than not. It tells us that they might want to take our possessions away or even hurt us, so we lock our doors and roll up our car windows in an effort to further separate ourselves from our brothers. As we do this, our heart silently begins to ache, for separating ourselves from a brother is not a natural reaction. Our hearts feel empty and we wonder why, for we are following the ego's laws, the laws that the ego swore would make us happy and whole. We feel as if we've missed opportunities, and deep down in our spirit, we know we have. We pass by a homeless man and feel as if something stays with him, almost as if our spirit is reaching back trying to embrace our brother. Our body begins to walk away but our spirit holds on to our brother for as long as it can. It holds on while it tries to remind us of the truth within us both.

But the ego is watching, and we won't have others judge us for doing something out of the norm. So we walk away, and we dismiss our heart's appeal by rationalizing that whatever assistance we would have offered would have made no difference, or would have been misused. We think we would have made no difference, but out of six billion people, God chose us, be it for a moment in time, to be with our brother, to assist our brother. Out of six billion people, God chose us.

The ego tells us that our behavior is normal, that this is safe, that we will not be judged if we follow the norm. And yet after following the ego's rules, are we still not judged every day of our lives by others who also see themselves as being normal? Has the world, that is ruled by the ego, truly found peace by following the ego's rules? Is the world any better off if we step away and turn our heads the other way as we walk by homeless brothers? Yet, isn't this what the world would have us understand to be a normal reaction, a reaction that will be less judged by our brothers?

So my friend, I ask your heart, for only your heart can answer these questions truly: Who is really homeless here? Is it the person who is asking for assistance, or is it the person who will not assist? Is it the person on his knees reaching out for you or is it the person who, as he walks by, turns his or her head the other way in order to not be bothered? Is it the person who has lost everything, or is it the person who will not search his or her soul? My friend, your heart knows the answers to these questions because your heart holds on to the truth of who you are. The ego would have you look away from your heart, but where has this thought system ever truly gotten you? Has it offered the world peace? Has it even offered you peace?

The time is coming when we will choose to look within. The time is coming when we will look into our brother or sister's eyes and see ourselves reflected in them. For when we truly look at a brother or sister, when we look closely into his or her eyes, do we not see ourselves reflected in them? Does this mean nothing to us? My friend, if there is one thing I can promise you it is this: The time is coming when we will turn to our brother or sister, take his or her hand and smile.

The following quote by Norman Cousins author of "Human Options," illustrates how every situation presents an opportunity to demonstrate compassion to our brothers and sisters.

8Compassion is not quantitative. Certainly it is true that behind every human being who cries out for help there may be a million or more equally entitled to attention. But this is the poorest of all reasons for not helping the person whose cries you hear. Where, then, does one begin or stop? How to choose? How to determine which one of a million sounds surrounding you is more deserving than the rest? Do not concern yourself in such speculations. You will never know; you will never need to know. Reach out and take hold of the one who happens to be nearest. If you are never able to help or save another, at least you will have saved one. To help put meaning into a single life may not produce universal regeneration, but it happens to represent the basic form of energy in a society. It also is the test of individual responsibility.

Service

Martin Luther King Jr. once said:

9"Everybody can be great because anybody can serve. You don't have to have a college degree to serve. You don't have to make your subject and verb agree to serve. You only need a heart full of grace. A soul generated by love."

I once read that service is love put into action. Yet if we ourselves are love, and love put into action is service, then any time we're in action we're in service. Service, as defined by the ego, has boundaries and parameters that the ego's world decided fit or didn't fit its definition of service. The ego says we're being of service if we do A and B, but not if we do C and D. It tells us that those who are doing A and B have bigger hearts and are better people than those who do C and D. The ego tries to have us believe all this to further separate us from our brothers and sisters.

8See Notes, page xv.
9See Notes, page xvi.

The Godself knows that every moment we're interacting with another human being, regardless of its physical manifestation, is a moment of service. When we smile at one another, we are being of service. When we pray for one another, we are being of service. When we give hope to one another, we are being of service. When we are assisting or being loving to one another, we are being of service. Any moment when we are being who in truth we are, we are being of service. This point was driven home to me when I experienced the second OBE offered for this chapter, which is described below.

Will I Ever Make a Difference?

I have always wondered whether I would be able to make a difference and be of service to others. I wanted to be like my uncle, who has been a very successful businessman, creating thousands of jobs for people in Venezuela. As a young man, I remember thinking that to earn that kind of respect and make that kind of difference, I would have to equal or exceed my uncle's accomplishments. It was always such an exhausting mental exercise to even imagine closing the difference between his accomplishments and mine. In my mind at the time, if I did not come close to his accomplishments, my life might be seen as a failure by me, my family and the outside world.

I remember at the beginning of my business career, praying to God to allow me to become a great business leader. That way, I too could create a great number of jobs and lead a great number of people. At the age of 30, I had completed my college degree, had gotten my MBA, and had worked in the family business for a few years. I had completed the plan the world, my family and I set up for me. I had done everything right. Yet I still felt that I was not in or heading to a satisfying place. How could I be doing everything right if I was not comfortable or at peace with where I was? It just did not make any sense! How could I not be in the "right" or "good" place if I was taking the "right" path?

Soon after my 30th birthday, I started to become very concerned with my progress. Although I had everything that a 30 year old could possibly want, I was still dissatisfied, and my idea of greatness, of making a difference, was not materializing. I was upset at my lack of progress. Internally, I blamed my uncle for not making "it" happen for me. I began to wonder if anything that I was doing was making a difference.

One night after my frustrations peaked, I decided to take my complaints to the man upstairs. No, not my uncle, but to God Himself! Although I did not have an institutionalized, religious-based relationship with God, I did feel that I had enough of a personal relationship with Him that I could file a complaint. I got into a meditative state, quieted my mind and began my inquisition (sorry, I meant to say I began my prayer). I vocalized all my feelings, and became quiet in order to hear the response. I waited and waited, got nothing, heard nothing and fell asleep.

The next morning, right before awakening, I got a response that would forever change my life. It was a simple message, yet with this thought form came such a profound understanding that my life would be eternally affected. The message, or thought form, was as follows: "Concern yourself not with leading a great number of people but learn to lead by example every day." That was it. Yet from that thought form it became crystal clear that we all touch and serve an innumerable number of people during our lifetime; that we can and do, in every single individual interaction, lead people to a more happy, peaceful and beautiful world or lead them to an angrier, more stressful, more confusing and chaotic world; that we all can be and are great leaders; and that we all literally create the world we live in by our interactions with each other.

In this OBE, I was given an example where I was led through an individual interaction where I offered love and peace. The example felt like it lasted just a moment in time and yet it seemed to forever flow through eternity. I was shown how one individual interaction touched not only the person with whom I interacted but flowed to those with whom they interacted and so on. I wondered how many people my one interaction affected, and in that one moment I was brought into a stadium full of people. I was in such awe of the number of people that single interaction in one way or another touched, that I had to hold back the tears. An angel smiled at me and said, "No, not yet." He lifted me above the stadium and there I saw what seemed to be a thousand more stadiums filled with those my one interaction had in one way or another touched. I could no longer hold back the tears. Before this thought form, I believed that the only way I could make a difference in the world was by directly leading or serving a great number of people. But it was there that I learned about the magnificence of the moment, the importance of even the shortest conversation, the beauty of a kind glance, the value of a caring smile, the substance of a gentle touch, the magnitude of an honest compliment and the magnificence of a warm hug.

Before that thought form, I went through the day without noticing the splendor of the great service that could be provided in the moment. Today I'm eternally grateful for even the shortest of interactions, and now, like a small child on Christmas Eve, I look forward to each and every moment as a present waiting to be unwrapped, experienced and shared.

Before that thought form, I would open doors for people or give away my seat on the bus simply because I was taught that it was the right thing to do. Today, I experience great joy in such actions and thank God for being able to be there for the interaction. I now see any moment that I can be of service as offering a great service to humanity.

Before that thought form, I found silence boring, and tried to find something to drown it out. Today, I use those moments to fill my body and soul with a light filled with absolute peace and gratitude that I then use to expand out into the world. And as the world breathes a little easier, so too do I.

Before that thought form, I fought to better myself and directly lead and serve a great number of people. Today I find peace and love in the moment. This expands to everyone I touch and with whom I interact, and they in turn expand what I offer them to others. By doing so, I serve the world. By simply knowing the truth about my brothers, sisters and myself, I help lead the world to a more peaceful and joyful place.

My friend, you touch the world on a much deeper level than you currently perceive. Do not concern yourself with the number of people you believe you need to lead or serve at one time to make a difference. For knowingly or not, you change the world with every interaction you have with a fellow brother or sister. Lead by example, it is truly that simple. Offer love and you will find your world more loving. Serve the person in front of you and you will find the world a more caring and hopeful place. Smile and laugh with the person you interact with and you will experience a happier and more peaceful world. Do whatever brings you joy, and the same world that you once cried in, you will now smile and dance in.

A fulfilling life also comes as a result of loving and serving others. Author Leo Buscaglia puts it this way in his book, "Born for Love:"

> [10]*We all have so many possible occasions for loving and yet there is so little demonstrated love in the world. People are dying alone, crying alone. Children are being abused and elderly people are spending their final days without tenderness and love. In a world where there is such an obvious need for demonstrated love, it is well to realize the enormous power we do have to help and heal people in our lives with nothing more complicated than an outstretched hand or a warm hug. Day's end is a good time to reflect on what you have done to make the world a better, more caring and loving place. If nothing springs to mind night after night, this can also be an excellent time to consider how you can change the world for the better. You need not perform monumental acts, but act on the simple things which are easily accomplished: the phone call you have not made, the note you have put off writing, the kindness you have failed to acknowledge. When it comes to giving love, the opportunities are unlimited and we are all gifted.*

I am ending this chapter with a favorite short story that I first

---

[10]See Notes, page xvi.

read in the book "Chicken Soup for the Soul." It illustrates the point that one person, by his actions, can make a difference.

One at a time

[11]*A friend of ours was walking down a deserted Mexican beach at sunset. As he walked along, he began to see another man in the distance. As he grew nearer, he noticed that the local native kept leaning down, picking something up and throwing it out into the water. Time and again, he kept hurling things out into the ocean.*

As our friend approached even closer, he noticed that the man was picking up starfish that had been washed up on the beach and, one at a time, he was throwing them back into the water.

Our friend was puzzled. He approached the man and said "Good evening, friend. I was wondering what you are doing."

"I'm throwing these starfish back into the ocean. You see, it's low tide right now and all of these starfish have been washed up onto the shore. If I don't throw them back into the sea, they'll die up here from lack of oxygen."

"I understand," my friend replied, "but there must be thousands of starfish on this beach. You can't possibly get to all of them. There are simply too many. And don't you realize this is probably happening on hundreds of beaches all up and down this coast. Can't you see that you can't possibly make a difference?"

The local native smiled, bent down and picked up yet another starfish, and as he threw it back into the sea, he replied, "Made a difference to that one!"

[11]See Notes, page xvi.

5

WORK ON YOURSELF FIRST

Friend, the world we see outside of ourselves is simply a reflection of the world that we have shaped and supported within. The world we experience is simply an extension of our minds. The level of stress or peace we experience in the world is in direct correlation to the level of stress or peace within our minds. The more at peace we are with ourselves, the more peaceful the world will appear to be. The more peace we have in our inner world, the more peace we will experience and extend to the outer world; whereas, the more stress we feel within, the more stress we will experience and extend into the outer world. The correlation here is not what is occurring in the world, but how we feel about ourselves within our minds. My friend, it is for this reason that we are asked to work on ourselves first. If we work on our minds, the rest will follow. As we change our thoughts and minds, we change our perceptions of the world and the way we react and participate in it.

Throughout this book, I will make the following points repeatedly as I have done already: joy and peace are our natural states. If, in any situation, we are not at peace, it is because we have misperceived reality. We have lost our peace of mind, not because of some external force, but because of a simple misperception of reality. A reinterpretation of reality is all that is needed to obtain peace. Our interpretation of an event, not changing the event itself, accomplishes this. Realizing and acknowledging that we can do this with one event brings us closer to the realization and understanding that we can do this with all the events in our lives. Again, if we can find inner peace in one event by reinterpreting reality through our Godselves, the possibility becomes real that we can do this with any event in our lives.

The following words were written on the tomb of an Anglican Bishop (1100 AD) in the crypts of Westminster Abbey and illustrate how one man recognized the importance of working on himself first:

> [12]*When I was young and free and my imagination*
> *had no limits, I dreamed of changing the world. As I*
> *grew older and wiser, I discovered the world would not*

[12]See Notes, page xvi.

change, so I shortened my sights somewhat and decided to change only my country.

But it, too, seemed immovable.

As I grew into my twilight years, in one last desperate attempt, I settled for changing only my family, those closest to me, but alas, they would have none of it.

And now as I lie on my deathbed, I suddenly realize: if I had only changed myself first, then by example I would have changed my family.

From their inspiration and encouragement, I would then have been able to better my country and, who knows, I may have even changed the world.

Working Through the Illusion

As we continue to work on ourselves, understand that if something is causing us anger, stress, unhappiness, regret or any other "negative" emotion, we are, by definition, experiencing an illusion. We will experience the illusions we still think are real. We will do so because we have made the unreal - real, and the best way to understand that what we see as valuable is actually valueless is to experience its valuelessness. Many times, when people awaken from a particular illusion, they hold themselves in judgment for having so viciously defended it. I gladly and gently remind them that they should not judge themselves, but should be grateful for the experience, and proud of their awakening. My friend, it is an awakening once we realize that the unreal, regardless of how real people want to make it, is unreal. The greatest gift any illusion can offer is the opportunity to let us see it for what it truly is.

Trying to be who we are not is hard. Negative and judgmental thoughts, emotions and reactions, simply aren't who we are. Because we're acting as someone we are not, this will drain us of energy. Spending time protecting and defending valuelessness, what we are not, is draining. Release these emotions, and we will be set free. Release these emotions, and we will have more energy than we ever thought we could have.

Understand that as we continue to work on ourselves, the ego will not sit quietly in the corner. It has invested a lot in making us the way we are. It has taught us how to be "normal." It has taught us how to judge and how to be stressed. The ego has taught us and most of the world that the unreal is real. It has created a chaotic thought system that it makes us call normal. Seeing the unreal as real creates a delusional state. Living in a delusional state creates confusion and finally chaos. For example, a mad man, or someone in a delusional state believes that what he sees is completely real. Regardless of how much sense it makes or how much pain and confusion it brings, he will defend his state as real. The ego has us call this painful and confusing state "normal" or "real life." This is the one reason we find difficulty in achieving lasting peace in our everyday experience. This world calls chaos peace, which is why we have not experienced lasting peace.

The ego tells us that, if we disagree with it, we are by its definition not "in the norm," or, in other words, not normal. The ego has us silently and secretly question ourselves for not being normal. It has us question the direction in which we're headed, and also our sanity. The ego then makes it acceptable for those in the norm to judge those outside the norm. Remember that the ego's ultimate goal in any situation is to separate us from our brother or sister. If we dare to disagree with it, it encourages us to feel like fools for having believed that the unreal was real in the first place. If we don't see ourselves as fools, it encourages us to look upon our brother or sister as a fool. If we finally see the unreal as unreal, it tries to make us believe that we are more spiritually advanced than our fellow brother and sister who still see the illusion as real. Even when it compliments us, its main goal remains to try to separate us from our brother or sister. It tries to sell us that because we're more spiritually advanced, we are also better. It tells us that we should be on a high pedestal, so that more of our brothers and sisters are able to hear and see us. This is all in an effort to further separate us from our brother or sister. But, my friend, an awakened spiritual teacher would never think or speak of himself or herself as a higher spiritual being than anyone else. Such a teacher knows that the simple act of leading by example is a great gift to offer the world. And he or she is as equally honored to talk to one child of God as he or she is to talk to thousands of people on the highest of podiums.

The ego has the world judge and criticize us for not being like it, and the ego has us judge and criticize the world for judging us. Decide not to play the ego's game. Do not judge the world for judging us. We release the world by forgiving it of its judgment of us. As a small child would judge us for taking a knife out of his hands, so will the world judge us for thinking unlike itself. Put the knife in a safe place where the child will not be able to reach it. The young child will not be able to reach the knife, and neither will the world be able to reach us with its judgment, for we are now in a higher place where we realize that what the world judges in us does not exist. Now, when the world attempts to judge and criticize us for our non-conformity, we smile, but not from a sense of superiority or importance, but from the relief and freedom we receive by not having to play the ego's game.

Former President Theodore Roosevelt said the following on handling critics:

[13]*It is not the critic who counts, not the man who points out how the strong man stumbles or where the doer of deeds could have done them better. The credit belongs to the man who is actually in the arena, whose face is marred by dust and sweat and blood, who strives valiantly, who errs and comes short again and again because there is no effort without error or shortcomings, who knows the great devotion, who spends himself in a worthy cause, who at best knows in the end the high achievement of triumph and who at worst, if he fails while daring greatly, knows his place shall never be with those timid and cold souls who know neither victory nor defeat.*

[13]See Notes, page xvi.

Thought, Action, Faith and Gratitude

I have mentioned before that the world we see outside our-selves is simply a reflection of the world that we have shaped and supported within. As the ego has trained our minds to react in a judgmental and stressful manner, so too can we retrain our minds to act and react with peace and joy. There are four steps to retraining our minds in order to obtain and experience peace and joy in every situation. They are:

Thought - Align ourselves with God and clarify the goal.

Action - Act with unconditional love.

Faith - Trust that the moment is perfect.

Gratitude - Give thanks, enjoy and rejoice.

Thought - Align ourselves with God and Clarify the Goal

My friend, it is only at the thought level that we can exercise choice. Just as what we see comes from what we value, so does what we do come from what we think. My friend, we are in paradise, but if we choose to believe that we are in a dump, then that is where we'll find ourselves. Where we stand is not nearly as important as where we think we stand. Where we think we stand unconsciously comes from where we want to be standing. Where we want to be standing, comes from where we believe we deserve to be standing. It is this belief; it is what we value that we will see. We could stand in the middle of heaven surrounded by angels, but if we consider ourselves not worthy enough, we will never see it or them. Again, we could stand in the middle of heaven surrounded by angels, but if we believe we deserve hell, then that is what we will see. In the end, it is our choice to make.

If, through our perceptions, we are experiencing any type of negativity it is due to negative conditioning by the ego. The ego will always respond first in any given situation, because this is how we have been trained and taught. We have been taught that the ego's world is the real world, and thus we think like it, and think it normal and correct to behave this way. If instead of listening to the ego, we align ourselves with God first, we can gain clarification about what it is that we want to accomplish, which will allow us to take control and handle any situation in a way that serves our highest good. I like to ask myself what Jesus would do in my place. What would Jesus' goal be in this situation? How would Jesus think, act and react? Again, I would like to remind you that Jesus is simply the example that I use because I feel a connection to Him. You can also use Him as an example, or you may equally and just as successfully use whichever "self-actualized being" you feel the most connected to.

Let me offer you three small but personal examples of how I worked on myself to undo the negative conditioning taught to me by the outside world and the ego in my life.

My Big Toe

I'm not sure what the record is in the "Guinness Book of World Records" for stubbing your toe, but there was a time during a two-month period when I had to be close to that record. Every time I stubbed my toe, I uttered an expletive, or at least thought an expletive. I had been taught by watching others react this way. It was the "normal and acceptable" way to react to such an incident. It was the way I had been unconsciously trained to react. My friends reacted this way, so I felt that it was fine. Yet, little by little, I became uncomfortable with such a reaction. One day, I decided that there must be a better, more positive way to react to such an incident.

I needed to clarify my goal - I want a more peaceful and positive way of reacting to the act of stubbing my toe. So I'm walking my dog Texas, thinking about how I can react more peacefully in such an instance, and all of a sudden, within my head, I hear "Thank me!" It literally sounded like I had a small stereo installed in the middle of my brain. The echo of those words was so clear that I felt it touch every cell in my head. I turned to Texas, hoping he had heard it too. Just as I did, I tripped on a crack in the sidewalk, and to my amazement, the words that came out of me were not expletives, but "Thank you God!" "Wow," I thought to myself. "That's a real nice thing to say in response to such an event." I then decided that I would train myself to thank God every time I stubbed my toe, so little by little, I did just that. Before I knew it, I was thanking God for the times I tripped and almost fell. In every situation that I used to react with some kind of expletive or negative thought, I retrained myself to simply thank God for the situation. Immediately, without thinking, I said, "Thank you God" every time I tripped or stubbed my toe, and I felt really good about it. Wouldn't you know that soon after I learned this, I stopped stubbing my toe and tripping. Now, whenever I trip or stub my toe (I'm glad to report that the incidents are now under the national average), I simply thank God, and this reaction feels natural, positive and peaceful.

Sarcasm

Another example of how I have untrained my ego-self and aligned myself more with my Godself is in forgiving people immediately. Whenever someone, even a friend, was sarcastic or said something mean to me, I immediately responded by saying or thinking something sarcastic or mean in return. I'm sure that you have joked with friends, only to cross the line where you teased them with a statement that made everyone laugh. Everyone laughed, including you and your friend, but deep inside you felt bad for having made your friend the butt of the joke, and you felt that he or she, deep inside, was hurt. There are even times when you're angry with someone, so you choose to hurt that person with words. You use a sarcastic, indirect statement that outwardly does not sound bad, but inwardly you know it has stung the person. You could use the excuse that this is how people interact with each other; you could say to yourself that this simply is the way things are. I have also used these excuses. However, there came a time in my life when saying something that could be interpreted as hurtful or sarcastic by another became painful for me. I teased a friend with a statement, and everyone laughed, including the person being teased, but deep within I could feel his pain, and his pain became my pain. I again had to go deep within to ask myself for a better and more peaceful way of co-existing with my brother. Once again I clarified the goal, which was how I wanted to react in those instances and what I wanted to say in response to such comments. My goal became to obtain peace in such circumstances, extend it to all those around me, and be equally funny but without using sarcasm.

At first, it was not easy to allow those cheap shots to go undefended, especially when I had a beautiful comeback. But interestingly enough, I felt much better for not defending myself against cheap shots and simply forgave my friends. Whenever I began to feel hurt, I simply forgave. I forgave and I was set free from the cheap shot. I forgave the insult and backhanded compliment, and became free from them. When an easy, sarcastic, cheap shot came to my mind, even when I thought it was funny, I simply kept it to myself, reminded myself that this was not who I wanted to be and released the thought. Although it might have been funny, I knew it would also bring pain. Inwardly, I felt very good about what I was doing. If a sarcastic thought came to mind that I knew had the possibility of hurting someone, I simply corrected it in my mind before letting it out. Interestingly enough, people who took cheap shots at me in the name of humor began apologizing for their comments. If they did not apologize, I could look deep within them and feel their regret for expressing the comment. After hearing the comment, I would always inwardly and sometimes outwardly forgive the individual, and by doing so I was released from feeling the sting. It almost became part of the norm and people would look at us funny whenever one of my friends forgave another for making a humorous but mean-spirited comment. I must admit that I was quickly forgiven a couple of times for jabs I took at friends, and I must say my friends found that when they forgave me it was extremely funny. Now if you were ever to walk into a restaurant or bookstore and see a bunch of people sitting around a table, laughing and forgiving each other, don't be apprehensive - it's just us.

In the end, I ended my use of sarcasm, yet I was just as funny, but not at anyone's expense. My heart reminded me that humor, if expressed at someone else's expense, wasn't humor but hurtful.

When I learned to follow my heart and align myself with God, not only was my humor more appreciated, but I also became more at peace with myself.

The "God Bless You" Kid

Some time ago, I boarded a plane headed back to Miami. I was on the right side of the plane, in a three-seat row, seated in the window seat. A woman I did not know was sitting in the aisle seat, and there was no one sitting in the middle seat. Being in tourist class, and being 6'4" and 220 pounds, I was hoping that either a model would sit next to me or that no one would sit in the middle seat. As soon as I silently expressed my hopes to God, a woman and her eight-year-old child dashed them. The mother told the young boy to sit in the middle and that she would sit a few rows back. Normally, I would have offered my seat to the mother and let her sit with her child. But two things stopped me from doing this: one, the mother really seemed to be relieved that she would have some time to herself, and two, the kid seemed to be a little hyper and complained about sitting by himself. I figured I could give the mom some rest and, at the same time, teach this brat a little courage and independence. Because I was doing two good deeds with one action, I figured that if the plane went down, I would definitely have a better chance of surviving than those people who had not done their good deed for the day! Plus, I was now sitting next to a child, which in and of itself, spiritually speaking, has to offer more protection.

The boy sat next to me, and immediately started talking. Of course the first thing he mentioned was that he gets sick on planes. "Just wonderful," I thought. So I psychologically started convincing him that the plane was safe by telling him that I fly this route all the time, that the ride was always smooth and that he would be perfectly fine on the flight. He seemed to be content with my past experiences and prediction so he then began to share his life story. Thank God he was only eight! In general, the kid seemed to be pretty cool. He would share some of his views about life with me, then would turn to the lady on the other side of him and share his views with her as well. He was a very considerate young man, I thought.

It must have been cold and flu season because there were many sneezes on the way to Miami. On average, I am not someone who notices or cares about people sneezing on the plane, but today I had the "God Bless You" missionary sitting next to me. Yes, every time someone sneezed, regardless of where in the plane he or she was sitting, the kid responded with the words "God Bless You." Now I'm not sure if the Green Berets trained this kid, or if he simply had bionic ears, for regardless of where a person was on the plane, if they sneezed, this boy could hear it! Not only that, but the farther he perceived an individual to be, the louder he would bless them. After the first few "God Bless Yous" the people on the plane, regardless of their location, answered him with "thank you." This created a comfortable and friendly feeling on the plane.

The experience made me think back to the days when I was a kid and young adult, and I would also answer a sneeze with "God Bless You." Somewhere on my journey to adulthood, not only had I dropped the "God" from my response to someone sneezing, but many times after hearing a sneeze I wouldn't even reply with "bless you." This experience got me thinking about how beautiful that response was, and how great it would be for me to bring it back into my life, and the life of all sneezers. I silently promised myself that, regardless of whether or not I felt comfortable responding in such a manner, I would reintroduce it into my life. It was a beautiful response and I now knew that I wanted to use it in my life and share it with others.

The plane landed safely, and the kid who at first I perceived to be a brat, I now saw as a great being. I told him that I thought he was a great kid and that I really enjoyed my time with him. In the end, I was the one who learned a powerful lesson from him. I was richly blessed by his presence. I finally told him that I would miss him, but deep in my heart I knew that somewhere, sometime, on a future flight, I would again hear those precious words coming from a seat way in the back of the plane. The people on this future plane ride will smirk and some will laugh at this response to someone's sneeze. As for me, I gladly look forward to a reencounter with this great teacher.

These three small examples - stubbing my toe, forgiveness and the "God Bless You" kid - are provided to show you how I chose to put aside what the world taught me to be normal, and remembered what my heart said was true. In aligning myself with God, I made peace the basis of all my thoughts, actions and reactions.

Do you want peace? This is simply what you must ask yourself in every situation. The clarification of the goal comes at the beginning of every situation. If your goal is peace, you will experience peace.

Please remember that I'm not saying, in this or any part of this book, that my way is the way. I am simply providing you with a few examples of how I have found peace of mind and joy. You might need to experience something totally different and that is fine. Do whatever brings you peace and you will find peace. There is nothing else that needs to be said. If you do not know what brings you peace, then experiment and understand how what you think and say affects your emotional state.

Action - Act with Unconditional Love

We will know when we act with unconditional love because when we do, we will experience peace. Peace is the result of unconditional love. Unconditional love is its own reward.

We all make attempts at kindness and forgiveness. At times, we have also been surprised at what little gratitude and outward praise we receive when we offer kindness and forgiveness. Sometimes, we might even become angry or sad at the lack of response to our gift or action. But is anger or sadness really the way we should react to such a beautiful offering? How do you feel when reacting in such a manner? I've already mentioned that there are two ways you can respond: one is with your ego-self, and the other is through your Godself. One has been taught to us by society, and one has been birthed in us by God. One has to be learned, and the other simply needs be remembered. One feels wrong and makes us feel heavy, sad and upset. The other feels right and makes us feel joyful and peaceful.

The ego's goal is to separate us from our brother and sister. Regardless of the manifestation of the situation, if separation is its final outcome, the ego has reached its goal through us. As an example, in the act of giving, the ego has different levels of illusion that it uses in order to achieve its goal. All illusions, regardless of their manifestation, have as a final result separation and loss of peace. The ego will sell us one illusion after another in order to keep achieving its purpose through us. We see the ego's illusions as different manifestations with separate outcomes. Yet there is one outcome to truth, and one outcome to illusion. In any situation, it is the outcome that we value most that we will experience.

If illusions are by definition nothing, then different illusions can only be encountered through our attempts to separate nothingness into parts. Only the delusional mind can see different levels of nothingness as separate and real. We can stack up our hundreds of thousands of personal levels of illusions and still not come close to the height of an atom. Only a delusional mind can believe that it needs to fight through different levels of nothingness, with different levels of answers, to obtain peace. The ego supports the efforts of a delusional mind, for the ego is the father and creator of the delusional mind. And a creator will support his creations. Although there are countless levels of illusions that the ego supports, there are four main illusionary barriers that the average delusional mind passes through in order to find the truth about the subject of giving. I offer these four, not only because they are the ones I personally had to pass through, but also because I have seen many of my friends and family members experience them. They are:

- If we give, we lose.
- If we give, we must get something of equal or greater physical value in return.
- If we give, we must at least get something of mental value in return.

- If we give, all situations must be judged as separate and given separate consideration with regard to getting something or anything in return.

Let's discuss these points one by one. First, at the height of its control, the ego would have us believe that to give is to lose. It tries to convince us that if we give, we will also lose something and there is no way to get it back. If we lose something, then we become less than we were before, or we will have less than we had before. We have fewer things, thus we are lesser people. The world teaches that when we give something away, we lose it, and if we don't get anything in return, we are less complete, less whole. The world also teaches that, when we lose something, we must become upset. So it is not a stretch to say that the world teaches us that becoming upset is a normal and proper reaction to giving something away and not getting anything in return. Yet, we know that being upset is not the natural reaction of a child of God, because a natural reaction of the child of God is to be at peace. Therefore, there must be another way of looking at the beautiful offering of giving.

Second, if the ego can no longer make us believe that to give is to lose, it tries to make us view the giving of anything as a trade. If we still choose to give, the ego will let us know that we must, at the very least, get something of equal value in return. Therefore, in the ego's calculation, although we have lost something, we have also gained something and we come out equal. Of course, the ego will then make us analyze whether we came out on top or not in the trade. If we come out ahead, the ego will congratulate us and allow us to do it again, as long as we always come out on top. If, in the ego's estimation, we come out on the bottom of the trade, it tells us "told you so" and that we should have never given in the first place. It encourages us not to make the same mistake again. However, if we continue to play the trade game, it will have us make sure we come out on top in our next trade. Here, the ego makes a mental list of who we can "beat" in such tradeoffs. We continue to play with those we can beat. Those we can't beat are either erased from our list or put at the very bottom.

Third, the ego understands that eventually we will no longer believe that to give is to lose. It also understands that we will not see giving as a physical tradeoff. So it allows us to give without the tradeoff, meaning we don't really need to get anything physical in return. But it makes sure that at least we get a thank you from the receiver. If we don't get a thank you, it makes us upset at the receiver's inconsideration. Out of our beautiful offering, what we get in return is anger at our brother's inconsideration. The ego laughs when we get offended, for it knows that it still has control over us. It still has control because, in the end, it made something ugly out of something beautiful, and it separated us from our brother or sister. In the end, it wins by separating us from our brother or sister.

Fourth, the ego understands that, for the most part, it cannot control our thoughts, actions, or reactions. But this does not stop it from attacking on all three levels on a case-by-case basis, looking for weaknesses in our thought systems. The individual at this stage knows that giving is its own reward. The individual gets satisfaction in the thought and act of giving and does not need anything physical or mental in return from the receiver. At this stage, the individual receives as he gives, and need not ever hear from the receiver to be gladdened, because he understands that all receivers, regardless of outward manifestations of gratitude, are grateful for the intention and action.

Would God not be thankful for any offering, regardless of how small it is? Would God not be thankful and proud of one of His children offering a gift, or even a kind word to another of His children? Would He not acknowledge the purity of our thoughts, the kindness of our actions? So what does it matter if another person outwardly thinks of our gift as worthy, or does not even acknowledge it? For the truth is, and this I believe with all my heart, that in the receiver's mind there is a part of him or her that joins with God in thanking us. There is a part in our brother or sister that joins with God in saluting our actions. There is a part in every single person, regardless of how hard they've tried to hide or forget it, where God resides, and this part blesses every gift we offer.

Every gift we offer a brother or sister is given and received by God. Thus, what we give away, we keep. And in the end, only what we give away do we ever truly keep. No gift is ever lost; no gift is ever left thankless. And know that I thank you, because every gift you offer to your brother or sister, you offer to me.

Faith - Trust that the Moment is Perfect

Increasing our faith is a part of the process of changing our world from the inside out, changing our attitudes and perceptions and changing our lives. So what happens when we have a problem, we know the solution to our problem, we execute the solution, but nothing within us changes? Here is an example. I was in a group once where a woman (let's call her Jane) was involved in a custody battle with her husband (let's call him... Tarzan) and his lawyer for visitation rights with their fifteen-year-old child. Jane shared her story by describing Tarzan as passive aggressive, and his lawyer as a bitch. Jane explained how this was draining her, and asked how she could see her situation differently. Many people gave very good and spiritual advice, explaining to her that what she was seeing in another was simply a projection of who she believed herself to be. They tried to explain to her that what she was experiencing was really an illusion; they told her that she needed to forgive and pray for her husband and his lawyer. Jane explained that she understood what people were saying. She said that she agreed with them, and that she had tried many of those suggestions, but she still could not find peace. She had the answer, she made an effort to execute the solution, but she still could not find peace.

Before I continue, let me say this: My friends, we bless this world by allowing our brother or sister to experience the illusions he or she still sees as real. Imagine, if you will, Jane walking in a garbage dump. Jane knows she is walking in a dump, she can smell it and feel the instability beneath her feet, but she still chooses to walk in it. Jane feels unstable and insecure, so she asks her friends to help her and they tell her that she is walking in a dump. Jane agrees with them. They show her the way she can walk to get outside the dump. Her friends even remind her of a beautiful park just outside the dump. Jane believes that what they are saying is true and it feels right to her. Jane follows her friend's advice and walks on the path her friends tell her leads out of the dump. Jane can see the park in the distance. She understands that she has a choice. After many, many circles around the dump she finally makes the choice to follow the path and walk out. She finds herself outside the dump, yet she cannot stop thinking of the dump. Although she now walks in a beautiful flower-filled park, she can't stop thinking of the dump. Just the thought of the dump brings back the smells, and although she sees herself walking on firm ground, she feels unstable and insecure. Jane looks back and can't see the dump anymore, but she imagines the many people still walking in circles in it. She cannot understand why she still feels a part of the dump even though she has physically left it. She has done the right thing and she knows she made the right decision. She feels proud of having made the choice to leave the dump; however, like flies in the dump, those thoughts and feelings of insecurity and instability still surround her.

Jane believes she knows her highest will. She listened and did what she knew was right and what would bring her peace. Yet, somehow she believes that she needs to add something to her highest will to make it complete, and because of this she lacks trust. For Jane, and all of us, a lack of trust will never be a consequence of doing our highest will. Our highest will or His will is perfection and perfection needs nothing added to it. As long as we believe that something needs to be added to perfection, we will not find rest or peace, because we will be on a continuous search for something that does not exist. My friend, even if you choose to transplant a rhino's tusk onto a horse you will not get a unicorn. Do what brings you peace; do what you believe to be right, and then trust. It is truly that simple.

My friend, listen carefully, for I have experienced this on many occasions. You will be lifted as high as you choose to go. You will choose to go as high as you believe you deserve and have the right to go. You will go as high as you trust Him to take you. No one else will make that decision for you. You will be taken by the hand and lifted toward God and only you will stop this process. You may create a gate, paint a wall, or simply believe yourself not worthy enough, but only you can block your connection to Him. If you actually had faith in your connection to Him, you would never need to worry about a gate. As the river flows into the sea, so too do you naturally flow to God. You need do nothing but simply allow. It is only your choice to hold onto a branch of the riverbank that will delay your conscious unity with God.

As our trust in God lifts and unites us with Him, our faith in His plan and in His will, will bring us absolute peace. I have said many times before that God's will and our highest will are one and the same. If we trust this, we will find peace. If we fail to trust this, we can do all the right things for the right reasons and stand in the most beautiful of places on this planet and we will not find peace. My friend, peace is our natural inheritance, but it is only when we choose to accept our inheritance that we allow ourselves to receive, experience and enjoy it.

We truly have only two choices: illusion and truth. We can either try to add to perfection, or we can experience perfection. The only thing that Jane lacked was trust. Jane did all the right things, said all the right words, but in the end she did not have full faith in what she was doing. She was looking to add to perfection instead of simply experiencing it. If we are looking to add to perfection, we will not find rest. We will not find rest from continuously looking for something that does not exist.

If our brothers or sisters want to add, or believe they have to add to perfection, then let them. They must look outside themselves to find they are missing nothing. And they will find nothing real, because nothing real is missing. They will find a lot of illusions and make them real, only to find out later that they were illusions and nothing else. They will not find rest, for they will never find what they are searching for. They will search until they realize that what they were looking for does not exist. My friend, it is exhausting to try to be who you are not. Once we recognize this, we will look no more and finally find rest.

The most difficult step in obtaining peace lies not in remembering truth, but in faithfully executing its principles. Peace of mind lies not only in the execution of the principles, but also in your absolute faith in them. One of the main methods of obtaining peace of mind is your ability to forgive. If you know that peace of mind is given to you when you choose to forgive, and you want peace badly enough, you will forgive. But, and this is a big but, if you do not have absolute faith that what you are doing is the right thing and that it will bring you peace, you will not find ultimate peace. Ultimate peace of mind comes when you can forgive someone and have absolute knowledge that it is God's and your highest will to do so.

Gratitude - Give Thanks, Enjoy and Rejoice

What if any and every moment we experience anger, frustration and stress could be reinterpreted through understanding, forgiveness and love? Would we not be grateful for such a shift in our perceptions?

Remember in the Godself's view, there is no experience or expression other than that of love or a call for love, a call for assistance. Thus, if in any moment we perceive that our brother is doing something that is causing us anger, frustration and stress, then understand that not only is he asking for assistance, but that we ourselves are asking for assistance. Yes, we have unconsciously asked our brother to help us bring forth to our conscious mind those areas in our lives where we still perceive that reactions and expressions of frustration, anger, and stress are correct and proper responses to God's creation.

Where the ego-self has trained us to act and react with frustration, anger and stress, the Godself is trying to remind us of the true gift that our brother is offering. Remember that every moment that the ego-self defines with frustration, anger and stress, that same moment is seen by the Godself as a gift to be grateful for. The gift is allowing us to consciously bring up the blocks to our awareness of love's presence. The blocks must be brought to the surface, seen, experienced and understood before they are dismantled, and that is what our brother is offering us. Once the blocks to our awareness of love's presence are dismantled, all that is left is the awareness of love's presence in every moment. Would we not be grateful to our brother or sister for this offering? Would we not be grateful to them once and for all for assisting us in dismantling the blocks of frustration, anger and stress and showing us the moment as it truly is? Is not the replacement of anger, frustration and stress with love a wondrous gift? Would gratitude not be the proper response to such a gift?

So forgive your brother or sister for what you think they have done to you. Forgive the moment for your interpretation of it. In truth, your forgiveness is a way of saying thank you for your brother or sister's participation in your remembering process. Thus, instead of using judgment as a response to your brother or sister's action, understand and remember what your brother or sister is truly offering, and forgive and thank him or her for it.

If you were awake, you would be thankful for each and every moment. Gratitude is the knowledge that God's will is being done. My friend, if we can take any of the ego's efforts and, instead of judging or cursing them, offer gratitude for them, the shift we will feel and experience will be not only noticeable, but life changing. It will be life changing, for if we can see one of the ego's efforts as an illusion that we can simply forgive, it will open the flood gates to the knowledge that we can treat all of the ego's illusions the same. My brother and sister, imagine for a moment how our lives would change if what we once cursed and judged we now forgive and bless? How would this change our lives? Would gratitude not be our response to such a change?

My friend, try shifting your perception from a thought system based on lack and scarcity to a thought system based on kindness, abundance and gratitude. What do you have to lose? You have likely tried it the ego's way and have been rewarded with judgment, sorrow, regret, animosity, hostility and pain. Know that God is in you, as well as in your brother and sister. Know that the part of you and your brother and sister that is God recognizes, acknowledges, salutes and blesses even the smallest gifts or the slightest kind word you offer. Believe me when I say that even the most Lilliputian of efforts to be kind and loving to your brother and sister is honored by God.

Continue to work on re-training your mind, for as your mind begins to heal, the world itself will begin to heal. There will be days when you experience life through the ego. There will still be days when you allow the ego to tell you what is right. On those days you will experience judgment, stress and pain. But now there will also be days when you will simply listen to your Godself. These days, you will experience love, peace of mind and joy. Do not judge yourself for listening to the ego, but simply stop when you experience judgment, stress or pain and ask yourself if this is truly what you desire. Regardless of what kind of day you are choosing to experience, offer gratitude for it, for it is bringing you into closer alignment with your Godself. As author Dan Millman writes in his book, "No Ordinary Moments:"

> [14]*Life has cycles. Whatever goes up, comes down, and what falls can rise again. Progress can be slow: We remember, then we forget, then we remember; we take two steps forward, then one step back. No matter how enlightened we become, we still face the realities of daily life.*
>
> *A lesson on enlightenment may be learned from the following anecdote:*
>
> *A young man had spent five arduous years searching for truth. One day, as he walked up into the foothills of a great mountain range, he saw an old man approach from above, walking down the path carrying a heavy sack on his back. He sensed that this old man had been to the mountaintop; he had finally found one of the wise-ones who could answer his heart's deepest questions.*
>
> *"Please, Sir" he asked. "Tell me the meaning of enlightenment."*
>
> *The old man smiled, and stopped. Then, fixing his gaze on the youth, he slowly swung the heavy burden off his back, laid the sack down and stood up straight.*

[14]See Notes, page xvi.

"Ah, I understand," the young man replied. *"But, Sir, what comes after enlightenment?"*

The old man took a deep breath, then swung the heavy sack over his shoulders and continued on his way.

Socrates (character in the story) once told me, "A flash of enlightenment offers a preview of coming attractions, but when it fades, you will see more clearly what separates you from that state - your compulsive habits, outmoded beliefs, false associations and other mental structures." Just when our lives are starting to get better, we may feel like things are getting worse because for the first time we see clearly what needs to be done.

"After illumination," Socrates continued, *"difficulties continue to arise; what changes is your relationship to them. You see more and resist less. You gain the capacity to turn your problems into lessons and your lessons into wisdom."*

6

TRUSTING GOD

Lily Tomlin once said: "Why is it that when we talk to God we're said to be praying, but when God talks to us we're schizophrenic?"

Do you trust God? If you were asked this question, your immediate response would probably be, "Yes, I do trust God." If you were also asked: Do you ever worry? Your answer would probably be, "Yes, I worry sometimes." My friend, allow me to say that if you truly trust God, then you would never worry. If you choose to worry in any situation then know that you are not fully trusting in God.

Trust God or worry. These are the two choices that we have in every situation. Trust God and be at peace. Worry and experience stress. Our choices are that simple, and we make our lives as peaceful or stressful as we choose to make them. Trust God and be at peace. This is all that is asked of us. Yet, over and over again, we choose worry over trust, and make our lives a living hell.

Our level of peace is directly related to our level of trust in God. The more we trust God, the more peace we experience. The less we trust God, the less peace we experience. If we choose to completely trust God, then stress will not be a part of our experiences. If we experience any level of stress, it is because we have chosen not to fully trust God.

You might be trying to convince yourself that you can trust God and worry at the same time. Yet, my friend, if you consider the irrationality of that possibility, you may reconsider your thinking. How could you fully trust the Creator of the universe with a specific event in your life and also worry that He is not carrying it out with your best interests in mind? You could say that the Creator does not have your best interests in mind and therefore you are worried, but somewhere deep within, you know that this is not so. How could the father of peace, happiness, kindness and love have anything but your best interests in mind? It is this that you need to remember when you experience worry or stress in any situation.

In her book, "The Christian's Secret of a Happy Life," Hannah Whitehall Smith writes:

*[15]And remember, there are two things that are more
utterly incompatible than even oil and water, and these
two are trust and worry. Would you call it trust if you
should give something into the hands of a friend to
attend for you and then spend your nights and days in
anxious thought and worry as to whether it would be
rightly and successfully done? And can you call it trust,
when you have given the saving and keeping of your
soul into the hands of the Lord, if day after day, and
night after night you are spending hours of anxious
thought and questionings about the matter? When a
believer really trusts anything, he ceases to worry about
that thing which he has trusted. And when he worries,
it is plain proof that he does not trust.*

Trusting "God's Plan"

Any situation in our lives that we regard as a problem can be
perceived in two ways, one is through our ego-self and the other is
through our Godself. We can let our ego-self take control and allow
it to grow this problem into the most chaotic situation imaginable.
We can stress and worry, and blame and separate ourselves from our
brothers and sisters for what we think they did to us. Our ego-self
will let this problem or issue grow, even affecting relationships with
those around us who had nothing to do with it in the first place.
Like a virus, the ego-self will have us infect them, making them a
part of the problem, having them take sides, having them separate
themselves from their brothers and sisters, and in turn creating an
even more chaotic situation. Or, we can choose to trust God. If we
work through our Godselves, we will understand that this problem
has been presented as an opportunity for growth. We can forgive
ourselves, and our brothers and sisters and be grateful for the experience and their participation in it.

The more we choose to judge an individual or situation, the
more an individual or situation will consume us. The more we
judge a brother, sister or situation, the less joy we will experience in

[15]See Notes, page xvi.

our lives. This happens regardless of whether we believe ourselves to be "in the right" or not. Judgment consumes joy. Again, in any moment, we have a choice, and it is between judgment and joy. The one we value more, in any situation, is the one we will end up experiencing.

Let's take a personal example and work through it. Several years ago, I began judging a situation that involved my uncle who I had perceived as not using his power to offer me a better position in his company. In my perception, I had all the credentials necessary to reach the next step on the ladder and he could, because of his position, give it to me. This did not happen as I envisioned it would and I became quite upset. As I thought about the situation late one night, I understood that the emotions I was feeling were childish, so I quieted my thoughts, prayed and asked for clarity and peace in regard to this issue.

As much as I wanted to fantasize and bring the past into the present in order to make myself the victim, make myself justified in being upset and make him the bad guy, in a moment of clarity I finally understood what the underlying issue was. The answer I received was simply this: "Trust our plan."

The problem with my uncle was, in fact, a very simple one. The bottom line was that I did not have faith in God's plan for my life. The problem was not created by my uncle or his action, but by my unwillingness to trust God and to trust that He had a better plan for my life. Again, and throughout this book, I say that God's plan for your life and your highest will are one. This was what was meant by "trust our plan." This statement was inviting me to put aside my ego-self, to put aside what was bringing me judgment, stress, worry, blame and separation and to allow the real message of the moment to come through. This statement was inviting me to put aside the veil of the ego-self so that I could see and allow the true gift that was presenting itself through the manifestations of the present moment. This gift, once illuminated in love, allowed peace and joy to once again be experienced. However, prior to this realization, I had decided that my ego-self's plan for my life was better suited for me than God's plan for my life. I had decided that I knew more about what was best for me than God did. I had decided to trust my ego-self's plan for the universe instead of God's plan. The only real problem was my lack of faith in God's decision-making skills. I mean, He could create the universe and all living things in it, but He could not take care of my little personal family issue, right?

From this example, you can see that whenever the emotions or incidents you experience are perceived with aversion, you have chosen to trust your ego-self's plan for the universe over God's plan. You have chosen to have faith in the way you believe life should be, rather than faith in God's offering. You have chosen to depend on your perception over God's knowledge. You probably don't know what you are going to have for lunch tomorrow, let alone what is in the best interest of the universe!

In every circumstance, in every instant, we are gifted with the free will to choose how we will react. We can choose to react with worry, conflict, chaos and confusion, or we can choose to react with trust, peace of mind, love and joy. Every instant, regardless of its manifestation, allows us the opportunity to begin anew, to experience life with peace of mind, love and joy. The knowledge that we have the power to react to any circumstance, any time, and in any way we desire, is the beginning of understanding the absolute power of free will.

When we say the words "Thy will be done" we are equally saying "May my highest will be done." There is no difference. Trust, peace of mind, love and joy will come about by choosing to have faith in God's plan for our lives. Our highest will and God's will are one. God's plan for our lives is our highest will for our lives.

You are the vehicle God uses to express Himself on this planet. Allow Him to flow through you. It is only by allowing this that His expression can be experienced. Believe it or not, we have the final decision on what will flow through us and into the world. Not even God would force Himself through us, unless we allow Him to. When we allow God to flow through us, this is our natural flow, this is our trueself, and this is our Godself. My friend, if we allow God to flow through us, we would want no other way. When we allow God to flow through us, peace, love and joy extend through us and into the world. Forgiveness and love are offered immediately to our brother and sister. And what we offer our brother and sister, we experience ourselves, for it must first flow through us. If we allow ourselves to see and feel His expression being expressed through His other vehicles, all we will ever experience will be peace of mind, love and joy.

Everything that happens to us, every situation we regard as a problem, regardless of how negatively we choose to perceive it, is of our will. We have chosen our experiences in order to assist us in our learning process. In a gentler light, problems or difficult situations can be seen as lessons, learning opportunities and gifts presented to us by our Godselves in order to remember our perfection and our brother and sister's perfection.

We have the absolute power and free will to perceive every situation in the light we wish to see it. The light in which we view and experience these situations and problems is simply a reflection of the light within our minds. For we know best what will help us listen, learn and grow. The light we use is not a reflection of the truth about us. It is simply a reflection of what we believe to be the truth about ourselves.

The gift offered to us by God is the free will to choose how we will perceive the situations or experiences in our daily lives. Every day of our lives, we can choose to live in heaven or hell. Every day of our lives, knowingly or not, we make that choice. How much we choose to suffer is, in the end, up to us.

The poem that follows, "An Unknown Confederate Soldier, A Creed for Those Who Have Suffered," is one that so eloquently summarizes our desire to follow our own plans based on what we think is best for our lives. The author shows us that when we trust God's plan, the result is a life with much more meaning than we could have possibly imagined.

[16]*I asked God for strength, that I might achieve.*

I was made weak, that I might learn humbly to obey...

[16]See Notes, page xvi.

I asked for health, that I might do great things.

I was given infirmity, that I might do better things...

I asked for riches, that I might be happy.

I was given poverty, that I might be wise...

I asked for power, that I might have the praise of men.

I was given weakness, that I might feel the need of God...

I asked for all things, that I might enjoy life.

I was given life, that I may enjoy all things...

I got nothing I asked for - but everything I had hoped for.

Almost despite myself, my unspoken prayers were answered.

I am among men, most richly blessed!

Trusting God Through "Accidents"

We have been taught to believe in such things as good luck and bad luck, in accidents and coincidences. Well, I am here to remind you, as well as myself, that there are no such things. All these things are inventions of society, made in the hopes of explaining events that just didn't fit into a "normal everyday experience." Centuries ago, what most people today call bad luck or an accident was explained by saying that the gods were disappointed or angry. But there was usually a way out. They simply made a sacrifice to the gods, an offering to the high priests, or to someone else in power, to guarantee that no such thing happened again. These rituals worked until bad luck or an accident came knocking on their door again.

Most of us have stopped making sacrifices or offerings in order to avoid apparent hiccups in our daily experiences. As always, I remind you that I personally have nothing against such rituals. People, in my opinion, should do and believe in whatever they wish, whatever brings them peace. I am simply offering another way of looking at such events. Most of us no longer believe that the gods are responsible for accidents and bad luck, but we still believe that control of these hiccups is out of our hands and that we have absolutely no connection to their manifestation. We still believe that we have little or no control over what happens to us. I remind you that this isn't so. We not only have control over what happens to us, but we also have control over our attitude and reaction to these circumstances or events.

The following short story speaks to the issue of accidents, good luck and bad luck. I first read this story in Dan Millman's book, "Way of the Peaceful Warrior."

> [17]*An old man and his son worked a small farm, with only one horse to pull the plow. One day, the horse ran away.*
>
> *"How terrible," sympathized the neighbors. "What bad luck."*
>
> *"Who knows whether it is bad luck or good luck," the farmer replied.*
>
> *A week later, the horse returned from the mountains, leading five wild mares into the barn.*
>
> *"What wonderful luck!" said the neighbors.*
>
> *"Good luck? Bad luck? Who knows?" answered the old man.*
>
> *The next day, the son, trying to tame one of the horses, fell and broke his leg.*
>
> *"How terrible. What bad luck!"*
>
> *"Bad luck? Good Luck?"*
>
> *The army came to all the farms to take the young men for war, but the farmer's son was of no use to them, so he was spared.*
>
> *"Good? Bad?"*

[17]See Notes, page xvi.

There are literally no such things as accidents. For example, let's take the extreme case of a life-changing or life-ending car crash. Obviously, a car crash of this magnitude is a major event. If someone you know has died in such an incident, let me sincerely say, before I go any further, that I am sorry for your loss. I understand that in this world, such an event would be perceived with sadness, anger and pain. The ego would have us experience anger, sadness and pain and call it normal and correct responses. Later, the ego would have us blame and judge. Finally, it would have us carry this anger, sadness, pain, blame and judgment for as long as possible. This is the ego's solution for us. This, in short, is what we have been told and taught to be proper responses to such incidents. The ego also tells us that if we follow its laws, we will find happiness and peace. Can we allow our minds to be open to the possibility that the ego's answer is insane? My friend, the ego's insane solution only sounds sane to an insane world.

God is love and only love. God is all knowing. We are God's creations. The only barriers between us and God are those we believe exist. Even if we do believe in these so-called barriers, deep within, we believe that we are somehow connected to God. If we can open ourselves to believing that we are connected, then what God knows, we also know. If God is all knowing, then he knows what is going to happen to us. If He knows what is going to happen to us, then somewhere within, we know what is going to happen to us. Yet, even if we know what will happen to us, we still need to make choices. God's greatest gift to us is that of free will. We have been given the opportunity to experience what we wish and believe we need to experience in order to grow. Earth is a school. We get to choose the classes we believe will best help us grow. God knows us, he knows our curriculum and he knows that we will make it back to Him. How and when we choose to experience our curriculum is up to us, it is our free will.

Back to the case of the fatal car accident. Before I begin to offer the Godself's way of viewing an individual's passing, I will first say this: let each of us feel and experience whatever it is we think we need to feel and experience without judging ourselves for the way we feel or grieve. Do not ever judge anyone else for the way or amount of time they choose to grieve. If they believe they need a few months or years, let them have the time they need. Do not try to force your beliefs on someone who is not ready for them, for all you will find will be a brick wall. The best thing you can do is to be there for them, pray for them, and most importantly, continue to work on bettering and advancing yourself. You can serve someone better by learning to love yourself and others more. The more you learn to love yourself and others, the less you will be bothered by how others choose to experience life and grow. The more you learn to love yourself and others, the more at peace you become, and the more peace other individuals will experience in your presence.

Individuals who pass away suddenly - be it through a car crash, murder, heart attack, etc. - simply choose to pass on this way. Quite simply, there were no further lessons for them to experience during this life. Their physical lives end when they choose to go home. They have successfully accomplished their life purpose. Please understand this one thing: they will not pass away alone. There will be souls that will assist them during the time of transition. They will be supported and great love and friends will welcome them home. Often, in the case of a sudden exit, a guide will immediately be available to the individuals to remind them that all will be okay. The individuals might at first be upset because of their quick exit and because of things they believe might have been left unsaid or unfinished. If this is the case, their guides will offer them a preview of the lives of those who stayed behind. If the person is a father, he will be shown how his kids will move forward. He will find peace in what he is shown. Even his style of exit will offer all who knew him new opportunities for growth. It will be more productive for his kids and all those affected by his passing to learn the lessons they came here to learn without his physical presence.

As a soul group, all those involved will understand that his passing was simply another step in the learning process, and that his choice to move forward and return home allows those left behind opportunities for growth that would not have been available if he had physically stayed on Earth. For that reason, his passing is really a great gift, and not a curse to those left behind. They will grow in many ways because of the physical absence of this individual. This individual will continue his lesson plan at home for now. He will be available to those left behind. He will come to them in dreams, when the body sleeps and the mind is quiet, and reinforce to all that he is okay. He will offer guidance, be it through dreams or other means, to those who wish to receive it. If one of those left behind is advanced enough, he can appear to them in meditation. Whether through meditation or dreams, our brothers or sisters, if we are open to it, will appear to us and tell us that they are fine and at peace. They will watch over us and be proud, and they will offer us guidance whenever we ask. My friend, our brother or sister is still with us, and somewhere deep within we know that this is so.

In "Emmanuel Book 1," the channeled spirit (through Pat Rodegast) talks about "accidents" and "accidental" death:

> [18]*There is no such thing as an accident. When your soul chooses to leave your physical body, it will leave. Life is not an amateur circus tent where those who enter are individual, lonely performers with no script and no director - only a tumbling about, a fling through the air, and then a crash. No, that is false. As souls, you are self-determining. You decide when to be born. You create your life every minute of every day by what you choose to believe. You decide when to die. All things evolve around the total truth of love, balance, order, cause and effect. These are Divine laws.*

Accidents and Choice

An excellent book on the subject of what happens to us in between incarnations, or our life between lives, is titled "Journey of Souls," by Michael Newton, Ph.D. By regressing 29 people, Dr. Newton literally takes the reader on a journey describing what occurs from death to rebirth. One example that I found very helpful in reinforcing my belief that there are no accidents is that of case number 26. This case involved an athletic woman who enjoyed

[18]See Notes, page xvi.

sports, despite having been bothered all her life with reoccurring leg pain. She had been to many doctors for this pain, yet nothing physically wrong was ever found. The following excerpt of the session is taken directly from "Journey of Souls:"

> [19]*Almost at once, the woman dropped into her most recent past life, and became a six-year-old girl named Ashley, living in New England in the year 1871. Ashley was riding in a fully loaded, horse drawn carriage, when suddenly she opened the door and tumbled out and under the vehicle. When she hit the cobblestone street, one of the heavy rear carriage wheels rolled over her legs at the same point above her knees, crushing the bones. My subject re-experienced a sharp pain in her legs while describing the fall.*

> *Despite efforts from local physicians and the prolonged use of wood splints, Ashley's leg bones did not heal properly. She was never able to stand or walk again and poor circulation caused repeated swelling in her legs for the rest of her rather short life. Ashley died in 1912, after a productive period of years as a writer and tutor of disadvantaged children. When the narration of Ashley's life ended, I returned my subject to the spirit world.*

The following is a transcript of the session with Dr. Michael Newton and his subject, Ashley. Ashley had experienced lives as a crippled woman and as Leth, a strong Viking.

Dr. N: In your history of body choices why did you wait a thousand years between being a physically strong man and a crippled woman?

S: Well, of course, I developed a better sense of who I was during the lives in between. I chose to be crippled to gain intellectual concentration.

Dr. N: You chose a broken body for this?

S: Yes, you see, being unable to walk made me read and study

[19]See Notes, page xvi.

more. I developed my mind... and listened to my mind. I learned to communicate well and to write with skill because I wasn't distracted. I was always in bed.

Dr. N: Was any characteristic about your soul particularly evident in both Ashley and Leth the Viking?

S: That part of me which craves fiery expression was in both bodies.

Dr. N: I want you to go to the moment when you were in the process of choosing the life as Ashley. Tell me how you decided on this particular damaged body.

S: I picked a family in a well-established, settled part of America. I wanted a place with libraries and to be taken care of by loving parents so I could devote myself to scholarship. I constantly wrote to many unhappy people and became a good teacher.

Dr. N: As Ashley, what did you do for this loving family who took care of you?

S: It always works two ways - the benefits and liabilities. I chose this family because they needed the intensity of love with someone totally dependent upon them all their lives. We were very close as a family because they were lonely before I was born. I came late, as their only child. They wanted a daughter who would not marry and leave them to be lonely again.

Dr. N: So it was a trade off?

S: Most definitely.

Dr. N: Then let's track this decision further back to the place of life selection, when your soul first saw Ashley's life. Did you see the details of your carriage accident then?

S: Of course, but it wasn't an accident - it was supposed to happen.

Dr. N: Once you came to earth, who was responsible for the fall? Was it your soul-mind or Ashley's biological mind?

S: We work in unison. She was going to be fooling with the carriage door handle and... I capitalized on that.

Dr. N: Tell me what was going through your soul-mind in the life selection room when you saw the scene of Ashley falling and being injured.

S: I thought about how this crippled body could be put to good use. I had some other choices for body injuries, but I preferred this one because I didn't want to have the capability for much movement.

Dr. N: I want to pursue the issue of causality here. Would Ashley have fallen anyway if she had a soul other than your own?

S: (defensively) We were right for each other.

Dr. N: That doesn't answer my question.

S: (long pause) There are forces beyond my knowledge as a spirit. When I saw Ashley for the first time, I was able to see her without me... healthy, older - another possibility.

Dr. N: Now we are getting somewhere. Are you saying if Ashley had begun her life with another soul entity that she might not have fallen at all?

S: Yes, that's a possibility... one of many. She could have also been less severely injured, with the ability to walk on crutches.

Dr. N: Well, did you see a physically healthy Ashley living happily without your soul?

S: I saw a grown woman... normal legs... unhappiness with a man... frustration at being trapped in an unrewarding life... sorrowful parents... but easier. (Voice becomes more firm.) No! That course would not have worked well for either of us - I was the best soul for her.

Dr. N: Were you the prime mover of the fall, once you elected to become Ashley's soul?

S: It... was both of us... we were one at that moment... she was being naughty, bouncing around in the carriage, playing with the door handle when her mother said she must stop. Then I was ready and she was ready.

Dr. N: Just how rigid was your destiny? Once you were Ashley's soul was there any way you could have backed out of this entire incident in the carriage?

S: (pause) I can tell you I had a flash just before I fell. I could have pulled back and not fallen out. A voice inside my mind said, "It's an opportunity, don't wait any longer, take the fall, this is what you wanted - it's the best course of action."

Dr. N: Was that particular moment important?

S: I didn't want Ashley to get too much older.

Dr. N: But, the pain and suffering the child went through...?

S: It was horrible. The agony of those five weeks was beyond belief. I almost died, but I learned from enduring it all, and I now see that the memories of Leth's capacity for managing pain helped me.

Dr. N: Did your inner mind have any regrets during those moments when the pain was most severe?

S: As I slipped in and out of consciousness during the worst of the ordeal, my mind began gaining in power. Overriding my damaged body, I started to better control the pain... the lying in bed... the doctors helpless. The skills I developed in managing pain were later used to concentrate on my studies and my counselor was helping me, too, in subtle ways.

Dr. N: So you gained a lot in this life by being unable to walk?

S: Yes, I became a listener and a thinker. I corresponded with many people and learned to write with inspiration. I gained teaching ability with the young, and felt guided by an internal power.

Dr. N: Was your counselor proud of your accomplishments after you returned to the spirit world?

S: Very, although I was told I had become a little too indulged and pampered (laughs), but that's an okay trade-off.

Dr. N: How does your experience with the strong body of Leth and the weak one of Ashley help you today, or is this of no consequence?

S: I benefit every day by my appreciation of the necessity of a union between mind and body to learn lessons.

During my client's reliving of the street scene, in which her legs were broken, I initiated desensitization measures. At the close of our session together, I then deprogrammed her generational memory of leg pain entirely. This woman later notified me she has had no further pain and regularly enjoys playing tennis.

Asking God for Inspiration

Several years ago, I was traveling through the south and stopped in North Carolina to visit a friend. I met a young woman who was trying to start her career as a gospel/rock singer. One night we had a conversation on forgiveness and before the night was over she asked me to write a song for her on the subject. I explained to her that I had no knowledge of how to write songs but that I would try to put some words together. Again, I promised her nothing but that I would try. For more than an hour before I went to sleep, I tried putting some thoughts on paper but nothing really came to mind. So, I did what I always do when I am stuck or looking for some sort of answer or inspiration - I prayed. Soon after, I meditated for a few minutes, then fell asleep.

The next morning as I was in the state right before waking, I heard and felt a knock on the top of my head. It literally felt as if someone took a knuckle and tapped me on my head. I had never had such an interesting direct physical sensation. But as I began opening my eyes I had this strong need to pick up a pen and write. The poem below is what came to me. In about ten to fifteen minutes I had it all written on a piece of paper.

Love Your Brother

On my journey through darkness,
Judgment dropped me to my knees,

And when I would not take another step,
I met the light within me.

He said: "Fear not for I am your brother,
I am the mirror of you."
In His eyes I remembered my glory,
And in His arms I remembered my home.

He said: "There is strength in forgiveness,
There is truth in His Love,
Find your power in silence,
and in peace, your inheritance."

I had built many walls around me,
I had built many illusions of stone.
But as the light shined on me,
Cracks of hope found my soul.

I had chosen to forget the light,
Yet it never disappeared.
And in blaming my brothers,
It was I that I feared.

Now all my brothers I treasure,
All are diamonds to me.
And through their search I remember,
The truth of love within me.

On your road through the darkness,
Know that your light I shall be.
Until that day of your waking,
Rest your shoulder on me.

And now I say:
"Fear not, for I am your brother,
I am the mirror of you.
Through forgiveness remember your glory.
Through love remember your home."

That morning I gave her the poem. She read it, looked confused (which I first interpreted as looking impressed), looked at me and said, "What does it mean?" I said, "I think it's for you, you'll have to decide what it means." Later that day I got back in my car and continued my journey. We e-mailed each other a couple of times but soon lost contact and I have not seen her since.

Remember Your Perfection

I received the following message the morning after spending a good part the previous night questioning certain aspects of my life.

Brother, I know you question your mission in life. So let me simply say this: You have fulfilled the plan for your life to perfection. Every moment of your life until this moment has been perfect. And I offer you a promise: Every moment until your return to Me will also be perfect. There has not been, nor will there ever be, a moment in your life that has not been chosen by you to experience your perfection, your peace, your truth, or the perfection, peace and joy offered to you by your brother. By recognizing this in your brother, you will recognize this within yourself.

Brother, I know you question your relationship with your parents. So let me simply say this: I was with you when you chose your parents. I was with you when you chose to be reborn into the world of illusions in order to remember that there is no such thing. Your parents were and are your perfect choice to assist you in remembering that this world is an illusion. Your parents were, are, and will be the perfect choice to assist you in remembering your perfection.

Brother, I know you search for peace. So let me simply say this:

Peace is offered to you in every moment. This is a simple recognition you can make. Pain, being the opposite of peace, is a choice you may also make in experiencing the moment. But understand this clearly, pain is a choice, an illusion you choose to make real. You manifest pain by making it real in your mind.

Brother, I know you look in the mirror, and see something other than perfection. So let me simply say this: Close your eyes and look through mine. Choose, for a moment, to see yourself as I see you. Do this honestly once and the joy you feel would flood your body, bringing tears of happiness cascading down your cheeks. You would see My face reflected in each drop of joy, and you would hear angels sing in honor of your glory.

Brother, you look toward the heavens and wonder how I feel about you. So let me simply say this: I am proud of you. I rejoice in you. You are the expression of the mind of God. God expressed Himself and created you. Can you even begin to allow yourself to understand what I am saying? God expressed Himself and created you. Please listen carefully: God expressed Himself and created you.

Through free will, you express your desire to remember your trueself, and create that which you are now experiencing. Listen carefully: You are the creator of the expression of your experience.

God expressed Himself and created you. Love expressed Himself and created you. Peace expressed Himself and created you. Joy expressed Himself and created you. You are the son of Love, Peace and Joy. The truth of who you are is love, peace and joy. You need know nothing else.

We Were Created in His Image

We were created in His image! Just saying this makes me feel good. Any time I even begin to think of judging another human being, I remind myself of this phrase, and I am again connected to my source. I remind myself that the true essence of every individual, regardless of how well he chooses to hide it, is that he was created in His image, that he is the physical manifestation of God on Earth.

This is a beautiful and powerful statement. This single thought feels right to many of us, and therefore we are at peace with it. But I do see a division between what people believe "His image" is, and how they live their lives. This to me is one of the most important questions we will ever answer to ourselves. The answer to this question then becomes the basis of our belief system. Is God a God of love or fear, of pardon or punishment, of peace or pain, of forgiveness or judgment? These are the questions we must search our heart to answer. The answer can be that either God is a God of love, pardon, peace and forgiveness, or He is a God of fear, punishment, pain and judgment. It can be either one of those two, but not both; for what is all encompassing can have no opposite. It can only be answered by our hearts, for it is a place untouched by this world, a place that remembers its source. This question, if asked of most people's hearts, is quickly answered. Most people answer that God is a God of love, peace and forgiveness. Yet, if our hearts answer this way, and we live our lives another way, it creates confusion. Such confusion is disguised by many other names such as judgment, stress, regret, sadness, anxiety, uncertainty and anger. All of these emotions have the state of confusion as their source. Confusion is the result, when we react to love with such emotions.

We have been taught that there are times when it is okay, when we have every right to judge, fear and punish our brother or sister. When we realize that the way the world would have us live is not the way we want to live, we will search for another way. This search will bring us back to our true source. Our source is not this world, our source is God, and there exists a place in our hearts that, when asked, will acknowledge this.

In her book, "The Christian's Secret of a Happy Life," Hannah Whitehall Smith invites us to trust our source with the management of not only the universe, but also of our personal lives. If we choose to do this, faith will begin to slowly dissolve our difficulties away. She says:

> [20]*You find no difficulty in trusting the Lord with the management of the universe, and all the outward creation, and can your case be any more complex or difficult than these, that you need to be anxious or troubled*

[20]See Notes, page xvi.

about His management of you? Away with such
unworthy doubting! Take your stand on the power and
trustworthiness of your God, and see how quickly all
difficulties will vanish before a steadfast determination
to believe. Trust in the dark, trust in the light, trust at
night and trust in the morning, and you will find that
the faith which may begin by mighty effort, will end
sooner or later by becoming the easy and natural habit
of the soul.

Why Are There So Many Religions in the World?

Many people have asked the questions, "How can I trust God when there are so many religions in the world?" and "How do I know which religion is right and which religious teachings are right?" Growing up, I too pondered questions about the religions of the world. As always, when I have a question that I want answered, I pray. I pray with all my heart, and somehow, someway, the question is answered.

The answer to this question came when reading Betty Eadie's book, "Embraced by the Light." In this book, Betty died and went to heaven, where she encountered Jesus. Before this encounter Betty had been a devout Catholic and believed that only those of the Catholic faith had the chance to go to heaven. She asked Jesus this question, and in her book she writes:

> [21]*I wanted to know why there were so many churches*
> *in the world. Why didn't God give us only one church,*
> *one pure religion? The answer came to me with the*
> *purest of understanding. Each of us, I was told, is at*
> *a different level of spiritual knowledge. All religions*
> *upon the earth are necessary because there are many*
> *people who need what they teach. People in one religion*
> *may not have complete understanding of the Lord's*
> *gospel and never will have while in that religion. But*

[21]See Notes, page xvi.

that religion is used as a stepping-stone to further knowledge. Each church fulfills spiritual needs that perhaps others cannot fill. No one church can fulfill everybody's needs at every level. As an individual raises his level of understanding about God and his own eternal progress, he might feel discontented with the teachings of his present church and seek a different philosophy or religion to fill that void. When this occurs, he has reached another level of understanding, and will long for further truth and knowledge, and for another opportunity to grow. And at every step of the way, these new opportunities to learn will be given. Having received this knowledge, I knew that we have no right to criticize any church or religion in any way. They are all precious and important in His sight. Very special people with important missions have been placed in all countries, in all religions, in every station of life, that they might touch others. There is a fullness of the gospel, but most people will not attain it here. In order to grasp this truth, we need to listen to spirit and let go of our egos.

"Daddy Loves Me Best"

Do you believe God loves the person who says four Hail Mary's a day more than the person who says two? Do you think God loves the saint more than the sinner? If a Buddhist, Hindu, Muslim, Catholic and a Jew stood in front of God, who would you say He loves most? These three questions are really just one question, and it is this: Have you actually convinced yourself that God plays favorites?

Only the ego can create actual wars out of a children's game of "Daddy Loves Me Best." From this simple ego belief comes one of the greatest mass illusions in the history of man. And we need not have killed in His name to participate in this illusion. Anytime we put ourselves above a brother or sister, or put down a brother or sister, anytime we judge a brother or sister, we participate in this illusion. God has no more or no less love for all of His creations. Regardless of their participation in illusions, God loves all, equally, and always.

Only in the delusional mind can there exist levels of illusions. In the world of illusions, there are many steps we can take. All directions, regardless of their outward manifestations, lead to truth. There is not, and this I repeat with absolute respect and love, there is not, nor will we ever take, a step back on our journey. My friend, we have been taught that we can take two steps forward and one step back, and that we can regress from our path. In the world of illusions this is true, but in the world of truth this is an illusion. My friend, it is in part a result of this learned belief that we sometimes judge ourselves, our brothers, our sisters and God. My friend, every single step we take regardless of the number or outward manifestation is a step toward knowledge and truth. Regardless of the time it takes and distance we choose to travel, all roads lead to truth. Regardless of where we are on your journey, be it on the hills of the Himalayas, or inside prison walls, all journeys can end with the simple recognition that there is nowhere else we need to go. Any and all journeys end with the recognition that we need not take one more step. And we will not curse the journey for having us search for so long, but we will bless it, for we will know that it is because of it that we are now home.

7

FREEDOM THROUGH FORGIVENESS

If we forgive our brothers and sisters, we will set ourselves free. We will set ourselves free from all that we thought they did to us. They need not ask for forgiveness to be forgiven. They might even believe that there is nothing for which they need to be forgiven. That is fine. We do not need to concern ourselves with how they choose to experience reality, for it has no effect on us, unless we allow it to. For something or someone to affect us, we must first allow it to affect us.

We can also choose not to forgive our brother. But what good has such behavior ever brought to our lives? We might be trying to consciously or unconsciously punish a brother by not forgiving him. But who are we really punishing? Who carries that judgment with him wherever he goes? We might not consciously recognize that we are carrying this judgment, but it does simmer below the surface, coloring everything and everyone with whom we interact. Little by little, these judgments add up and weigh us down. We may be quick to anger, feel tired or stressed, and not understand why. Comments to other brothers and sisters may become nasty and our patience may fade. All this is due to our attempt to punish our brother by not forgiving him. My friend, again I ask you, who are you really punishing?

Do you realize what anger can do to you? Max Lucado says it best in his book, "No Wonder They Call Him Savior:"

> [22]*Anger. It's a peculiar yet predictable emotion. It begins as a drop of water. An irritant. A frustration. Nothing big, just an aggravation. Someone gets your parking place. Someone pulls in front of you on the freeway. A waitress is slow and you are in a hurry. The toast burns. Drops of water. Drip. Drip. Drip. Drip. Yet, enough of these seemingly innocent drops of anger and before long you've got a bucket full of rage. Walking revenge. Blind bitterness. Unharnessed hatred. We trust no one and bare our teeth at anyone who gets near. We become walking time bombs that, given just the right tension and fear, could explode.*

[22]See Notes, page xvii.

*Now, is that any way to live? What good has hatred
ever brought? What hope has anger ever created?
What problems have ever been resolved by revenge?*

Forgiveness: The Key to Knowledge, Peace of Mind and Joy

Forgiveness is the key that opens the door to knowledge, peace of mind and joy. The door itself is the stumbling block, or judgment. The door maker is the ego. Each individual ego builds and decorates its own door. The door and the door maker represent the illusion of who we think we are. Forgiveness is only necessary because we have chosen to believe that the door and door maker are real. Once our belief in the door and door maker are released and disappear, so will our need for a key. What good is a key if there is no door?

We have been offered a smooth road, and yet, what we see is a road full of holes. We sometimes talk a good talk, yet there are crevices in our minds, hearts and lives that although not real, we have made them real by our belief that we are something less than what we truly are. We are so richly blessed, but we continue to perceive holes in our roads, and so we secretly and silently look to fill these holes with materials that cannot last. Soon our roads become brittle and crack, and we must again make repairs. We complain about how incredibly bumpy our roads are, yet we cannot see, nor will we admit, that it is because of our own selves that our roads are bumpy. We continue to try and fill these holes with illusions and lies that will not stand the test of time. We curse the road, and curse and judge those we believe are responsible for its condition. We choose to look anywhere but within, and blame everyone but ourselves. My dear friend, we will never fix our roads with the same material that has helped us create the problem. Once we look within and realize that it is our own minds that create the holes, we move from trying to fix the road to trying to better understand our own minds. Once we obtain clarity in our minds, the holes in our roads magically disappear. They disappear because, they were illusions that we had simply chosen to believe as real.

Knowledge, peace of mind and joy are available in every situation. We can recognize this and obtain them through forgiveness or we can focus on judgment, their opposite, and obtain its result. The choice of which road we take and experience is ours.

If you have obtained peace of mind and joy in a situation, congratulations - no further instruction is necessary. If you have not obtained peace of mind and joy in a situation, then the following 10 steps may be helpful to you in changing directions:

- Accept responsibility. Acknowledge to yourself that, at this moment in time, it is your perception that is resulting in your lack of peace.

- Acknowledge that your lack of peace is not due to the external environment but to your internal reaction to it.

- Acknowledge that thinking with the ego, and judging the situation, has brought about a lack of peace.

- Do not condemn yourself or your ego for feeling the way you do.

- Acknowledge to yourself that there is another way, a more peaceful way to perceive this situation.

- Choose to see it as a learning experience, an opportunity to better understand how to choose peace.

- Offer gratitude for the experience and your inner shift.

- Forgive yourself and everyone else involved in the situation.

- Send love to yourself, your ego and everyone else involved in the situation.

- Be grateful for the opportunity that you have offered yourself to once again choose peace.

Ego-Self, Godself and Forgiveness

Forgiveness is not a natural reaction for the ego-self. If the ego-self even considers forgiveness, it might do so saying that our brother deserves forgiveness because he was simply in an immature or insane state at the moment when the "infraction" or "error" occurred. The ego's sense of forgiveness is to look upon our brother as insane or immature. By saying this, the ego is implying that the infraction or error is real; that there is something to forgive; and that somehow we are more or better than our brothers - that we're "bigger than they are" because we can forgive. It is also saying that our brother is capable of insane or immature behavior, thus making insanity, immaturity and their consequences real. Even in forgiveness, the ego's secret and silent goal is separation.

The Godself simply overlooks error because it knows that the child of God is not, nor ever could be immature or insane. It knows that the child of God is perfect because he comes from perfection. The Godself's sense of forgiveness is that an insane brother or sister does not exist. The Godself simply overlooks insanity or error because it knows them as illusions, as unreal. The opposite of error is perfection, but if perfection is all, then error cannot be anything but an illusion. The Godself not only does not judge nor have a need to forgive error, it does not see the error because it can only see what is real. For the Godself, to forgive is to overlook, because it is only interested in seeing the truth in a brother or sister. Thus the whole idea of forgiveness (the key) itself is an illusion, because, in truth, there is not nor will there ever be anything (the door) to forgive. If truth or perfection needs forgiveness, then the only value forgiveness holds is to recognize that it is not needed.

We attach to the act of forgiveness whatever value it holds for us. We should love our brothers and sisters for the truth in them; they are God's creation. Disregard their errors, and all of our brothers' errors are undone by seeing the truth in our brothers and accepting them as they were created.

Forgiveness is simply a step in the recognition that our brother and sister are perfect. We see in our brother what we believe about ourselves. So by seeing him as perfect, we recall the perfection in ourselves. By forgiving a brother or sister, we recognize that we too, can be forgiven, and this brings us a quiet and personal sense of peace.

In actuality, we never have to forgive anyone because there is nothing to forgive. This sounds strange. But the thought will be only as strange or as foreign as we allow it to be. Whenever I feel someone has done me wrong, I forgive quickly, thus releasing judgment and obtaining peace. Looking back, I can say that the ability to forgive someone offered me power over the illusion. But it was a power over nothing. I became good at forgiving, and it brought me peace. To forgive and release became an effective tool in my fight against illusions, in my fight against nothing.

To forgive nothingness, we simply need the understanding that it is nothing. Today, I know that there is nothing to fight against, nothing to ever forgive. My next step will be to not have to forgive people and to simply see the truth in them. To see the truth in all my brothers and sisters, regardless of what illusions they or I choose to value, seems like an interesting challenge. Then again, the challenge itself is but an illusion.

If an individual needs to hear the words "I forgive you" to feel better, or if I need to offer these words to feel closure, then I will offer them, but I will try to simply overlook the bothersome action from now on. This seems like a big step, yet I know that the step is only as big as I make it, and that in truth there is no step. To actually see the child of God as the child of God in every instance will bring total peace once we understand what it is we are truly doing. There is nothing easier than to see the child of God as the child of God. If we are open to this, we can be open to the idea that there is nothing easier than to be at peace. There is nothing easier than to be in our natural state.

Forgiveness is a very useful tool in obtaining peace. But it is just that - a tool. What tool would we ever need to offer what we already have? If we were able to perceive the truth in every moment, in every brother and sister, do we truly believe that a tool would be necessary to obtain peace of mind and joy? Truth simply is. Peace of mind and joy are always present in truth, because that is what it is. There will come a day when forgiveness will simply be seen as an unnecessary step in obtaining truth, in obtaining peace. Yet until that day comes, forgive and experience peace.

For author Corrie ten Boon, the ultimate lesson in forgiveness came at a very unexpected time. In her book "The Hiding Place," she writes the following:

> [23]*It was at a church in Munich that I saw him, the former S.S. man who had stood guard at the shower room door in the processing center at Ravensbruck. He was the first of our actual jailers that I had seen since that time. And suddenly it was all there - the roomful of mocking men, the heaps of clothing, Betsie's pain blanched face.*
>
> *He came up to me as the church was emptying, beaming and bowing. "How grateful I am for your message, Fraulein," he said. "To think that, as you say, 'He has washed my sins away'!"*
>
> *His hand was thrust out to shake mine. And I, who had preached so often to the people in Bloemendaal on the need to forgive, kept my hand at my side.*
>
> *Even as the angry, vengeful thoughts boiled through me, I saw the sin of them. Jesus Christ had died for this man; was I going to ask for more? Lord Jesus, I prayed, forgive me and help me to forgive him.*
>
> *I tried to smile; I struggled to raise my hand. I could not. I felt nothing, not the slightest spark of warmth or charity. And so again, I breathed a silent prayer. Jesus, I cannot forgive him. Give him Your forgiveness.*
>
> *As I took his hand, the most incredible thing happened. From my shoulder along my arm and through my hand a current seemed to pass from me to him, while into my heart sprang a love for this stranger that almost overwhelmed me.*
>
> *And so I discovered that it is not on our forgiveness, any more than on our goodness that the world's heal-*

[23]See Notes, page xvii.

ing hinges, but on His. When He tells us to love our enemies, He gives, along with the command, the love itself.

Invitation #5 -
How to Forgive a Brother or Sister

Many people ask the question, "How can you begin to heal a relationship with someone who you believe has caused you pain?" How about trying a case of amnesia. Remember that what you choose not to forgive will weigh you down as long as you choose to carry that thought with you. Regardless of how right you thought you were in defending your position, regardless of whose fault you perceived the situation to be, you will carry the pain until you are able to forgive your brother or sister. As the great "philosopher" Buddy Hackett once said, "Don't carry a grudge. While you're carrying the grudge, the other guy's out dancing." Forgive your brother, release him and you shall set yourself free.

When God looks at you, He sees His perfect expression manifested in you. He has no need to see your past, or imagine your future, for that which is perfect, simply is, and will always be. You need do nothing but feel His presence to remember that this is truth. If you allow yourself to look into His eyes, you will remember all that you have always been and will always be. He has offered you a present, and that present is your brother. If, in the moment, you allow yourself to see your brother as God sees you, all illusions of the past or future will simply disappear. They will affect you no longer, and they will be gone.

For a moment, let go of all things that you believe your brother or sister has done to you. Let go of all thoughts that have brought you pain, all thoughts that have weighed you down. For a moment, let go of the past and look at your present. Ask God to lend you His heart, and open your mind and spirit to seeing the perfection in your brother or sister. In this moment, you will remember your perfection. Ask God to be with you in this moment and you will feel His presence. For a moment, ask God to reveal all the love He has for you and your brother or sister. Pour out this love on your brother or sister.

What do you have to lose? Offer God a moment of your time, and look upon the brother you once judged, with absolute love. Forgive all your brother's past illusions of himself, and see him as God does. Offer this one moment to yourself, and you will be set free forever. Ask God to assist you in looking through your brother's actions and into his soul. Truly offer yourself this moment, and it will change your life.

It will change your life, because it will allow you to see and acknowledge that regardless of what you think a brother has done to you, there is another way of looking at him. It will change your life because you will encounter a moment that extends forever. In this moment, you have the ultimate power to see life and your brother as you wish. Your brother is God's perfect expression and not what you perceive he did to you. The ego has taught you to take an action that you thought a brother did to you and to judge him for it. The ego has you replace your brother's truth with an action and judgment. Your brother no longer truly exists, but your judgment of his action now lives in his place.

Again, your brother is not what he did to you. Look for a moment through the Godself and see the truth shining through. In the moment when the ego-self advises judgment, the Godself offers forgiveness. In the moment, you have this one choice. It is a choice between peace and pain, forgiveness and judgment, and simply put, between heaven and hell.

This simple invitation will give you back the power and understanding that it is up to you to choose how you see your brother in any moment of your life. You will remember that if you truly desire, you can choose forgiveness, peace of mind and joy in any instant, in any situation, and with any brother or sister. You will remember that God is always with you, and that you need only to call upon Him. Call upon that part of Him that is in you to set you free. God's present to you is your brother, and your brother's present to you is the opportunity to choose peace in any moment.

Your present to God is seeing and remembering that perfection in His creation.

Throughout your life, you have most likely tried it the ego's way. Allow yourself, if only for an instant in time, the opportunity to try it His way. The ego's way has offered you suffering, judgment, sleepless nights, stress, resentment and pain. His way promises you peace of mind and joy. The ego's way is based on illusions of who you think you should be and how you think you should act and react. It is a false way, a dead end road made up of lies you have been taught to believe are true.

His way is your true way. His will is your true will. The moment is God's present to you. It is the eternal gift. It is always available, offering peace of mind and joy. It has never left you and never will. You will always be offered the opportunity to choose the moment, to choose peace instead of pain. The moment is at your disposal to do with it as you will. Your true will brings forth peace of mind and joy. Your false will brings forth judgment and pain. Yet, free will is your right, and it is you, in every moment, who will choose what you will bring forth and experience.

OBE Given for Chapter Seven: Experiencing Only Love

The same night I wrote the amnesia - forgiveness exercise, I had an OBE, and found myself assisting lost souls (souls that are dead, but don't know it). I was having problems getting their full attention, so I started praying to God for assistance from Jesus. Suddenly I turned around and there He was, dressed in a white robe. I remember that my first thought was, "Wow, Jesus has really nice hair." I mean, he had a full head of long thick hair, more like a woman's than a man's thinner long hair. Yes, I admit this was not the most impressive and enlightening thought; then again, if you had my hair, or lack thereof, the thought would not be so foreign. Anyway, I'm sure He got a good laugh out of it. He began guiding me into an auditorium, so I followed. I had had a few conscious past experiences with Him. Nevertheless, I got overly excited at being in His presence, and found myself back in my body. You see, when you're out of the body, you travel by thought, and so you have to be focused on the moment or else you're back in your body or off somewhere else. I became a little upset at my lack of focus but I knew He would understand and that sooner or later I would experience Him again. I would not have to wait long.

The next afternoon I began meditating and again left my body. Interestingly enough, I suddenly found myself outside the same auditorium that I had visited the night before. This was not one of those ancient Greek auditoriums full of light that you might envision Jesus teaching in. It was a modern-day auditorium with modern-day chairs and a large screen in the front. I went inside and saw Jesus again. This time he had on short and tight fitting clothes and was saying strange things - statements full of judgment and pain that you would not associate with Jesus. He was saying things that I definitely didn't agree with and the people around him were doing things that were not spiritual in nature. I asked myself what was actually going on in my mind to create such an image, especially since all prior images and experiences with Him were so spiritually uplifting. Then I looked into His eyes, and I got the message He was trying to send!

The message was "Love me for who I Am, not for what I might say, look like, or do." In that moment I found myself loving Him not for what He was saying, not for what he looked like, and not for what he was doing. I loved the Christ in Him, who He in truth, is. He is like us, and we are all God's children. That is what I loved about Him. It had nothing to do with what He can say or do, and nothing he says or does changes anything about the truth in Him. Just as I believe that nothing anyone on this planet can do or say can change the truth of who that person is.

We are here to love people for who they truly are, and not for who they think they are. Their projection of themselves and our interpretation of that projection has, in actuality, nothing to do with the truth in them.

I believe that all people were created from perfection and in perfection, and there is nothing they can do to change their essence. They can try to add or subtract from who they truly are, but you can't truly add to or subtract anything from perfection. Perfection simply is, period. So if in the moment you were to actually have a true vision of any human being, perfection is all you would see. Any judgment you would have in regard to what that individual says or does can only come from your past perceptions of how one should react to anything someone says or does. If you don't bring that judgment from the past, then you experience the present, and your present is the person in front of you, whoever that might be. Anytime you judge someone, you are bringing your past and theirs into the present. As a result, you miss the present by choosing to experience the past in its place.

When you experience Christ, you experience absolute love, and that is a love that has nothing to do with His past, or what you think He did or did not do. It is a love you experience simply in His presence. This you can accomplish with all people, for if you can judge all, you also have the ability to love all.

Let's go back to my meditation in which I saw Jesus. The whole point was that judgmental words were being said and uncomfortable actions were occurring all around me. But I just looked into His eyes and I knew that none of that mattered. I looked into His eyes, and I "got it," and the only thing I felt was love for who He really is - that and nothing else. If you can experience love with Him, and everyone comes from the same source, why can't you experience that same love with everyone? If you can see God in one person's eyes, then you have the opportunity and ability to see Him in all people. My friend, there is no difference between your best friend and worst enemy, except your willingness to see the truth in both of them.

I remember smiling at Jesus during the experience, and mentally expressing to Him that I "got it." And I remember Him smiling back at me, mentally expressing to me that He knew I did. In a time of chaos, I found a moment of peace. Once this moment was recognized, it became all there was. It was I who had made the chaos real by focusing on it, and it was I who released this chaos by focusing on the truth. In any moment, you have a choice. Focus on the illusion and you will experience it; focus on the truth and you will experience it. As you grow, fear and chaos will be released, and peace and harmony will take their place. It will be these moments of growth that will lead you to experience more consistent peace and harmony in your life. It will be experiences such as these that will remind you that the choice to focus on fear and chaos or peace of mind and joy are yours.

Speaking with Anger vs. Speaking Our Truth

There is a difference between speaking with anger and speaking our truth. When we speak with anger, know that the ego-self is speaking. Know that we're reacting to and focusing on an illusion we see as real. When we speak with anger we bring forth, knowingly or not, emotionally repressed feelings from the past. We replace the present with the past and we lose the opportunity to experience what is really going on.

When we speak with anger, we are not really concerned with how those listening to us will feel. All we really care about is that our point of view is heard. When we come from such a place, all we are doing is making the listener defensive. The listener then puts up a wall to defend himself or herself against the perceived attack. As a result, we end up arguing or shouting at a wall with the hopes of being heard. Regardless of how smart or right we believe ourselves to be, we will not be heard by a wall. Obviously, a wall is not a good listener, which creates frustration. The frustration leads to confusion, which then ends in regret. This person, knowing that he cannot communicate with us, will move on to someone he believes will listen to what we did to him. This creates more frustration and miscommunication on everyone's part. In short, whenever we speak with anger, regardless of whether or not we believe we have every right to do so - frustration, confusion, separation and regret are the end result.

Before making an effort to speak our truth, we must first understand how the ego has trained us. It has trained us to believe that defense is a proper response to a perceived attack. Thus it has taught us that when people begin to either disagree with us or raise their voices, we are under attack. The ego has taught us that it is right and honorable to defend ourselves, and so we do. We put up a wall, defending ourselves against the perceived attack of a brother or sister. The ego has reinforced in us that these actions are an attack, yet if we listened to our Godselves, it would remind us that these actions are simply calls for help, calls for love. Yes, any and every time that our brother or sister raises his or her voice to us, he or she is really asking to be loved.

When a baby or young child cries, what is he or she asking for? What do we usually offer? What is the result of your behavior toward your child? Do you not offer the child comfort and love? Does the child not respond by becoming calm, feeling comforted, smiling, laughing and continuing his or her play? Can you not see that this result is absolutely possible with all our brothers and sisters if we offer love and comfort instead of confrontation and defense? My friend, this offer of love and comfort is the Godself's answer any time we perceive a brother or sister attacking us, regardless of the manifestation. Thus, if we choose the Godself's way of reacting to a brother or sister's perceived attack, we will create a safe place where two or more individuals with different points of view can come together. In other words, we can come together in a place where people agree to speak and listen with an open mind, as non-judgmentally as possible, so that all points of view can be discussed, heard, understood and respected. In order to create this place, try the following five steps:

- Be quiet. Understand that the ego-self will try to answer first by attacking and defending. The less insane person in any argument takes control of it by being quiet.

- Bring your thoughts into your Godself. Understand that your brother or sister is simply asking for love in the best way he or she knows how, in the moment.

- Send your brother or sister peaceful and loving thoughts. Surround yourself and him or her with light and invite God to enter the situation.

- Listen non-judgmentally to whatever your brother or sister believes he or she needs to express. Give your brother or sister the time he or she needs.

- Go to your Godself and ask it how you should deal with the situation, what you should say, and when and how you should say it.

Understand that there are those who are so invested in the ego's thought system that they believe that if we do not get physically upset, shout and argue with them, we do not really care about them or love them. Sit quietly for a moment and understand what this says about those individuals. Imagine how lost and confused they must feel. They equate love with being physically upset, shouting, arguing and regret. But do not judge them, for they simply have bought the ego's fairy tale as true. My friend, only small children believe fairy tales are true. Thus, if we encounter such beings, simply offer them even more comfort and love, and one day they will realize that comfort and love are the only sane responses to comfort and love.

Reacting to an Immature Action

My friend Mike has a four-month-old daughter with a woman from Costa Rica. They are not married and he's had trouble seeing his daughter. Mike was upset about the situation. Then Mike found out that his sister had called both the mother of his child and the child's grandmother to tell them how badly they had been treating Mike with regard to the baby. Apparently, Mike's sister had angrily expressed the way she felt about them and the situation. Obviously, this action did not make the situation better. Both women told Mike how his sister acted which made Mike mad at his sister. He was so upset that he was planning to cancel his visit with his sister once he got to Miami for his birthday.

In handling the incident, Mike had two choices. One, he could allow the ego-self to dictate the situation, and react with anger, judgment and condemnation, thus separating himself from his sister. Two, he could recognize that his ego-self would try to answer first, and pause. Mike could then bypass this effort by his ego and go to his Godself for guidance. If Mike makes the latter choice, he would see that the Godself would always ask him to act with compassion. In return, he would receive peace.

People who have not yet remembered their perfection will, from time to time, act and react in an immature manner. Mike's sister's feelings were hurt by her brother's situation and she reacted immaturely and with anger.

The ego-self will always answer first because it has made itself our programmed response. We have been trained by it and thus we react as we were trained. Speaking with anger and condemnation is a natural response of the ego-self; it makes us right for doing so. Anything that differs from our point of view of how the world and those in it should behave and react is taken by the ego-self as an attack upon us. And the ego-self continually tells us that it is right and honorable to defend ourselves against an attack.

When we are angry our actions are not constructive. We become angered by others' actions, which because of their immature nature, they had little control over. Our anger now becomes an immature reaction to their immature action. So we need to ask ourselves, where does this leave us? Definitely not in a peaceful place! A peaceful place is found by reacting with compassion and love toward our brother or sister. This peaceful place can be our goal in every situation. This peaceful place is our natural state, and our natural state is not temporal in nature.

Reacting with anger and condemnation might bring us a false and very temporary state of peace from the simple misperception that we are right and the other person is wrong, and that the wrong deserve to be punished. Remember our ego always answers first, and its primary goal is to separate us from our brother or sister. We need to ask ourselves: Would we rather be right or happy? Would we rather express false power or experience everlasting peace?

If we listen to our ego, we will react with condemnation and judgment, for they are among the ego's favorite tools in its effort to separate us from our brothers and sisters. As surely as the sun rises in the east, so does reacting with our ego-selves bring us a lack of peace. You and I know this very well, for we both have experienced situations like this when we've reacted with anger to another person's action, and later felt badly and saddened by the way we reacted and dealt with the situation. We feel badly because we've lost our peace of mind, which is our natural inheritance. We feel badly because we have tried to attack and separate ourselves from our brother or sister who is a part of God. But we cannot attack and separate ourselves from our brother or God and still feel whole. Trying to do something that is impossible creates frustration. Frustration leads to confusion and confusion to chaos. Because we, our brother and God are one, what we do to our brother we do not only to him but also to God and ourselves. If we attack ourselves without knowing it, we create confusion. At first, it may be difficult to see that this confusion is self-inflicted. If we are not currently aware of this confusion we will soon be, for the number of times that we unknowingly attack ourselves may be high but they will not be without limit.

I am simply here to remind you and myself that there is another way. Through compassion and understanding, we can choose peace instead of anger. We can choose a peaceful mind instead of an anxious mind. We can choose happiness instead of sadness and we can choose compassion instead of condemnation, anger and regret. We are all spiritual beings, having a human experience. We have yet to remember our perfection, and that is why we are here. Someone with whom we may be angry is here to assist us in remembering our perfection. He or she is our teacher, as well as our student. All of his or her actions and reactions offer us an opportunity to choose peace in a situation where we once found the possibility of peace unobtainable. This person offers us another opportunity to forgive what we once found unforgivable, and to love who we once found unlovable. In making these choices we remember our own perfection, and in remembering our perfection, we find peace, forgiveness and love within ourselves.

That "immature" person, in truth, has offered us the gift of remembering our perfection, that we can choose peace in any situation. What else but gratitude would we offer someone who is teaching and reminding us that peace is available in every situation? Would gratitude not be the sane response to such a wonderful gift? There is a place in your heart that understands what it is I am sharing. I know this of you, because I now know this of myself, and you and I are one and the same.

After remembering all this, how will you now react to your brother or sister's next immature action? Will you react with condemnation, anger and an anxious mind or with compassion, gratitude and a peaceful mind? Will you choose to be right, or will you choose to be happy?

As it turns out, after the initial anger that Mike experienced, we talked about it, and he was able to deal with his sister with compassion. He understood that people sometimes act in an immature manner, and in order for him to keep his peace of mind he had to forgive her action, and understand where she was coming from. He had to understand that his sister simply made an error in judgment. He remembered that the sister he loved was not represented by that immature action, but was a spiritual being on her journey to remembering her true self. He understood that her action deserved understanding and his sister deserved compassion.

On our journey toward achieving peace of mind, it is very important to understand that there is a difference between an action and the person performing the action. An action happens at a moment in time and regardless of how we have been taught to see it, it is an opportunity. The opportunity shows us where we are within our minds. It teaches us who we truly believe ourselves to be. We can choose to react with peace now, or we can choose to react with peace later. Sooner or later we will find peace. Because of free will, we can choose when we want to experience peace. Also understand that the belief that peace is not immediately available to us does not in any way interfere with the fact that peace is always available. The time it takes us to react with peace is up to us, and will be measured not only in time, but in pain. For if we do not have peace about a situation, then we are experiencing some level of pain about it.

When we choose to act with compassion and forgive a brother or sister after an immature action, we receive peace as our gift. We can also choose not to forgive a brother or sister for an immature action for a lifetime, and our gift will be a lifetime of carrying in our hearts and minds a lack of forgiveness for that action. This lack of forgiveness will weigh on us, for it is unnatural not to forgive. We can forgive a brother or sister and in doing so release ourselves from that action, or we can choose not to forgive and carry that painful action with us until the end of time. In the end, it is we who have the power to resolve the issue. We have the power to react to every situation with or without peace. We have the power to carry it with us as long as we want. We have the power to release it as quickly as we want. It is our choice to be weighed down or released, to be right or to be happy, to live in pain or in peace, to react with condemnation or compassion.

Dealing with Negative Emotions or Feelings through the Ego-self

It is a part of everyone's development to react with negative emotions or feelings toward their brothers and sisters. In fact, it is the ego's hope that we judge every brother we meet, and blame every brother for how we feel. The ego tries to make our brother responsible so that we will not take the time to look within. The ego hopes we will judge our brother any time he acts in a way that differs from our belief system. Yet the ego's hopes are also its demise, for the more it gets us to react the way it wants us to, the more we realize that it is a fruitless, insensitive and agonizing method of existence.

The world is governed by rules enacted by the ego for the ego. One of the rules that this world tries to constantly reinforce in us is that there are times when judgment is a proper response. But would we judge a tourist from a foreign land for being lost? And isn't this all our brother really is, a tourist in a foreign land? Aren't we all just tourists in a foreign land? Every time a brother walks up to us, he is asking for directions, and it is up to us to react with judgment and send him to hell, or to react with love and remind him of heaven. And understand this: Every time we communicate with a brother, we are giving him directions to where we secretly live.

Another one of the rules that the world tries to reinforce in us is that it is right and fair to judge a brother who judges us. But why does reacting with judgment even when this world tells us that it is right, proper and fair cause us regret, resentment and pain? If, in the ego's world, what is right, proper and fair causes us regret, resentment and pain, then how can we ever truly find peace of mind and joy? If, in the ego's world, reacting in a right, proper and fair manner causes us regret, resentment and pain, then what would reacting wrongly, improperly and unfairly bring to us? Certainly not peace of mind and joy! In the ego's world, there is no way that we can truly win. What the ego masks as happiness is regret, resentment and pain. Can we really believe that we will ever find true happiness by living a life full of regret, resentment and pain?

The ego has made us believe that it has laid a never-ending path of red rose petals for us to walk on. It has made us believe that it is the only safe path on which to travel. It has taught us its rules and warned us not to look elsewhere for guidance. Yet if for a moment we realize and feel what we are doing, we discover that beneath those rose petals are millions of rusted nails lining the path, ready to tear the flesh from our feet. We then see that what we thought were rose petals are actually torn pieces of flesh from those who traveled this same path. And the pieces of flesh are red with our brothers' blood.

In moments of reflection, we have felt judgment's pain, but we could not believe it had been self-inflicted because we did everything the ego said that we needed to do. We did everything right. So with every judgment, we took another step on the ego's path.

The ego smiles and tells us that we also should be smiling, and so we go ahead and smile that false smile we have so often performed with. We become weaker with every step and cannot understand why. We have not quite realized that every time we judge a brother we slowly cut into our own spirits, our trueselves. We do not look at ourselves, but we are slowly losing blood. We do not know why, but we understand that something has to change. Somewhere within, we understand that, for our own survival, a change must take place.

Dealing with Negative Emotions or Feelings through the Godself

Instead of reacting to negative emotions or feelings with judgment as the ego has taught us, how would the Godself invite us to react? The Godself would invite each of us to take the following three steps:

- Bring any negative emotions or feelings to the surface.

- Release any remorse or guilt that you once chose to believe in these illusions.

- Release your negative emotions or feeling. Thank them for what they have taught you and let them go.

First, bring any negative emotions and feelings to the surface, for it is in walking the ego's path that we will truly recognize that it will get us nowhere.

We have been walking on the ego's path because it has convinced us that it will take us where we want to go. We have made ourselves respond with negative emotions and feelings, because the ego has taught us that judgment is a "natural and right response" to a brother's words and actions. But judgment never offers us peace of mind and joy.

Do not resist negative emotions or feelings because it is healthy to feel and experience them. This was very much an issue for me. There was a time when I believed that it was "not spiritual" to deal with negative emotions or feelings. I forgave many illusions before really understanding and acknowledging their illusionary nature. I swept them under the rug; and when it was time to clean up, there was a lot of dust to deal with. I truly believed that all negative emotions and feelings were illusions and, when involved in an argument, I would simply release them by forgiving the person in my mind so that the argument would not escalate. I would immediately release all negative emotions and feelings because I understood that what the individual was really looking for was love. This, in its purest form, is the Godself's way of dealing with an individual. This, in its purest form, will always bring peace. All this is great as long as we bring to the surface what it is we are feeling. So don't feel like we're not being spiritual simply because we feel or express negative emotions. It is simply a part of our journey, and all of the journey's parts are necessary for its completion.

The value of an illusion is to have the opportunity to realize that it is an illusion. The one value of all illusions lies in understanding and acknowledging their lack of value. The more we value an illusion, the more we defend it and try to protect our beliefs. If we do not physically experience its lack of value, then we will truly never believe that it is valueless. How many times in our lives have we tried to explain something important that happened in our lives only to resort to the phrase, "you really had to be there." For most of us, this is how we learn that our illusions are valueless. We have to experience them ourselves to learn that they have no value. A guru or spiritual teacher can tell us that to find peace, we need to forgive and release our anger, but it is only by holding resentment that we can truly experience, appreciate and acknowledge its valuelessness in our lives. It is only through holding onto such resentment that we can experience its full weight, its energy drain, the absolute worthlessness that such emotions bring to our lives.

If we can understand that everything a brother says to us comes from either love or a call for love, then congratulations and God bless. But most people will need to experience the valuelessness that illusions offer them in order to cease choosing them. So feel free to bring to the surface, experience and feel whatever it is we think we need to experience and feel. If these feelings are manifested as negative emotions toward your brother, then sit with them. But for your own good, for your own growth and peace of mind, ask yourself how these experiences are making you feel. Ask yourself how much peace of mind and joy they have brought to your life. Truly look inside and see what you are doing to yourself by choosing to react this way.

Second, release any remorse or guilt that you once chose to believe these illusions. Remorse and guilt are themselves illusions, and knowledge of this fact turns them into gifts. Knowledge turns all illusions into miracles. Knowledge turns hate into love, fear into freedom, judgment into forgiveness and pain into peace. Knowledge frees the prisoner and forgives the jailer. Understand that these illusions or trials have come to offer you an opportunity to choose again. Let remorse and guilt turn into a prayer of gratitude, for the experience that you once believed was true is true no more. As "A Course in Miracles" states:

> [24]*Trials are but lessons that you failed to learn presented once again, so where you made a faulty choice before, you can now make a better one, and thus escape all the pain that your previous choices brought to you.*

Third, release negative emotions or feelings, let them go. Do not exaggerate the act of letting them go, because this only gives them the importance they no longer deserve. Be thankful that illusions you chose to see as real are now seen as the illusions they have always been. Be thankful that what once caused you so much judgment, regret, resentment and pain now simply dissolves in your light. Be thankful that the truth has set you free.

Forgiving Parents and Other Family Members

Many people still find some kind of comfort and safety in blaming their parents for how they feel about themselves. Even as adults, they blame their parents for self-esteem issues. Understand that it was not what our parents did to us, but how we choose to carry the past that affects us now. My friend, you might now find it difficult to believe, but some day we will completely forgive and love our parents. In our perception, our parents may have acted in ways we once believed impossible to forgive and love. But as we grow, we

[24]See Notes, page xvii.

will begin to understand the lessons that came to us as a result of their behaviors. With understanding comes peace, and with peace comes gratitude. With gratitude our hearts open, and we will grow spiritually by learning to forgive behaviors we once found unforgivable, and love those we once thought were unlovable.

Before we were born, we chose the individuals who became our parents. We were aware of the issues we would face, and the environment we were coming to experience. Yet, we came to Earth understanding the environment in which we were placing ourselves. We also came to Earth to learn about love, forgiveness and service. The first people we came to love, forgive and serve were our parents. We now believe that some women choose to have relationships with emotionally and physically abusive men because their father was an emotionally and physically abusive man. If they do not learn to love the truth of who their father is, then they will choose men with his characteristics to assist them in learning to love, forgive and serve such beings. There may be something about their father's behavior that has blocked their awareness to the presence of love, the truth in him. If they do not choose to work with their father and his characteristics, then brothers with the same characteristics will offer themselves to them in order to assist them in releasing these blocks. They will offer themselves to them and they will not only accept them, but they will strangely be attracted to them, because deep within, they know that there is something that they need to learn that only these men can teach.

Another lesson that they might have come to learn is that they don't need to be treated in this abusive manner, that they should be treated with love, honor and respect. If they do not learn to stand up for themselves and be treated with love, honor and respect by their father, then they will choose individuals like him to stand up to, in order to learn that they can stand up to these kinds of beings. When they finally stand up for themselves, and acknowledge and demand that this is not how they want to be treated, the lesson is complete and the pattern ends. The pattern ends because their lessons are complete. There is nothing else this type of individual has to teach them; there is nothing else for them to learn together. And the next time an individual like this appears, they simply bless him and move on. There is no longer a secret need to come together. There is no need to repeat the grade once the lessons are fully learned.

Now we arrive at the most important point of this example: We cannot release an individual or situation unless we have done so with forgiveness and love. When we express ourselves through judgment and anger, we will feel worse afterward. We will have a feeling of incompletion, as if something still remains to be said or done. We will carry with us, the individuals or situations in which we expressed ourselves through judgment and anger. We will feel weighed down and not know why. And the individuals or situations will reappear in the future. It may not be the exact form, situation or individual, but we will re-create the environment to allow ourselves the opportunity to resolve it with forgiveness and love, and obtain peace. Again our patterns will be repeated until we release them with forgiveness and love.

If you see yourself attracting the same type of person, or experiencing the same kind of stress in your everyday life, I recommend that you:

- Thank yourself for bringing that situation to your life, for there is something for you to learn from the individual or event.
- Thank the individual or event in your life for its participation in your lesson plan.
- Ask your Godself why it is that you are choosing to repeat this pattern.
- Take time to analyze the pattern. Write down all your thoughts and emotions relating to this pattern. Invite your friends and family to comment on this pattern.
- Ask to be offered guidance on how to resolve this issue with forgiveness and love.
- Pray that you'll be offered the strength and clarity to act with forgiveness and love.

- Acknowledge that every moment in your life is a learning experience created by your higher self to teach you how to be a more loving being.

- Acknowledge to yourself that you are not reacting in the most constructive and loving way possible.

- Forgive yourself for reacting in this manner.

- Forgive everyone and everything else involved in the situation.

- Acknowledge to yourself that there is another more peaceful and mature way of looking at this situation.

- Ask yourself what is more important: to be happy or to be right?

Forgiving vs. Not Forgiving

Think of moments in your life and remember the times that you chose not to forgive. Then think about the times when you chose to forgive. You need not look far into the past to remember them. You probably do not need to look to the past at all. Today, in the present, you might recall someone who you have forgiven and someone who you have not yet chosen to forgive.

Sit still for a moment with the memory of how it feels not to forgive. Does it seem to cloud the mind? How do those thoughts affect your body? Does it feel as if something heavy or uncomfortable is living within? Do you believe that holding on to those physical, emotional and mental sensations affect you in a negative way? Are these sensations hurting you, or are they hurting the person you have not forgiven? Who does your inability to release these thoughts and forgive affect more?

You think that by not forgiving, you hold a power over that individual, yet now you can begin to realize that, by choosing not to forgive, this individual holds that power over you. And to go one necessary step further, it is not the individual himself who holds a power over you, but those negative thoughts that you choose to hold on to that hold you captive. You hold yourself captive. These are the thoughts you created through your perception of the situation. This perception, which has made you a prisoner, can also set you free, for it is you that holds the key.

You have carried this weight and suffered long enough! Forgive, and you will see things differently. Forgiveness will give you power over all the people and events that seem to now have power over you. Remember how it feels to forgive, to truly let go. It literally feels as if a weight has been lifted off your shoulders.

Forgiveness is in you, and as hard as you have tried to forget, you know it is available. Blessed is this day, for you have finally chosen to see what has always been.

You can choose not to forgive. You can carry stuff from your past with you all you want; that is your choice. But sooner or later, your shoulders will become heavy with the burden. So, heavy in fact, that you will fall to your knees. Once on your knees, you will release this weight, and for the first time in a long time, you will truly feel rested and at peace. You will ask yourself: Why do I choose to carry this weight, for the past is gone and the future is imagined. Now you realize you have a choice, and now you truly understand how each choice feels. One weighs your shoulders to the ground, and the other lifts you up. One makes you worry and stress about the past, present and future; the other offers you peace. Through your own judgment one jails you, and the other, through forgiveness, sets you forever free.

Kneel for a moment, my brother, and ask that this weight be lifted. Kneel for a moment my sister, and feel the weight lifting off your shoulders. Kneel for a moment, my friend, for today you have chosen peace.

Invitation #6 - Exchanging Pain for Peace

Read completely through the following invitation a couple of times to get a feel for it. Then, put the book down, find a quiet place, sit down, close your eyes, relax and give it a try.

This, as with other invitations, asks that your complete heart be engaged during the process. (The invitations are heart-centered, meaning you must use your heart and soul to guide you through the process.)

If you are currently emotionally, physically, or spiritually tired, you may want to wait for another day. Yet if you feel tired and still want to try it, please do as your instinct tells you. Finally, do not judge yourself if you feel "nothing happened." Many times, progress does not come in the form that the ego expects. But I promise you that progress will be made, for I have witnessed how one moment spent with God completely raises the vibration of not only this planet but also of all its inhabitants.

- Get into a meditative state.

- Speak, pray from your heart. When you're done speaking, just breathe and allow for quiet time.

- Listen.

- Give thanks. End meditation.

Before going to bed one night, go to your room. Sit on a chair and take about a minute to breathe. Breathe deeply; close your eyes. With every breath you take, feel God getting closer.

Visualize yourself on a chair, sitting in darkness. Then visualize a fog coming toward you; the fog is full of white light. This white light represents God's love. Feel His light and love slowly surround and envelop you. Give Him permission to enter and ask your guardian angels and guides to also come in. Surround yourself with the white light of protection and feel the light surrounding you, protecting you. Tell God, Jesus, and your guardian angels and guides that you are now ready to exchange pain for peace. This pain can be anything from an emotionally trying time to an individual you have yet to forgive. Go back to a time when you once experienced pain. Understand that you are now completely protected. Understand that nothing can hurt you any longer, because you are now completely surrounded by your spiritual family. They are here to assist you, to protect you from your own thoughts. Bring that pain into your thoughts and offer it to God. See yourself handing all the pain you experienced over to God. A little willingness is all it takes. Visualize yourself slowly and deliberately grabbing all of the dark pain out of your body and mind, and putting it into a bag. Feel the weight of the pain that you are extracting from your body. Feel the bag getting heavier and your body getting lighter. Hold this bag in front of you and offer it to God. Feel the weight of the pain that you are extracting from your body. See the bag turn black as you continue to release your pain into it. Feel the bag getting heavier and your body getting lighter. See God gladly take this bag from you, and as He does, see it being slowly dissolved into His light. As the bag begins to dissolve, feel yourself becoming lighter, for you have finally chosen to let it go. The weight has been lifted. As you begin to feel lighter and free, feel God filling those now open spaces with His light. Feel His light expanding throughout your body, filling up all the crevices that were once dug up by the ego. By your choice, His truth now replaces your illusions.

God will gladly take all memories of pain from you because He loves you. See your pain being dissolved in His light, and feel His peace enter you. Let His love enter you; feel the waves of love entering your spirit. You and God are one. He has absolute love for you. Let Him forever take the pain away and replace it with His love. Feel His love filling that place in you where pain once lived.

He is so grateful for the exchange because He knows that one of His children has just taken another step toward Him. He is so grateful for the exchange because He knows that one of His children has just exchanged the illusion of pain for the truth of peace. He is very grateful to you and I know you'll be grateful to Him. Thank Him with all your heart and feel Him receiving your love and thanks. Send waves of love and light into His light that you now are. Thank Him for being there for you. Thank all of your spiritual family for their protection and support. Spend some time in the light and in quiet gratitude. Say goodbye and let God, your guardian angels and your guides go with the understanding that they are always with you and that any moment you ask them to be with you, they will be there. For today, you have rediscovered a moment in time that had been hidden from you but you now acknowledge is always available. All you need to do now is ask, and Heaven will gladly come to you. All you need to do is ask for peace, and as you ask for it, you will remember its ever present availability.

For a moment, choose to put aside all of your complex and heavy questions and learn to be silent. Replace all of your questions with two simple words: Thank you. Be silent for a moment, my friend, and you just might hear "You're welcome!" You might ask: How far am I away from God? And you just might hear:

> *"How far do you believe your brother to be from Me?*
> *How far do you believe your neighbor to be from Me?*
> *How far do you believe your enemy to be from Me?*
> *For that is how far you are from Me!"*

The following quote comes from Anne Frank's "Diary of a Young Girl." I use it to end this chapter on forgiveness simply to show the power of the Godself. This young child, living in the most difficult of circumstances, held onto her belief that people are really good at heart. There is also a place within your heart that, when asked, acknowledges this. It is this place that is your foundation. It is this place that whispers throughout eternity that all will be all right. It is this place where you'll rediscover the freedom forgiveness has to offer.

> [25]*It's really a wonder that I haven't dropped all my ideals, because they seem so absurd and impossible to carry out. Yet I keep them, because in spite of everything, I still believe that people are really good at heart. I simply can't build up my hopes on a foundation consisting of confusion, misery, and death. I see the world gradually being turned into a wilderness; I hear the ever-approaching thunder, which will destroy us too. I can feel the sufferings of millions and yet, if I look up into the heavens, I think that it will all come right, that this cruelty too will end, and that peace and tranquility will return again. In the meantime, I must uphold my ideals, for perhaps the time will come when I shall be able to carry them out.*

[25]See Notes, page xvii.

8

BEING IN THE NOW

My friend, if we're not in the now, we are lost. We bring judgments of the past into the present and question why we don't understand what is really going on. We look at a brother or sister, call him or her a stranger instead of a friend and speculate as to why we live in fear. My friend, we live in fear because we bring all of our past judgments into the present moment.

We extend our past into the present, creating a future like our past, and thus we never really experience the present. Living this way, we can not experience the perfection of the present moment. The present is God's eternal gift to us. It is when we look at a brother or sister without past judgments and see a friend. When we see our brother or sister as God's perfect creation, we are experiencing the present moment. It happens when we look into our brothers and sisters' eyes and see ourselves reflected in them. We need only do this once and we will want no other way. If we see our brother or sister as something other than God's perfect creation, know that we are exchanging our past judgments for the present moment.

The present moment is perfect. If we see anything other than perfection in the moment or in our brother or sister, it is because we have veiled the present with past judgments. When enough veils are placed on top of each other, they become as thick as a wall and obscure the light of truth. We might add or subtract a veil and thus change our perception of reality, but it is still just that, a perception of reality. The truth is simple, but it can be as complicated as we wish to make it. As long as we bring any judgment into the present, we color the present with the past and thus change the present's true color. This creates confusion, and ultimate peace cannot be experienced as long as we are confused.

Allow the simplicity and truth of the moment to manifest itself, or choose to replace it with the complexity and confusion of what we think we wish to see. This is the one choice we make in every moment. The present moment simply is. It is free from past judgments or future imaginings. We can find peace by allowing the present moment to be what it is. We can experience peace by simply doing two things:

- Having faith that the moment is perfect.
- Being thankful for however the moment chooses to manifest itself in our minds.

The present moment is perfect and this simple recognition is all that is asked of us in order for us to experience its perfection. It is in allowing the present moment to be what it is that we find peace. And as we recognize the present as God's gift, we replace our judgment of it with gratitude.

If we do not experience peace in the present moment, it is because we have substituted the ego's illusions for the present moment. The ego will invite us to believe in a thousand different ways in which we can lose our peace of mind. The ego will also offer us a thousand different solutions, which only ends up adding to our confusion. Yet, if one of the ego's illusions or solutions is unreal, then all of the ego's illusions and solutions are unreal. For the ego's illusions and solutions, in and of themselves, are nothing. And regardless of how many times we multiply nothing, we will still get nothing.

You might ask for an example to clarify this point. The manifestation of that example might clarify a small number of similar illusions. This is exactly what the ego would offer, because it gives more than enough wiggle room to offer us a thousand different illusions and a thousand solutions to those illusions. And as long as we have use for the ego, it can remain alive, well and in control of our perceptions. And so I offer no specific examples to cloud your thoughts. I do offer that all illusions, regardless of their manifestations, will result in a loss of peace. There is really only one illusion, one problem, which is that we are experiencing the illusion as real. Call it your spouse's impatience, your boss' ruthlessness, traffic or your job. Call it what you will. If it takes away your peace, it is because you have seen the illusion as real. In their essence, all illusions are the same because all illusions are not real.

React as you will to illusions. Defend yourself against illusions if that rocks your boat. Hate, fear and punish that figment of your imagination that does not exist, if you wish to. Anytime that you relate to the present moment with anything but peace and gratitude, you have had a misperception brought on by a past judgment you thought had once served your purpose.

In order to live in the present moment, let go of past patterns that are inconsistent with the truth within you. Offer God the judgment of your brother or sister, the judgment that has brought you nothing but sadness, pain and regret. Let it go, and in turn, He will offer you eternal peace of mind and joy. Offer Him all of your past perceptions and He will offer you the eternal present moment. If you put aside the unfruitfulness of judgment, you could easily lift the many veils that you use to cover the present moment. Beneath the veils, you would rediscover the simplicity of faith, faith that the present moment is perfect. This rediscovery, that you need not add nor subtract or judge the present moment, will offer you total freedom and peace. And gratitude will become your only sane response to the offering of total freedom and peace.

Lay aside all judgment, and feel yourself lifted into another world, a world that you have not seen or experienced for a long time - but one that has always been and will always be available to you. If you offer God a little willingness to put your judgments aside, He will, in turn, offer you eternal peace of mind and joy. Do this for one moment in time and you will rediscover that this is all you desire. As you rediscover this, you will also find that this truth is available to everyone, at any time, and that a simple decision is all that separates those who have rediscovered their truth from those who are in the process of rediscovering their truth.

Knowledge that the perfection of the present moment is available to everyone all the time will fill your heart with an overflowing sense of gratitude and joy that even the most blind will see. Your heart will burst with rainbow-colored love that will touch everyone, and the judgment of your brother and sister will all but dissolve in its light. Your simple willingness to put judgment aside will result in the complete love of God flowing through your soul and not one cell in your body will be left untouched by His gratitude and love. You have dammed a once free flowing river, and as a result, you have not felt God's complete gratitude and love flowing through you. But by trusting the present moment, you are once again putting your trust in God. Once you have done so, thousands of illusionary bricks will fall, again letting the river flow free. The river will overflow its banks, and you too will overflow with God's gratitude and love. As the banks of a flooding river cannot contain its waters, your ego-self will not be able to prevent your Godself from extending and offering all that has been extended and offered to you. As you extend this love to your brothers and sisters, your gratitude and love toward them will grow. For as you extend love, so too will you experience it - its fullness, nourishment, beauty and purity. Simply put judgment aside and allow the present moment to be. If you do this, all your brothers and sisters' colors, races, religions, beliefs, actions and reactions will dissolve into an ocean of gratitude and love so nourishing that peace of mind and joy will forever feed your heart and soul.

You will live in gratitude, and others will be grateful to have you in their lives. Your brothers and sisters are also engaged in a search. They may not realize that they are searching, but they are also on a journey. It is the realization that they are not where they want to be that will awaken the memory of their own journey. You will be there as an example to them that the place they are looking for is within reach. And you will remind them that it is not so much a physical journey but a simple realization. It is a simple shift from coloring the present with past judgments, to one of being grateful and allowing what is to be.

Invitation #7 - Friend vs. Stranger

Allow me to offer you a way to live more peacefully in the moment. Try looking at a brother you have never met and instead of calling him a stranger, call him a friend. Instead of judging him for what he looks like, wears, does, acts or reacts, or who he seems to be, simply look at this stranger and know him as a friend, as God's child. Outwardly, you might consider this possibility and say, "big deal, what could changing one word and seeing a stranger as a friend possibly do?" I will share with you that this simple act would completely change your world. You might say that there is "no way that such a small shift could completely change my world." For on a foggy day not so long ago, I also verbalized these same thoughts. But today I invite you to give your heart honestly to this effort for just one moment in time.

This invitation will only be as difficult to accept as the denseness of the fog that surrounds the memory of who your brother or sister truly is. I know that while lost in the fog you have been confused and afraid. But the time has finally come when you will notice the twinkle of the lighthouse on the horizon. Congratulate yourself and know that it is showing itself now not because it is burning brighter, but because you have come to a place on your journey that allows you enough clarity to see. The light was there before the fog and it will be there long afterwards. It has brought many a lost ship safely home. And just as the people on these ships thanked God when they saw the light, so too will you one day breathe a sigh of relief and thank God for such a blessing.

The ego has taught us to call our brother or sister a stranger. The ego has taught us that when we first look at a brother or sister, we must immediately judge something about him or her. The ego does not explain why it has us react in such a manner. Yet we are trained so that our first reaction is not to question its motive, but to think like it thinks, and react the way it has taught us to react. The ego wants us to acknowledge it as our one confidant, the only one we can truly count on and trust. The ego will use words, it will use thoughts, it will use actions and reactions, judgments and blame. Its tools are as limitless as the illusions and the results they produce.

My friend, with one thought or action unlike that of the ego, the fog will begin to lift. Just as thinking with the ego-self produces confusion, judgment, separation and regret, so too does thinking with the Godself produce clarity, peace of mind, unity and joy. A moment is coming when you will look at the being the ego calls a total stranger and you will see him or her as God's child. The ego will defend itself against this perceived attack to its "reality" by saying that this is no big deal. But I offer you that this is the beginning of the end of the ego's grip on your perception of reality. As soon as you do this once with a completely open, love-filled heart and mind, the fog will immediately begin to lift. Simply lay your eyes on a brother or sister who in the past you would have immediately judged as a stranger, and see him or her as God's perfect creation.

Seeing your brother without judgment, with a completely open, love-filled heart and mind will fill you with so much compassion, love and joy that you will never again consciously choose to see another brother any other way. You will be so grateful for being able to see him as he truly is that you will look forward to doing this every day. Imagine the hundreds of judgments you will no longer need to support, digest and carry with you – simply because you are seeing your brother as he truly is. Imagine how much lighter and at peace you will feel. This is what your brother offers you each and every time you are gifted with his presence. This is the gift your brother and sister offer you every time you set your eyes upon them and simply see them as they truly are. The more you do this, the clearer your days will become. Day by day the fog will continue to lift, and as it does, clarity will begin to surround your every thought. You will quickly develop deep gratitude and respect for all your brothers and sisters. And as you do, the lines that separate your physical selves will begin to dissolve, merging into a oneness that is new to you, yet somehow quite familiar. As you continue to spend more time during the day remembering and acknowledging this oneness, the ego's attempts to have you fear and separate from your brother or sister will diminish, until one day the ego completely dissolves into the nothingness from which it came.

In Kahlil Gibran's book "Jesus the Son of Man," Kahlil discusses the concept that the "stranger" you see is much more like you than you realize, and the more understanding you receive, the more these so-called differences or barriers fall. Gibran explains this concept using an example of Peter's recollection of Jesus talking to him. Jesus says:

> [26]*Your neighbor is your other self dwelling behind a wall. In understanding, all walls shall fall down. Who knows but that your neighbor is your better self, wear-*

[26]See Notes, page xvii.

ing another body? See that you love him as you would love yourself. He too is the manifestation of the Most High, whom you do not know. Your neighbor is a field where the springs of your hope walk in their green garments, and where the winters of your desire dream of snowy heights. I would have you love your neighbor even as I have loved you."

Then I asked Him saying, "How can I love a neighbor who loves me not, and who covets my property? One who would steal my possessions?"

And He answered, "When you are plowing and your manservant is sowing the seed behind you, would you stop and look backward and put to flight a sparrow feeding upon a few of your seeds? Should you do this, you were not worthy of the riches of your harvest."

When Jesus had said this, I was ashamed and was silent. But I was not in fear, for He smiled upon me.

Invitation #8 - How Your Thoughts Affect You in the Moment

Sit alone in your room for ten minutes with a clock in front of you. For the first five minutes completely involve yourself in bringing to the surface any and all negative thoughts and feelings you have toward any individual in your life. Bring to the surface any negative thoughts you may be holding on to about strangers you have met, or someone on television, or whomever. Bring to these five minutes everything wrong you think they have done to you and judge, criticize and curse them for it. It is very important to feel how what you are thinking is literally changing your body, mind and spirit. For these five minutes dig everything out that you've been holding within the dark crevices of your mind and heart. But be aware of what your thoughts are doing to you physically and mentally. Do this exercise honestly and truly once in your life and you will never again question that your thoughts, even when they are directed at someone else - even a total stranger - will completely affect and change your mental, physical and spiritual state.

Now consider how your judgments of others and yourself throughout the day silently and viciously affect your mental, physical and spiritual state. These individual judgments might have a tenth of the venom of your thoughts during the five-minute exercise, but remember that there are 24 hours in the day. Imagine for a moment how all these "little judgments," when accumulated throughout the day, end up affecting your mental, physical and spiritual state. Now multiply that by 365 days, and then multiply that by the number of years you have lived. Can you now begin to understand the power of your own individual thoughts and judgments? This is how the ego is advising you to live! These are the tools the ego has used and is using to mold you into who it wants you to be. Is there any wonder why you now question who you have become? Will you not, if only for a moment, consider the ego's attempt and advice as corrupted, destructive and insane!

But rejoice my friend, for today you have arrived at a place in your heart and mind that desires another way of thinking, acting, being and living. This place has always been within you simply waiting for you to consider it as a possibility. Once this possibility is entered, light will again begin to freely flow from within you. This light, with your acceptance, will begin to fill your body. With your acceptance, it will completely fill you and even begin to overflow. As it begins to overflow, tears of happiness, peace and joy might need to flow. Soon this light will begin to fill and expand to your whole room, your house, your city, state, country and Earth. It will expand to every person, place or thing you set your eyes on, and you will begin to bless every moment and every circumstance. All things you once judged such as hair, skin color, the way people dress, weight, facial features, age, how they act or react, will dissolve in this light. You will put aside the ego's training and you will exchange it for knowledge, peace of mind and joy, all the things the ego promised you but never delivered. You will exchange all judgments for blessings and see strangers as brothers and sisters.

Quiet the mind, take some deep breaths and invite your guides and angels to be with you for the next five minutes. Completely reverse how the ego has trained you to think. For just five minutes, bring God into the room. Invite God to enter your heart, body, mind and spirit, and everyone and everything you judged in the first five minutes you now forgive, pray for and bless. Regardless of what you think they did or did not do to you, for the next five minutes forgive, pray for and bless them. Do this with every centimeter of your heart, with every ounce of your body, with all the love in your soul. Ask your guides, angels and God to assist you. Give God all your pain, anger and sadness and let it dissolve in His light. Ask your guides, angels and God to fill all those places within your heart that have been hurt with absolute forgiveness, kindness and love toward the brothers and sisters you once chose to judge.

Remember, you are participating in this invitation to assist you in understanding and acknowledging the power of your thoughts, both positive and negative. Once you have forgiven your brothers and sisters, once you have given and seen all the pain and anger dissolving in God's light, begin to pray for those you once judged. With all your heart and soul, pray for their well-being. Pray for their health, pray for their present and future. With all your heart and soul, ask God to help you hold them. Feel yourself holding your brother or sister and feel God holding you both. Ask and invite God to assist you in seeing your brother and sister through His heart from now on. Ask God to completely retrain your thought system from one based on judgment and pain to one based on forgiveness and love. Ask God to assist you in carrying this new thought system with you wherever you go and to let it touch whomever you see. Offer gratitude to God. Thank your angels and guides for their assistance, then slowly return your mind to the room.

You have now felt what five minutes fully dedicated to thinking negatively or positively can do to your body, mind and soul. Again, think of what a whole day of positive or negative thoughts can do. Think of what a whole day of the ego's thought system, immediately judging a brother or sister, can do. Think of what a whole day of the Godself's thought system, immediately seeing a stranger as a brother or sister - as the perfect creation of God, can do. Now multiply that by 365 days and then by the number of years you have lived. That is the power of one positive or negative thought when it is added to the next positive or negative thought and to the next, and so on and so on. Each thought occurs in the moment, and it is in the moment where your life is created.

Next time you judge a brother or sister, catch yourself doing this, and then forgive yourself and your brother and sister. Bless and pray for yourself and your brother and sister. Offer gratitude to them for assisting you in seeing where, through your thoughts, you were taking yourself. Offer gratitude to God and invite Him to remind you that the same light that exists within Him and you also exists within your brother and sister. My brother and sister, our lives are simply a reflection of what we choose to think in the moment.

We're Always in the Right Place at the Right Time

In order to experience peace of mind and joy in the present moment, trust and have faith that we are always in the right place at the right time. The following short story highlights this point and is taken from Lilly Walter's book, "One Hand Typing and Keyboarding Manual: With Personal Motivational Messages from Others Who Have Overcome."

> [27]*One of my joys and passions is my voice. I love to perform in our local community theaters. My throat became very sore during a particularly grueling show run. It was my first time performing an operatic piece, and I was terrified that I had actually done some damage to my vocal cords. I was a lead and we were about to open. So I made an appointment with my family doctor, where I waited for an hour. I finally left in a huff, went back to work, grabbed a phone book and found a throat specialist close by. Once more, I made an appointment, and off I went.*

[27]See Notes, page xvii.

*The nurse showed me in and I sat down to wait for
the doctor. I was feeling very disgruntled. I rarely get
sick, and here I was, sick when I needed to be healthy.
Besides, I had to take time out of my workday to go to
two different doctors, both of whom kept me waiting.
It was very frustrating. Why do these things have to
happen? A moment later the nurse came back in, and
said, "May I ask you something personal?"*

*This seemed odd; what else do they ask you but personal
questions in a doctor's office? But I looked at the nurse
and replied, "Yes, of course."*

"I noticed your hand," she said hesitantly.

*I lost half of my left hand in a forklift accident when I
was 11. I think it is one of the reasons I didn't follow my
dream of performing in theater, although everyone says,
"Gee, I never noticed! You are so natural." In the back
of my mind I thought that they only wanted to see perfect
people on stage. No one would want to see me. But I love
musical comedies, and I do have a good voice. So one day,
I tried out at our local community theatre. I was the first
one they cast! That was three years ago. Since then, I have
been cast in almost everything I tried out for.*

*The nurse continued, "What I need to know is how has
this affected your life." Never in the 25 years since it
happened has someone asked me this. Maybe they'll say,
"Does it bother you?" but never anything as sweeping
as, "How has it affected your life?"*

*After an awkward pause, she said, "You see, I just
had a baby, and her hand is like yours. I, well, need to
know how it has affected your life."*

*"How has it affected my life?" I thought about it a
bit, so I could think of the right words to say. Finally,
I said, "It has affected my life, but not in a bad way*

- *I do many things that people with two normal hands find difficult. I type about 75 words a minute, I play the guitar, I have ridden and shown horses for years, and I even have a Housemasters Degree. I'm involved in musical theater, and I am a professional speaker. I am constantly in front of a crowd. I do television shows four or five times a year. I think it was never "difficult" because of the love and encouragement of my family. They always talked about all the great notoriety I would get because I would learn how to do things with one hand that most people had trouble doing with two. We were all very excited about that. That was the main focus, not the handicap.*

"Your daughter does not have a problem. She is normal. You are the one who will teach her to think of herself as anything else. She will come to know she is "different," but you will teach her that different is wonderful. Normal means you are average. What's fun about that?"

She was silent for a while. Then she simply said, "Thank you" and walked out.

I sat there thinking, "Why do these things have to happen?" Everything happens for a reason, even that forklift falling on my hand. All the circumstances leading up to being at this doctor's office, and this moment in time happened for a reason.

The doctor came in, looked at my throat and said he wanted to anesthetize and put a probe down it to examine it. Well, singers are very paranoid about putting medical instruments down their throats, especially ones so rough they need to be anesthetized!

I said, "No thanks," and walked out.

The next day, my throat was completely better.

The ego insists that we can be in the wrong place at the wrong time. The Godself reminds us that we are always in the right place at the right time. If we were to open ourselves to the possibility of the previous sentence, moments of frustration during the day would turn into moments of peace and gratitude. There are no such things as accidents or coincidences. Could we ever truly believe that a person who is never sick, goes to her doctor's office, leaves after waiting for a little while, goes back to work, picks up the yellow pages, picks a throat specialist, and in that specialist's office there happens to be a new mother whose baby has only half of one hand? The nurse musters the courage to ask a very personal question, and a perfect answer comes back as if spoken by an angel. Of course Lilly chooses not to have treatment on her throat, which she was obviously concerned enough about to seek a specialist. Yet the next day after refusing treatment, she is perfectly healthy. Is that a coincidence or an accident?

Every situation, when properly perceived, is a gift to all involved. The above situation was as much a gift to Lilly as it was to the nurse, and even to the daughter of the nurse. The last thing Lilly believed during this particular day was that she was about to experience a gift such as this. Everything that was happening to her during the day was simply setting her up for this miracle. Imagine how the nurse's perception must have shifted after Lilly's response. Imagine how much the possibility increased that the nurse will raise her child with positive self-esteem now that she has seen a real life example of what her daughter can do and who she can become. Imagine all the self-imposed boundaries that Lilly expanded for this young mother and child. And, for the first time in her life, Lilly had the opportunity to answer a very basic question for herself, which was: how had this "disability" impacted her life? Was it really a disability, as society defines it, or was it a gift, as God defines it? Understand that what the ego's world defines as a disability, God defines as a gift.

There are no such things as disabilities. Disabilities, and terms such as these are creations of the ego, all made in an effort to further separate us from our brothers and sisters. It uses such terms to make us feel more fortunate and more able than our brother or sister. The Godself would remind us that regardless of physical manifestation, we are no more or less fortunate or able than any brother or sister. Children are not born with disabilities by accident. People are not in wheelchairs because of accidents, and Lilly did not lose half her left hand by accident. These were all events the individuals chose, and decisions they made in order to learn, teach and consciously expand.

We, at a higher level of consciousness before being born or during our lives, chose such events and circumstances. In actuality, they are not disabilities or accidents but gifts. Pure and simple, they are gifts we offered ourselves in order to grow through lessons that can best be learned through such experiences. So next time you see a person in a wheelchair or an individual or child with a "birth defect," do not feel sorry for them but understand that these are courageous individuals who have chosen their paths, just as you have chosen yours. Some have chosen to walk, others have not; some have chosen two arms, others have chosen one. We all have our individual lessons to learn, and we all individually understand ourselves well enough to know which specific circumstances and experiences are most useful to our personal growth.

Society has tried to teach us that two arms are better than one, that walking is better than not walking. Remember, though, that society had also taught us that slavery was acceptable and that white was better than black. As we know, teachings about slavery and discrimination based on the color of a person's skin are wrong. Some day we will learn that walking is not any better than not walking and that two of anything is not better than one of anything.

If you can walk, then that is what will best serve your growth. If you're in a wheelchair, then that is what will best serve your growth. Walking, in truth, is as much a gift as not being able to walk. Being black is as much a gift as being white. Be grateful for every second of the day, for you have given yourself exactly what you need. There will come a day when these thoughts will be natural to all of us, yet until that day comes, let them be natural to you.

Being in the Now on the Road

"Have you ever noticed... anyone going slower than
you is an idiot, and anyone going faster than you is a
maniac?"

George Carlin

The ego has taught us that if someone cuts us off in traffic, we should react with emotions such as annoyance, irritation, anger or even rage. The world considers these emotions to be natural and deserved responses. The world tells us that we have every right to be angry. It feels natural and right to react with anger because that is how we have been trained and what we are now used to. In fact, we often consider what is natural and what we're used to as basically the same thing. Yet, what we are used to and what is natural are usually two completely different things. Any time we react with anger, such a reaction occurs not because it is natural, but because it has become a bad habit. We have learned negative tendencies, have not corrected them and they have become bad habits that we now call our natural behaviors. We have repeated these bad habits over a period of time and they have now become "second nature" or natural tendencies. But many of the reactions we consider natural tendencies have, in truth, nothing to do with our true nature. When we were children, our parents, other family members and friends reacted this way. As children this type of reaction was often common, first with our parents and family members, then with our peers. As adults, they probably still react this way, and now we have probably joined them in their thinking. At first, such reactions probably did not sit well with us, but as we heard our families react over and over in such a manner, sooner or later we got used to the behavior, and let it be until their behavior became ours.

I remember as a very young child, driving with my mother in Caracas, Venezuela. Sooner or later, someone would cut her off, or something would happen on the road that she simply did not agree with. Her response was typically a negative comment regarding the other driver's skills. I remember hearing my mother say things she would never say outside the car. Needless to say, the first time I really remember arguing with my mother was in the car. She complained about someone's driving and I immediately came to that person's defense and explained to my mother what she could have done to avoid the situation. Let's just say that taking criticism about her driving skills from a seven year old child did not win me any brownie points! On the other hand, she was happy because she thought that it was only a matter of time before I would become a successful defense attorney. So on and on it went. My mother complained, I defended the other drivers, she came back at me telling me why I was wrong, and I offered driving advice on how she might avoid such situations in the future. She would say that I should be defending her and not the other driver whom I did not even know. Anyway, on and on it went, drive after drive, until one day I got so tired of the whole game that I figured it would be best for me to just fall asleep, or just keep my opinions to myself.

The reactions of my mother, which most people consider natural and correct responses, offer people a certain level of comfort. For if it did not offer a certain level of comfort, why would people continue to react this way? Attacking a brother or sister only offers a certain level of comfort because we believe that when we do so, we are released from the negative emotions we ourselves offer. Yet, if we were to look within, we would see that whatever we offer a brother or sister remains with us. If, in a car, we offer anger, that anger, as much as we want to believe that it affects the other driver, affects us more. We think that we experience release and comfort by attacking a brother or sister, but this is only a false release, a false comfort.

I invite you to look within. Does this so-called release truly bring comfort? True comfort manifests itself as the state of peace. Does attacking a brother or sister, regardless of how much we think we are right, offer us true peace? Shouldn't comfort and peace of mind go hand in hand? Do these "comfortable" feelings come from actual comfort, or from habits and illusions of comfort?

The ego would have us believe that if we "give it" to another driver, this action will make us feel better. The ego teaches us that what we give we lose. Thus, if we give a negative emotional response to another driver, this negative emotion will leave us and somehow stay with the other driver, thus releasing us from the response. This, the ego says, will make us feel better and will make the other driver feel worse. Not only that, but the ego also wants us to believe that this negative emotion will somehow stay with the other driver for a long time to come, thus making us believe that we got the upper hand.

The Godself reminds us that what we give - we keep, that what we offer a brother or sister - we gift ourselves. There is no way we can offer a negative emotion without feeling it ourselves. What we offer a brother or sister must first flow through us. There is no such thing as letting another driver "have it" without feeling it in one way or another.

Now try to remember all those times you reacted with anger out of habit. You will probably not have to think too far back. Has this habit ever brought you true peace of mind? And if not, has it ever brought you comfort? So isn't this habit of anger, with which we are now comfortable, really just an illusion of comfort? Haven't we suffered in our cars long enough? Would you like to change your way of reacting? Would you like to know what true comfort feels like? There is a way, my friend, to find peace and comfort on the road.

I used to react with a lack of peace on the road. I admit that even today, I slip every now and then and mentally let a driver have it. But the difference is that I now catch myself being out of peace with myself much quicker, and as I catch myself I correct the situation in my mind and find true comfort and peace.

Living in Caracas, Venezuela presents many opportunities to choose peace on the road. If you haven't been there, imagine Los Angeles with half to a quarter of the available traffic lanes, no real street police enforcing laws and stop lights which, on a good day, are perceived by fellow drivers as yield signs. If it rains, people are better off walking to work, regardless of the distance. This is a city where, if a survey were conducted asking people to find the turn signal in their cars, at least 90 percent would fail!

We have discussed that anger might seem to be a logical, comfortable response - one that we are used to, a habit. We have also discussed that this so-called comfortable response has truly never brought us comfort, and if it hasn't brought us comfort, it definitely hasn't brought us peace. In fact, we have tried it the ego's way over and over again, and what has it ever really brought us? Are you open to trying a new way? Good, because this has worked for me, and if it has worked for me then it can work for you.

Invitation #9 - Living in the Now: Four Steps to Choosing Peace on the Road

There are four steps that I have used and still use to obtain peace on the road. They are as follows:

- Learn to differentiate between the spiritual being driving and the action of cutting you off.

- Look at each driver on the road as the child of God and visualize someone you know, trust and love. I visualize Jesus, especially when I need His assistance with those who cut me off or drive recklessly.

- Pray for the safety and protection of every driver who cuts you off or is driving recklessly.

- Be a positive example on the road.

The first step toward choosing peace on the road is to learn to differentiate between the spiritual being driving and the action of cutting you off. We have all had bad days, or at least days we perceived as bad. We have all been late for a meeting, a date or work. We have all had plenty of excuses for not driving as carefully as we could every day. Having said this, would we like our lifetime to be judged based on one driving mistake, one careless act? Well, that is what we do when we call someone a jerk (or worse) for cutting us off. We judge that person's entire life by that one moment in time. We see this person as someone who has always been a jerk and will probably die a jerk. Not only do we punish this person for this one act, but we equally punish ourselves through our loss of peace.

Little do we know what kind of day or week this person has had or what kind of situation that individual is currently experiencing.

For all we know this person could be a great person who just happened to make an error in judgment while driving. We are always in the right place, at the right time. Thus, this person is offering us a gift, and this gift is the opportunity to remember and practice our perfection through the act of choosing peace on the road. As Plato once said, "Be kind, for everyone you meet is fighting a hard battle."

What a wonderful gift it is to be able to choose peace in such a situation. This child of God who has crossed our path is allowing us the opportunity to practice choosing peace. We have been taught the habit of choosing anger, and judging our brother or sister. This is a habit that will probably take time and practice to correct. Therefore, every opportunity that a brother or sister offers us is no more or no less than a beautiful gift. This individual is offering us the practice of choosing peace. There will come a time when we will no longer need to practice choosing peace, for we will be at peace and live in peace. Until that day comes, let us thank our brothers and sisters for their offerings, participation and assistance.

We, and our brothers and sisters, are the extension of God's love in action. When we see that in our brothers and sisters, we feel it. Every action, reaction and situation is an opportunity to remember this. There will come a day when instead of judging our brothers and sisters, we will thank them. There will come a day when, instead of reacting with anger, we will react with understanding. And there will come a day where, instead of seeing an error, we will see and meet the opportunity. That day is coming, for you have been led to this passage and in your heart you sense its truth. You have tried it your egos' way long enough. You have tried judging your brothers and sisters. You have tried anger and seen error. Now your hearts remind you that there is another way of looking at this. There is another way of reacting. There is a way to find peace in your brother or sister's action. There is a way to find peace in your reactions. There is a way indeed.

The second step toward choosing peace on the road is to look at each driver as a child of God and visualize someone you know, trust, respect and love. I visualize Jesus driving certain cars on the road, especially the ones that cut me off or drive recklessly. At first, you might feel a little strange doing this but this might assist you in getting past the illusion that the spiritual being who just cut you off is a stranger. For how could you ever truly be mad at God's child? There is nothing strange about a child of God, for you and he are one. You are a child of God; the stranger is a child of God. Both of you are part of the extension of God's love in action. Both of you have chosen this path, a path that will allow each of you to choose heaven or hell, peace or anxiety, forgiveness or judgment. Forgive his error and you will be released. Choose not to forgive, and you will add the weight of judgment to your heart.

To me, Jesus was and is a great teacher. He is the definition of love in action. In my heart, I know that He would want me to feel the same way about all my brothers and sisters. He would want me to see His perfection in everyone. He would want me to forgive and love my brothers and sisters no matter what, and to treat all my brothers and sisters as I would treat Him, and so I do. To me, Jesus is a child of God, and we are children of God. There is no difference between any of us, except for the fact that Jesus has remembered his perfection and we are in the process of remembering ours.

See who you will in the other car, but know this: that person is a mirror image of ourselves. There is nothing that we wish for that person that we do not experience ourselves. If we are angry with him, we will feel it within ourselves. If we forgive, understand and have compassion for him, we will also feel that within. There is nothing we do to another that we don't do to ourselves. We know this to be true because we have felt our own anger. Regardless of where and to whom we distribute it, we have felt its consequences.

The next time you become angry with another driver, feel what that does to you, not only to your outer self but also to your inner self. Feel the heavy fog roll through your heart, feel its denseness. Feel the tension in your body, the anxiety. Then listen to the sadness in your soul. Hear it for the first time asking you this one simple question: Why would anyone in their right mind do something like this to themselves over and over again? Ask yourself: "What am I doing to myself? What am I accomplishing?" Then, as the fog dissipates and the light begins to shine through, say this: "I simply choose not to do this to myself any longer! There is another way I can react. I will now choose to see God's child in my brother and sister!"

The third step toward choosing peace on the road is to pray for every driver who cuts you off or is driving recklessly. Replace the angry reaction that has brought you nothing but pain and sadness - with a prayer. Let that prayer come directly from your heart. Reach into your heart and pray that the individual gets home safely, that he or she has a great day, and that his or her kids and family are showered with love. With all your soul, pray for God to send angels to escort him or her home. Pray that they touch his or her heart so he or she might think of others and slow down. Pray that anything that is bothering him or her will be washed away through God's mercy. Do this for him or her and you will be set free. You will feel all that you have asked for them. What you will receive in return is a peace that will fill your drive anywhere you go.

The fourth step toward choosing peace on the road is to be a positive example for those on the road. It feels good and peaceful being a positive example, whether in life or on the road - there is no difference.

How Envy Keeps Us from Living in the Moment

Envy is another one of the ego's deception tools which keeps us from living in the moment or being in the now. I have a friend who, on many occasions, has told me that he wishes he had my life. This is a person who has a wonderful wife, two awesome kids, a supportive family and he is financially stable. I would usually smile and say thanks, but little by little, that comment began to bother me and I did not know why. So I prayed about why I was feeling this way and the next time he said it, I replied, "You really don't wish you had my life. What you truly desire is to recognize that you wish you had your own life." There is no life that is better suited for your own growth and development than your own. If you respect the way someone lives his or her life, by all means, follow his or her example, but don't envy him or her. If you had an inkling of knowledge of who you truly are, you would continuously praise God and thank Him for your opportunity and truth.

My friend, even those you perceive as having perfect lives are fighting their own battles. If you had knowledge of their personal battles, there would be a good probability you would reconsider changing roles. I have known many a great spiritual teacher whose personal life was far from perfect. I keep addressing my issues in order to grow as a human being. Those who know me know that I am far from perfect, but I continue to delve into my misperceptions and imperfections in the knowledge that I come closer to my trueself every time I try.

My friend, it is this life that counts. It is this moment that you can recognize as perfect and experience peace in. Ask and trust that all that can be done on the spiritual level to offer you a more fulfilling life is being done. Do not concern yourself with envy and wanting to be someone else, but work on your own misperceptions and imperfections, and you will obtain more peace of mind and joy.

My friend, you are exactly where you need to be, and you are exactly who you need to be. You have been offered more than you know and there will come a point in your life when you recognize that this is so. When you do, you will never look at another person and be envious.

9

CHOOSING ONE'S ATTITUDE

Attitude is a choice. The external environment in and of itself is neutral. The external environment's neutrality is broken by our perception and reaction to it. Our perceptions and reactions are colored by our past beliefs and interpretations. Past beliefs and interpretations are adopted from what we were taught, and have subsequently taught ourselves is the proper, normal, acceptable, agreeable, productive or comfortable way of reacting or being.

Some people believe that they have little or no control over how they react to their environment. These people do not understand that they have already established all of the parameters they will use to react to their environment. Thus, if in any situation we react in a negative, stressful or unproductive manner, we have already set up parameters that have made us react in this manner. We have control over the parameters we set; therefore, we have control over our final reactions or the attitudes we decide to have in relating to our environment. If we currently react in a negative, stressful or unproductive manner to certain situations and we truly want to react in a positive, peaceful and productive manner, all we need to do is change our parameters, the beliefs that generate our reactions. We can react peacefully to every situation.

We give our external environment all the meaning that it has for us. The assessment we place on the external environment is totally up to us. If we give it a positive definition, it is because we believe it is positive. If we give it a negative definition, it is because we believe it is negative. If we give it a stressful definition, it is because we believe it is stressful. If we react angrily, it is because we believe that the external environment deserves an angry response. Our reaction to the external environment is a reflection of the parameters we have consciously or unconsciously set up within our minds. The attitude we display toward our external environment is a verbal and mental manifestation of these parameters. Since we can consciously shift these parameters within our mind, we therefore have the final say as to what attitude we will use in any and every situation.

In his book, "Man's Search for Meaning," Victor E. Frankl illustrates that you can shift your perceptions, and thus choose your attitude even during the most horrific of circumstances. He writes:

28"We who lived in the concentration camps can remember the men who walked through the huts comforting others, giving away their last piece of bread. They may have been few in number, but they offer sufficient proof that everything can be taken from a man but one thing: The last of his freedoms - to choose one's attitude in any given set of circumstances, to choose one's own way."

I Have Two Choices

The following story illustrates one man's determination to choose his attitude in the face of seemingly insurmountable odds.

> Jerry was always in a good mood, and always had something positive to say. When someone would ask him how he was doing, he would reply, "If I were any better, I would be twins!" He was a unique manager because he had several waiters who had followed him around from restaurant to restaurant. The reason the waiters followed Jerry was his attitude. He was a natural motivator. If an employee was having a bad day, Jerry was there telling the employee how to look on the positive side of the situation.
>
> Seeing this style really made me curious, so one day I approached Jerry and remarked, "I don't get it! You can't be a positive person all of the time. How do you do it?"
>
> Jerry replied, "Each morning, I wake up and say to myself, 'Jerry, you have two choices today. You can choose to be in a good mood or you can choose to be in a bad mood.' I choose to be in a good mood. Each time something bad happens, I can choose to be a victim or I can choose to learn from it. I choose to learn from it. Every time someone comes to me complaining, I can choose to accept his complaining or I can point out the

positive side of life. I choose the positive side of life."

"Yeah, right, it's not that easy," I protested.

"Yes, it is," Jerry said. "Life is all about choices. When you cut away all the junk, every situation is a choice. You choose how you react to situations. You choose how people will affect your mood. You choose to be in a good mood or bad mood. The bottom line: It's your choice how you live life."

I reflected on what Jerry said. Soon thereafter, I left the restaurant industry to start my own business. We lost touch, but I often thought about him when I made a choice about life instead of reacting to it. Several years later, I heard that Jerry did something you are never supposed to do in a restaurant business; he left the back door open one morning and was held up at gun point by three armed robbers. While trying to open the safe, his hand, shaking from nervousness, slipped off the combination. The robbers panicked and shot him. Luckily, Jerry was found relatively quickly and rushed to the local trauma center. After 18 hours of surgery and weeks of intensive care, Jerry was released from the hospital with fragments of the bullets still in his body.

I saw Jerry about six months after the accident. When I asked him how he was, he said, "If I were any better, I'd be twins. Wanna see my scars?" I declined to see his wounds but did ask him what had gone through his mind as the robbery took place.

"The first thing that went through my mind was that I should have locked the back door," Jerry replied. "Then, as I lay on the floor, I remembered that I had two choices: I could choose to live, or I could choose to die. I chose to live."

"Weren't you scared? Did you lose consciousness?" I asked.

Jerry continued, "The paramedics were great. They kept telling me I was going to be fine. But when they wheeled me into the emergency room and I saw the expressions on the faces of the doctors and nurses, I got really scared. In their eyes, I read, 'He's a dead man.' I knew I needed to take action."

"What did you do?" I asked. "Well, there was a big, burly nurse shouting questions at me," said Jerry. "She asked if I was allergic to anything. "Yes," I replied. The doctors and nurses stopped working as they waited for my reply. I took a deep breath and yelled, "Bullets!" Over their laughter, I told them, "I am choosing to live. Operate on me as if I am alive, not dead."

Jerry lived, thanks to the skill of his doctors, but also because of his amazing attitude. I learned from him that every day we have the choice to live fully. Attitude, after all, is everything.

Changing Attitudes: Expansion of Human Behavior

Some people complain about today's youth. Some people complain about where they perceive society to be heading. They question the behavior in which people seem to be engaging. They comment that people are rude on the road, that there's too much sex on television and in the movies, that there is too much violence in the world.

In some ways, we can all recognize and sympathize with their perceptions of reality, with how they choose to view the world. I recognize their attitudes toward the world because there have been moments in my life where I, too, felt that way. And I am sympathetic because I understand where they are in their thought process, and the way they choose to view the world. But today, I respectfully choose not to share in their attitudes or join them in their thinking any longer.

Today I observe an expansion occurring. An expansion of all we think we are. This expansion simply teaches us the following: All that we think we are, we are not, and all that we ever wish we could be, we already are. There is a great strength and energy in the people leading this expansion.

At the same time, it takes a lot of strength and energy to subscribe to and follow illusions in our lives, on a daily basis. It takes a huge amount of energy to live out a lie and to keep expanding on a lie. The world of illusion, for those who believe in it, is hard, very hard. It is hard because it is unnatural, and because it is an unnatural way of living, it takes a significant amount of strength and energy to simply get through such days.

It is exhausting to try to be who you are not. Think about your toughest days. Weren't those the days you chose to believe and live the greatest illusions about yourself and your brothers and sisters? Think of any tough day you have had in the past and try recognizing how much of it you lived by buying into the illusions about yourself and your brothers and sisters, and by buying into illusions of your unworthiness and of others' unworthiness. Think of the time you spent buying into your illusions of fear, sadness, anger, anxiety, regret, distrust, rudeness, arrogance, materialism, faithlessness, and your inability to forgive and see the good in people. Weren't these truly your toughest days? Didn't these days take extreme strength and energy to get through them?

Why do you think that was? The answer is simply this: any time we are in any of these illusionary states, we are in an unnatural state, a chaotic state. Chaos can be defined as an utter state of confusion. It takes great energy and strength to live in such a manner.

We have learned certain ways to react and behave from society, family members, friends and peers. We might think that some of these behaviors are natural. We might even be willing to defend them as being the right behaviors and reactions. Yet, how could any behavior or reaction that causes us pain and suffering be right or natural? Could we not at least ask ourselves if there is a better way to behave and react? Is there not a way that could bring us peace?

The natural way of behaving and reacting will always brings us gratitude and peace. The unnatural way of behaving and reacting will always brings us stress, judgment, pain and regret. If we have reacted to a brother or sister in what we thought was a natural way and we experienced stress, judgment, pain and regret, then we must understand that our natural way of reacting is, in truth, unnatural.

The only value these behaviors hold for us and the world is for us to recognize them for what they are to us and the world: our unnatural selves, our false selves, our ego-selves. The only value they hold for us and the world is to experience them for a long enough period of time for us to get physically, mentally and spiritually sick of them. When we've had enough of them, we get to the point where we no longer choose or want to live this way. We no longer choose to support them and torture ourselves. We no longer choose to support them and torture others.

Growth can be a detoxifying process in which things will need to come up, out, and looked at before they are released. All these behaviors, all these illusions that we, as a society, as families and as individuals are choosing to go through at this moment in time are necessary to bring us to the point of recognizing and remembering that this is not who we are. The illusions are necessary for us to remember that this is not how we want to live our lives, not how we want to raise our children, not how we want to interact with each other, not how we want to spend our time, and that this is simply not who we truly are.

Understand that any day that we perceive as difficult is actually a gift that is offered by our higher selves. It is a gift because our Godselves are trying to physically and mentally show us the activities and parameters we are supporting that are "making us" react to the environment in such a manner. Sooner or later, we see what the Godself is trying to show us. When we do, these difficult days will turn into beautiful days filled with miracles. As Gregory M. Lousig-

Nont, Ph.D., put it in "The Best Day of My Life:"

[29]*Today, when I awoke, I suddenly realized that this is the best day of my life, ever!*

There were times when I wondered if I would make it to today; but I did! And because I did, I'm going to celebrate! Today I'm going to celebrate what an unbelievable life I have had so far; the accomplishments, the many blessings, and yes, even the hardships, because they have served to make me stronger. I will live this day with my head held high and a happy heart. I will take time to marvel at God's seemingly simple gifts, the morning dew, the sun, the clouds, the trees, the flowers, and the birds. Today, none of these miraculous creations will escape my notice. Today I will share my excitement for life with other people. I'll make someone smile. I'll go out of my way to perform an act of kindness for someone I don't even know. Today I'll give a word of encouragement to someone who seems down. I'll pay someone a sincere compliment. I'll tell a child how special they are. And I'll tell someone I love, just how deeply I care for them and how much they mean to me. Today is the day I quit worrying about what I don't have, and start being grateful for all the wonderful things God has already given me. I'll remember that to worry is just a waste of time, because my faith in God and His divine plan ensures everything will be just fine. And tonight, before I go to bed, I'll take a stroll outside and raise my eyes to the heavens. I will stand in awe at the beauty of the stars and the moon and the majesty of the universe and I will praise God for these magnificent treasures. As the day ends and I lay my head down, I will thank the Almighty for the best day of my life. And I will sleep the sleep of a contented child, and yet excited with expectation, because I know tomorrow is going to be the best day of my life, ever!

[29]See Notes, page xvii.

The Snowflake that Changed a Life

Everything that we see and experience is seen and experienced through our physical senses. The emotions and feelings we hold in regard to these forms and experiences make up our perceptions.

Let's take the example of snow. Snow is a phenomenon of nature and because it is a natural phenomenon, it is of God. The way we perceive such a phenomenon, the purpose and function we give it, and the attitude we have toward it is up to us, our free will in action. The following is a true story of how one man I encountered changed his world by simply changing his perceptions and attitude - toward a snowflake.

A heavy snowstorm fell throughout the day. As most of us know, when it snows, it takes more time to get to work. We become more concerned about possible car accidents, our ears, nose and feet freeze, the wind can reach into our bones and even walking becomes a hazard. On this particular day, I participated in "A Course in Miracles" study group and I could feel that the snowstorm had taken a toll on the energy of the group. It had taken a toll on all except for one of the students.

I wondered how he could be so upbeat after such a day, especially since this man had a job that kept him on the road. He shared with the group that on the way to the post office, he went into a coffee shop to get out of the storm and cold for a while. While sitting in the coffee shop he looked around and saw that most of the people there seemed miserable with red noses, sniffling, coughing, bundled up in layers of clothes. He too was feeling quite miserable. He too was sniffling, tired and cold. Then he remembered that in the Course, it stated that you are in control of your perceptions. Right then and there, he decided to do something about his attitude.

In an instant, he decided that on the way to the post office, each and every snowflake that hit his face would bring him joy; that those snow flakes would no longer cause him grief, that they would no longer make him curse the weather, or in any way negatively affect his state of mind. So after finishing his coffee, off he went walking to the post office.

As the first snowflakes hit his face, interestingly enough he also experienced his first smirk of the day. And as the snowflakes increased in volume, so too did his smirk, which turned into a smile. Soon joy became an actual thought in his mind. He began to sing "snow flakes are falling on my head" as he walked by so many other souls who had chosen, in their own way, to see the day and their walk as a hassle, inconvenience and a hazard. At first, he sang the song in his mind, then just loud enough for himself to hear it. As the snowflakes increased, so too did his volume. There he was, singing joyfully as other pedestrians probably wondered what this poor schizophrenic person was doing out in this kind of weather. The snowflakes kept falling on his face and now that his rendition of the song was a number one single in the charts of his mind, he could sing it loud, proud and with joy.

This action made adult pedestrians cautious and made children smile and laugh. Seeing that children, in their own way, were "getting it" made him more joyous and soon he began to be thankful to God for the snowstorm, for the cold, for the icy streets and for the children. The more he thanked God for the moment, the more perfect the moment became and the more joy he got from being in it. With an increased joy for the moment, there came an increase in his energy and stamina. To say that by the time he reached the door of the post office he was the happiest person ever to walk into a United States Post Office might not actually be stretching the truth.

What had begun as a hassle, inconvenience and hazard had become an energy booster, a spiritual high and a gift. Nothing in the physical environment had changed, only the way he had now chosen to perceive it. Only his perception and attitude changed. By changing his mind, he changed the world around him from one that was a hassle to one that made him happy, from one that was a hazard to one that made children laugh, and from one that was an inconvenience to one that became a gift simply because he chose to see a snowflake differently.

As he retold the story, tears came from his eyes, but they were not from sadness or fear. They were from recognizing that every moment, if looked upon from a place of love, is miraculous. And tears filled our eyes and joy filled our hearts, because as we listened, we too remembered this possibility.

I spent about two years going to those classes once a week. It was a beautiful experience and I learned and remembered a lot by interacting, listening and discussing our different perceptions. But never throughout all those years did one story or spiritual thought touch or stay with me as much as the story of the snowflake that changed a life.

In his book, "Something's Going on Here," Bob Benson offers another example of how an individual can completely change his thoughts and attitude about an event in his life by simply reinterpreting the event in his mind. Bob writes:

> [30]*"W.T., how did you like your heart attack?"*
>
> *"It scared me to death, almost."*
>
> *"Would you like to do it again?"*
>
> *"No!"*
>
> *"Would you recommend it?"*
>
> *"Definitely not."*
>
> *"Does your life mean more to you than it did before?"*
>
> *"Well, yes."*
>
> *"You and Nell have always had a beautiful marriage, but now are you closer than ever?"*
>
> *"Yes."*
>
> *"How about that new granddaughter?"*
>
> *"Yes. Did I show you her picture?"*
>
> *"Do you have a new compassion for people - a deep understanding and sympathy?"*

[30]See Notes, page xvii.

"Yes."

"Do you know the Lord in a richer, deeper fellowship than you had ever realized could be possible?"

"Yes."

"How did you like your heart attack?"

Silence was his answer.

A Brother in Pain

A friend of mine was going through a tough time, and I asked for a message to offer him in order to lift his spirits. The following message came to me in first person. I offer it to you the way I received it. If, for whatever reason, this use of the first person makes you uncomfortable, then feel free to skip it or change it in any way you wish. As I've mentioned before, do not be afraid to ask, the universe waits for you to ask. Any time that your attitude toward life is less than positive, ask for clarity. Sit down with a paper and pen, and through your heart, ask for clarity, and allow whatever wants to flow through to flow. Here is the message I received:

I feel your pain, yet all pain is self-inflicted. So if all pain is self-inflicted, how, you may ask, do I feel your pain? Ah, the answer is as simple as the question, for the answer came even before the question. There is nothing you can feel, nothing you can accomplish without Me, for there is nothing I can be, feel or accomplish without you. Herein lies the gift we hold for each other. At times, you might think this is not true, yet aren't those the times when you are at your loneliest? Be lonely, my brother, for that is your choice, but understand that you have chosen it and understand that you feel lonely, not because you are alone, but because you think you are. There is one thing that I know, feel and live, from the grandest of ballrooms to the smallest crevices in my heart. You may feel lonely but you are never alone. Simply remember this: You are never alone for I Am always with you. Choose to feel Me in the silence and I

Am there. Let Me cover you and no rain shall touch your head, not even in the grandest of storms, when you remember that I Am with you.

You might try to dim the light of your perfection, yet light surrounds you always, for I Am the Light, as you are My light. On occasion, you might choose to forget Me, but I know that forgetting is your way of remembering better. On occasion, you might choose to not love Me, but I sit with you in everlasting patience and envelop you with love, as I Am enveloped by love.

Do not choose to see Me with your eyes, or hear Me with your ears, for who I Am is who you are, and nothing else can surround All That Is. Never be lonely, my brother, and never search for Me in things. Do not search for happiness and love in that which you can touch with your hands or taste with your tongue, for you have already tried that, and where has that gotten you? Do not search for me outside yourself, for I Am in you, and I Am you. In times of insanity when illusions surround you, offer me an instant and sit in the power of your silence. Understand that I Am all that you need and that you are all that completes Me. For as you hold a place in my heart, so too do I live in yours.

Do not forget to bring your brothers and sisters, for they hold the key to the truth about you. And when you hold your brother or sister's hand, I'll be there, for I Am the forgiven and the forgiver, the Truth and the Light. Know that you, your brother and sister are one and the same. Forgive all who have chosen not to forgive you. Learn to love all who love you not. Serve all who would not serve you. This is the key to happiness, the release from all pain, the one lesson you came back to remember. Forgive, love and serve all always, and you will never be engulfed by judgment, loneliness, pain or regret.

That, my friend, is the story. The same simple story that has been taught by many to many, and from that teaching comes learning. From that learning comes the release from illusion and pain, and from this release comes union. Through union you will, for the first time, see your face reflected in God's eyes, and it will not surprise you to see your brother and sister there with you. For they have always been there, waiting for you to look, to truly see.

Dream Offered for Chapter Nine: The Smile

While writing this chapter on attitude, I received the following dream. This was a non-lucid dream, meaning that while I was experiencing the dream, I had no clue that I was dreaming nor did I have any conscious control over the events that were occurring. Even though the dream was a non-lucid one, the colors, emotions, environment, actions and reactions were so shockingly realistic that when I awoke, I had no problem recalling it and putting it down on paper. In the dream, I was an old man retelling and reliving the story at the same time.

It was World War II. Every day, while fighting the Nazis, my fear mastered most every moment. I knew I was fighting the devil. I knew that every day I was in hell. Yet, it was while in this hell that I met a very strange fellow who surprisingly ended up becoming my best friend. One of his peculiarities was that in the darkest of moments when things seemed hopeless, he did three pirouettes in the air like a ballerina and landed with the biggest smile on his face. I'm not sure what brought about that confident smile. Was it the guys breaking up with laughter, as this two hundred pound man danced in the air? Was it just a momentary shift into another world? I don't know what it was, but after he landed and gave us his smile, things became different. We began by calling it the BD/AD effect, the before dance, after dance effect. The BD/AD effect was upgraded to "dad" (from BD/AD which spells DAD) which was upgraded to "father." Thus, my friend was now simply known as "father." In the scariest of moments one could ever imagine, at times when the only natural emotion of a sane individual was total panic and fear, at moments when we were in hell fighting the devil - these were the times father did three pirouettes, landed and gave us a big smile. Regardless of the hell we were facing, the moment would be lost and all we could do was look at each other and laugh.

I had always believed that father was a little nuts, until the day he taught me the greatest lesson I have ever learned.

It was D-Day and a fierce battle broke out. I was driving a tank and providing cover for my men. It was looking very bad, and the Germans were giving us all they had. There was no retreat today, for this was hell and we were in the middle of it, fighting the devil 'til death. I just knew, had absolute knowledge that, today was the day I would die!

I was overcome by such fear during the battle that driving the tank and concentrating on covering my men was the last thing on my mind. Like flies on a trash can I could see, hear and feel bullets all around me, flying in every direction. I could see men exploding into pieces, some walking around without arms, some on the ground without legs. I felt like I had held back Satan for a long time and that I could hold him back no longer. I, in the most literal sense, saw myself on top of the tank holding a giant 10-foot tall, black, devilish, bat-like creature by its wings. I had grown so tired of holding it back that I knew I could hold it back no longer.

Father must have felt or somehow seen on my face that I was breaking. So, in the middle of the battle, during the worst part of the fight, he jumped on the front upper part of the tank, did three pirouettes and landed. The third time he landed, he did so with his face toward me. Suddenly I could see right through him! He had taken a heavy German round in the middle of his chest. As he leaned forward his hand gently touched my hand. Then he fell life-less onto the tank. Yet, when I looked at his face, I could see that he died with a smile, a perfect heavenly smile. And for some reason, I felt no sadness. All I could do was look at his smile. It was as if God had come down from heaven and offered humanity one last smile. Nothing else mattered, the beauty of his smile mesmerized me and all I could do was look at it, smile back and cry tears of joy. It was as if for a moment, the battle ceased and all I could see was the beauty and perfection of all men. That is when it hit me. My mind shifted, the devil disappeared and all I could see was heaven. Heaven was right in front of me and I released all the fear that I had been holding all this time. As I released it, something amazing happened. The 10-foot bat that I was holding off did not finish me off, but as I released it, it simply disappeared.

You see, in the darkest moment that any human could experience, father made me smile and think of heaven. In the darkest moment in my life, when not a drop of sanity was left in my mind, when not a drop of love was left in my heart, father showed me heaven. He had, in that one act, expressed to me that I could see heaven in any action. Regardless of the physical appearance of that action, I could see it as heaven sent. In a moment's time, I learned that God was in every action, that God was in each expression, that God was in each word, and that God was in each man. I learned that even in the scariest of moments you can see and experience God. Regardless of whether or not you thought you were in hell, you can still choose to see and experience heaven. Regardless of whether or not you saw your best friend blown away, you can still see God and the kindness of all men in one smile.

In that one moment when I should have cursed the Nazis most, I could not stop the tears from rolling down my face, for the absolute love I felt for them. In that one moment when I should have lost all faith in men, I gained absolute trust that what I was seeing was not what was truly there. In one moment's time, the devil disappeared, hell melted away and all that was left was the kindness, gentleness, courage and the friendship of men.

Yes, a part of me did die that day. It was the part of me that embraced fear, the part of me that harnessed hatred and reveled in revenge. The part of me that died that day was the dark, lonely and lost part of me that never wanted to live.

So with an absolute peace, I fought and drove through the battlefield taking the rest of my men to safety. Throughout the rest of the battle, my friend's lifeless body laid on my tank and every time I looked at his smile, I understood for the first time that there is God in all men. For me, there was nothing left to ever fear. There was no one else to ever hate. For in the darkest of hours, I found the light that exists within me.

Everything Happens for Our Own Good

Little by little, we hear people changing the way they talk. More and more, we hear people saying "everything happens for a reason." I remember, not so long ago, when most people just believed that "shit happens." They were basically saying that good or bad things happen and that's the way it is - and we just have to deal with it. Now we are in a time when I hear a lot of people saying to one another "everything happens for a reason." This means that good or bad stuff will happen but there is a higher purpose for why it happens and we should be patient and understanding. In the end, something good will come from the experience.

In order to encourage the people who are saying that everything happens for a reason to take it to the next level of evolution, I would like to offer the view that "everything happens for our own good." This means that everything that is happening to us now can be used for our development and growth now. We don't have to wait for the future to be grateful for what is happening to us now. If properly perceived, every moment, regardless of its physical manifestation, is a gift we have offered ourselves.

My friend, I understand that you might look back at your life, and tell yourself that this cannot be so. If you believe this to be the case, I have no interest in changing your mind about how you wish to carry your past. I have no interest, not because I do not care, but because I have an absolute respect for how you choose to carry your past and view your reality. The only thing that I do ask is for you to consider the possibility. It is in considering this possibility that you allow yourself to expand and develop. The acceptance of the possibility is not as important to me as your sincere consideration of it.

We may not yet believe that everything happens for our own good, because we still believe that sometimes growth comes through pain and struggle. We hear about pain and struggle, and negative connotations immediately come to mind. Yet we believe that this is what works for us, that this is what helps us get to the "next level." We may criticize ourselves, believing that this is the best way to get ourselves motivated and moving.

We can grow through pain or joy, that choice is ours to make.

But only the insane would prefer to learn through pain, rather than through joy. Yet, even in insane behavior, there is hope. For the more time we spend in insanity, the less we want to remain there. As we would not want to remain in a pool for an extended period of time because it is not our natural environment, neither would we want to remain in insanity. Growth through pain and struggle is insane, yet it is only because of our choice to grow through pain and struggle that we can recognize and realize this insanity. It is because of this that even insane behavior is a great gift we offer ourselves.

Thus, my friend, grow through pain and struggle if you still wish to, but understand that in doing so, you are coming closer to the realization that this is not how you want to grow. It is because of this that your perceived pain and struggle are great gifts and happen for your own good.

When properly perceived, all moments are opportunities to remember the presence of love. When things seem to be going against us, they are occurring in order to allow us to see and experience our personal blocks to the awareness of love's presence. The presence of love is available to us in every moment. Gratitude and joy are the only sane responses to the presence of love. If gratitude and joy are not our immediate responses to the moment, we are misperceiving reality. The unconscious misperception of reality produces confusion and stress. Any confusion and stress that we are experiencing are, in and of themselves, gifts because they make us aware of our personal blocks to the awareness of love. The moments when we experience stress and confusion can actually be used as opportunities to find and define our unconscious blocks. In finding and defining these blocks, we begin the undoing process. In the undoing process, we question why it is that we are choosing to act and or react in a manner that is causing us stress and confusion. Sooner or later, we acknowledge to ourselves that we do not want to act or react in a manner that causes us stress and confusion. By acknowledging behaviors we don't want to experience, we come to understand and recognize that there is another way, a more sane and loving way to experience the moment. We can then begin acting and reacting in this more loving manner and subsequently experience more love and joy in our lives. We can then experience greater peace in our lives. There will be moments when we forget and react and act with confusion and stress, but these occasions will slowly diminish and become a smaller part of our days. As they become a smaller part of our days, they also become a smaller part of our lives. The moments when awareness of the presence of love is experienced increases, filling a larger part of our days. Gratitude and joy become natural responses to having such daily awarenesses. The same moments in which we previously experienced stress and confusion, we now experience the presence of love, and we can simply smile at our past misperceptions. Not only can we smile, but we can also experience gratitude for them. We will know that it was only because we got tired of what they offered that we ever questioned their existence in our lives. And again, we can look back into our past and this time see every misperception as the true gift that it was. Once more, we can smile and be thankful in acknowledging the perfection of each moment in our lives. In this, we can find great peace, for we can understand that in all future moments, we will also have the opportunity to acknowledge the presence of love and be thankful for its perfection.

Turning Blocks into Blessings

Some of us currently believe that there are times where we can achieve a peaceful state and times when we can't. We might have already taught ourselves that we can remain peaceful if "x" happens, but not if "y" happens. My friend, the only difference in these circumstances lies not in their physical manifestation, but simply in our beliefs. It is because the work lies within, in modifying our beliefs, that only a simple reinterpretation is needed to obtain peace in any situation. When we lack peace in any situation, it is not because peace is not available, but because we have somehow blocked the awareness of the presence of peace. Once the blocks are dismantled, all that is left is the state of peace.

My friend, the universe is kind. It will offer countless opportunities to obtain peace in areas that we previously perceived peace to be unobtainable. Our Godself also knows that we can achieve peace in any situation. This knowledge is currently within us and it is only our willingness to consider it that is necessary. Currently, you may have blocks to this awareness and they manifest themselves as situations in which you believe that peace is unobtainable. Again, my friend, the universe is kind. It, along with your Godself, will assist you in bringing about situations where you block the awareness of the state of peace. This is done to allow you the opportunity and understanding that peace in such situations is indeed available and attainable. It is only by bringing these blocks up to your awareness that we will have the opportunity to choose once again.

My friend, if you look into your past, you will recall situations that once brought you thoughts and emotions of stress and pain that you now deal with in a more peaceful manner. The same situation may occur today, but your reaction to it is more positive. You simply realized that there was a better way of dealing with it. A better and more mature way of dealing with a situation brought you feelings of understanding and peace. Looking back, you see that the ability to choose peace in such situations had always been available. By dealing with the block, you were able to find peace in a situation where you once did not even consider peace as a possibility. In doing so, you dismantled another block to your awareness of the presence of the state of peace. As you continue to dismantle different blocks, you will find that the state of peace is always available to you in every situation, in every moment. It lies there waiting for your recognition of it. Once recognized, it is all you will desire. You will desire peace in every situation, and because you desire peace, you will obtain and experience it. Now and then, blocks may come up again, but you will quickly remember what it is you truly desire, and when you do, you will have it. Now when such blocks appear in your life, you will no longer curse their appearance or feel unlucky because of their manifestation in your life. In fact, once you see them, you will now thank and bless them, for you now have the knowledge that these blocks are really just offering you an opportunity to understand where the awareness to the presence of peace and love is blocked in your life. Once you understand and acknowledge this gift, these blocks will turn into blessings, and love will replace all that you once found unlovable.

As your sense of inner peace develops, you will become more and more confident that it has nothing to do with your outside environment. You will depend less and less on circumstances turning out a certain way, or on other people responding a certain way. As your inner peace develops, your outside world will also begin to change. Slowly, you will begin to realize that the world you experience outside of yourself is directly related to how you feel within.

To assist you in realizing the importance of attitude, consider the following statement on attitude from renowned author and pastor Charles R. Swindoll:

> [31]*"This may shock you, but I believe the single most significant decision I can make on a day-to-day basis is my choice of attitude. It is more important than my past, my education, my bankroll, my successes or failures, fame or pain, what other people think of me or say about my circumstances, my position, or me. Attitude is that 'single string' that keeps me going or cripples my progress. It alone fuels my fire or assaults my hope. When my attitudes are right, there's no barrier too high, no valley too deep, no dream too extreme, no challenge too great for me."*

[31]See Notes, page xvii.

10

TAKING RESPONSIBILITY
FOR OUR DESTINY

Our destiny comes about as a result of what we do now. We are responsible for what we do and experience now, therefore we are responsible for the destiny we will experience. We are in a constant state of creating our destiny. Every moment contributes to the destiny we will experience. What we are doing and experiencing now is our current reality. We have a great deal more control over our current reality than our egos have allowed us to remember. In fact, we are in a constant state of creating, manifesting and experiencing our reality. Each moment in our lives is created, manifested and experienced by us for our growth and development. Let me further explain what I mean.

Creation is the act of bringing a thought to your mind, forming a plan for its implementation and execution, and putting that plan to action. Manifestation is the physical result of your mental creation. Experience is the way you choose to see and react to your manifestation.

We create and manifest both in the conscious and unconscious state. Most of us have already created and experienced conscious manifestations. Choosing to lose 10 pounds and achieving it, or getting a college degree are two examples of conscious manifestations. If something did not exist in our lives, and we made a conscious decision to achieve it or not achieve it - this is an example of a conscious manifestation. It may have taken a moment, hour, day, month, year or more to create, manifest and experience our current situation, yet it was our choices that brought our experiences to us. The value in a conscious manifestation lies not in what we can manifest, but in the knowledge that we can manifest whatever it is we choose. Having physical proof, the knowledge that we have the power to manifest our reality allows us to begin opening our minds to the possibility that our physical experiences are created, manifested and experienced by us.

What we experience in our physical world is simply a reflection of what is in our minds. Simply changing the thoughts that we allow to enter our minds can change our reality. If our minds lack clarity, the circumstances that we will manifest in our physical world will also lack clarity. If thoughts of peace and love fill our minds, then the circumstances that we will manifest in our physical world will be equally as peaceful and loving.

Think back to times when you have been in either a good or bad mood, and recall how being in that mood colored your experiences for the day. The world feels tougher, less fair and more hopeless when you are in a bad mood. If you're in a bad mood, little things upset you much more than if you are in a good mood. Those little or not so little things are still the same; the only thing that changes the way you see them is the kind of mood you're in, or your mental state. Depending on whether you're in a peaceful or agitated mental state, those little things will affect you differently. Little by little, you start realizing that reality has nothing to do with what those little things are.

If you will, open your mind and entertain the possibility that it is your mind and not the outside world that needs changing. If the ego accepts this, it would want you to begin this process with the idea that you must improve yourself or become something better in order to have an improved or better life. For a moment, put the ego's demands aside and simply recognize that this change will not come about by becoming something more or better, but by simply bringing yourself into a closer realignment with who you have always been, your Godself. My friend, you will some day realize that there is nothing easier than being who you truly are. On the deepest level, it is an effortless accomplishment.

We have manifested and continually manifest into our reality certain situations and patterns that assist us in our learning or remembering process. By looking back at our lives, we can better understand which lessons we have chosen to learn, and which lessons we are still in the process of learning. Hopefully, we'll be able to see how perfectly we created our circumstances in order to learn our lessons and complete our patterns. Patterns or lessons repeat themselves because we have not learned from them. We make certain "mistakes" in our lives that we don't learn from and thus we repeat them until we learn to choose with love and forgiveness. Once we have learned what the pattern is about, it is no longer necessary to experience that pattern. Most patterns keep occurring in our lives because there is some kind of value they hold for us. Once the value is recognized, we are able to release ourselves from the pattern.

Only you can make the final choice of how you see life, of how you react to life, and of how you live life. You may attract others to your life to assist you in your learning process, but it is you who gets to make the final choice of what you will focus on and experience.

When I suggest that we attract others in our lives to assist us, I am suggesting that we and others make a spiritual commitment to assist each other in the learning and remembering process, and ultimately in the release of all fear and ego-based patterns. Every brother and sister in our lives has made a spiritual commitment to assist us, and we have consciously or unconsciously made a spiritual commitment to assist them in their growth and development. Thus, if our current perception toward any of them is anything but that of gratitude, we will create confusion. It is in the state of confusion that patterns and lessons are repeated.

It is our beliefs and perceptions that will drive our focus; and we will experience what we focus on. If this is difficult to grasp, take, for example, two types of people we have all met: optimists and pessimists. Spend an entire day with both of these types of people. If we do this once, we will never again question that a person's reality, how he or she sees and reacts to the world, is mainly in that person's mind and has little or nothing to do with the outer physical world.

When Bad Things Happen

Everything that we experience as real in our physical world must first be accepted as real within our minds. Thus even an illusion, if accepted as real within our mind, will then be experienced as real in our physical environment. When we accept the illusion that we will only really listen or learn by experiencing some level of pain, we make this belief real in our minds, which will in turn manifest into "bad things" in our lives.

Free will allows us to choose between learning through pain or joy. Whenever bad things happen in our lives, it is because we have chosen to learn through pain and trauma, instead of learning through peace and joy. "Bad things" happen because some fearful thoughts entered our minds. They entered our minds consciously or unconsciously, because we believed that such thoughts could be real. By believing in them, by entertaining those thoughts in our minds, we become witnesses to their reality. We then make them physically real by manifesting them as physical experiences in our lives. We bring such manifestations into our lives because there is some value we still hold in them. We keep bringing illusions back into our lives in order to bring the unconscious knowledge that they are illusions into our conscious minds. The ultimate value of each and every illusion is to realize its valuelessness in our lives. Once we realize that any specific illusion is valueless, we consciously end our negative and painful interpretation of it and substitute it with gratitude that we no longer need to be negatively or painfully affected by it. As much as we want to believe that we sometimes bring valueless moments and events to our lives, this is not so. We never experience a valueless moment in our lives. Every moment offers us some type of value. Even when the greatest value of the moment is to experience its valuelessness, that moment in and of itself becomes most valuable. Once the valuelessness of illusions is acknowledged and understood, there is no longer a need to manifest such an experience in our lives again.

When it comes to illusions, there is good news, which is this: there is only one real lesson we need ever learn. The lesson is that each and every fear-based thought that we choose to manifest into our physical experience is an illusion. There can be hundreds or thousands of fear-based thoughts that each individual can manifest into his or her life. Yet, when properly perceived, these fearful thoughts and illusions are the same. Regardless of how many fear-based thoughts we choose to manifest into our physical experiences, in the end, they are all illusions, and illusions are not real. They are, in truth, nothing.

The only reason one illusion bothers us more and seems to be more painful than the next one is because of the value we put on one over the other. There are some fear-based thoughts that we give more value to, yet regardless of how much value we personally give an illusion, it is still an illusion. Because illusions are, by definition, not real, they are, in effect, nothing. Once we acknowledge and understand this of one illusion, we have the ability to see the same in all illusions. This is the one lesson we need to remember in order to avoid "bad things" from coming into our lives. Learn through peace or through pain, through joy or through trauma, that is our choice. But once we remember that it is our choice, we will no longer want to learn through pain or trauma. This understanding will bring more learning experiences of peace into our lives.

The more at peace we are with our physical world and everyone and everything in it, the more peace we will experience in our lives. The more peaceful thoughts we have in our minds, the less fearful thoughts we have and the more peaceful a life we will experience. It is truly that simple. The more moments we spend having peaceful thoughts in our day, the less moments we spend having negative thoughts. The more time we spend having peaceful thoughts, the more peace we will experience. This might seem simplistic, and it is, for truth is always simpler than our egos allow us to imagine. The ego has no interest in truth and would have us believe that truth is complicated, inaccessible and unobtainable to mortal man.

Fear-based thoughts will be a bridge to our awakening. This awakening is indeed a great gift, but remember that the opportunity arose only because we once chose to experience the illusions as real. Herein lies the one great gift, the one lesson that all illusions teach. Be grateful for them; be grateful for our past pain and trauma, for it is because of them that we now understand that they are no longer necessary for our continued growth. When we acknowledge that they are no longer necessary for our continued growth, we will have no more need to experience them. Be grateful for them, for they have offered us a wonderful gift. The gift is the knowledge that there is a better way. We will now understand that we can equally and more harmoniously grow through peace and joy rather than struggle and pain. Thus, if properly perceived, whenever a "bad thing" happens, we should be grateful to ourselves for allowing it to happen. By allowing it to happen, we have given ourselves the opportunity to rediscover that it is not real and that our level of suffering is not due to the experience itself, but to the value we place on that particular illusion. If we can properly perceive moments when "bad things" happen as gifts to ourselves, then imagine how grateful we will become by simply experiencing all other moments.

Bad Things: Levels of Perception

In this section, levels of perception involving "bad things" that manifest into our lives are examined, not because there is in truth such an idea, but because these are some of the illusionary steps that we might experience during our journey. Within illusions there lies as many levels of perceptions as there are humans on this planet. We make nothing into something by giving it value. There are innumerable combinations of illusions. Yet, regardless of how much value we give to our illusions, they are still nothing but illusions. They are still, by definition, false ideas or conceptions, unreal or misleading images.

At the first level of perception, we believe that when "bad things" happen, we have no control over what is happening; that we have no control physically, psychologically or spiritually. At this level, we interpret bad things as negative. We are likely to blame others, blame God, or say it's bad luck. At this level of thinking, we believe that there is another force other than ourselves that has control over our lives and that we have little or no influence over what occurs in our lives. We might also believe that we have little or no control with regard to how we react to our brother's words or actions. When we're operating at this level, we might ask, "How can I choose peace, when others control everything around me?" This is yet another trick that the ego plays. It tries to convince us that our patterns cannot change unless the people around us conform to our way of thinking.

Other people's patterns will not change until we decide to change ours. Once we shift from a fear-based thought system to a love-based thought system, our outward perceptions will also shift. When this choice is made, and it is simply a choice, nothing others do will affect our peace of mind. When our minds reside in a state of total peace, it is impossible for us to experience anything other than peace, and we are likely to view everyone around us as existing within that same peaceful state.

At the second level of perception, we believe that when bad things happen, we do have some level of control over what is happening. We interpret the situation as something we brought upon ourselves in order to learn a lesson. At this level of thinking, we choose to see the situation as a short-term negative but a possible long-term positive, for the simple reason that we will, in the end, learn something from it. People at this level go through this because they believe that lessons are learned, for the most part, through unpleasant experiences. Thus, they bring those lessons to themselves to be experienced in that manner.

If we experience any unpleasantness in our physical existence, it is because our egos have placed some value on these experiences. Please understand this: the answer lies not in judging ourselves as bad or less developed for allowing these events to happen, but in seeing that what is occurring in our physical existence is simply a reflection of what is occurring within our minds. And if it's occurring within our minds, then understand that we have the power to change it.

At the third level of perception, we know that when bad things happen, we brought the situation on ourselves, and that as negative as it might look to the outside world, we have no doubt that it is a positive experience. We understand that the only suffering we will bear is the suffering we choose to bear.

And finally, at the fourth level of perception, we acknowledge that there are no such things as "bad things." Gratitude becomes our only response to each and every situation. At this level of thinking, we know with utmost certainty that nothing comes to us that is not held in our minds. If properly perceived, the previous statement offers absolute and total freedom. We understand that we do have the power to determine what will enter our minds. We know that there is no force outside of ourselves that brings lessons that should be experienced as unpleasant. When we are in touch with peace, which is our natural inheritance, we are in a harmonious state. As a result, we make requests from this state and the results of our experiences will be harmonious and peaceful.

Blessing Every Step of the Journey

I expect to pass through life but once. If, therefore, there be any kindness I can show, or any good thing I can do to any fellow being, let me do it now and not defer or neglect it, for I shall not pass this way again.

William Penn

We have the free will to either bless every step of our journey or to be annoyed and frustrated by them. The physical manifestation and expression of our mind allows us to see where we are in our development. If we have a peaceful mind, we will create peaceful experiences. Peaceful experiences are, more often than not, the result of having a peaceful mind. If we have a chaotic mind, we will create chaotic experiences. More often than not, chaotic experiences are a result of having a chaotic mind. When we bless each step, we acknowledge it as a useful part of our journey and, in turn, we receive peace. When we are annoyed and frustrated by a step, we create tension and anxiety which leads to stress.

Some people treat positive experiences in their lives as gifts, not as lessons. The same people have the tendency to treat negative experiences in their lives as lessons and not as gifts. Some say it is a gift if we learned a lesson. But if we do not learn a recognizable lesson from what we perceive to be a negative experience, is it still a gift? Sure it is! It is a gift regardless of whether we learned the lesson or not, because the experience itself has brought us one step closer to recognizing what it is trying to offer. Because of the experience, we are now a step closer to "getting it," and because we are now a step closer to "getting it" it was helpful and useful in getting us to the next step. As a result, it could be considered a gift.

Let's use an example of taking a flight from Miami to New York. For argument's sake, let's divide the trip into three parts, which include the ride from your home to the airport, the journey from the airport entrance to the gate of departure and the flight itself. You might perceive the most important part of the trip to be the flight itself, but you first need to get to the airport, go through the check-in counter and then to the departure gate. The walk from the airport's entrance to the check-in counter to the departure gate might be the shortest distance, but it could also be the most taxing and stressful part of the journey. All of these are necessary steps to get you to New York. Some steps might seem more important than others, but you need all of them in order to get where you want to go. And it is only by taking all of the steps that you will be able to reach your destination. On the surface, you might see the trip from the airport's entrance to your departure gate as the least important part of the trip, but it is still as necessary as the other two components of the trip. Regardless of which part of the trip you perceive as most stressful, it is still necessary and useful in helping you reach your destination. You can choose to see each part of your journey as useful and be thankful for having completed it, or you can choose to see it as stressful.

The plane ride, like all other parts of the journey, can be as stressful as you make it. On any given airplane, those on board experience different levels of stress, no matter how stable or unstable the plane ride is. Even when statistics show that flying is many times safer than driving, most people consider the plane ride more stressful than the car ride to the airport. For many, the level of stress during the flight itself has little to do with the statistical reality, but relates to how safe those on board perceive themselves to be. As you and others may have trained yourself to be fearful on planes, so too can you train yourself to be peaceful during any flight. You can, on any and every part of your journey, choose to be at peace, or you can choose to experience fear and stress. Focus your mind on what you wish to experience. Please understand that it is your choice, and that ultimately, it has little to do with the physical manifestation and more to do with how you choose to react to it.

The point is that you are exactly where you need to be and you are there because of everything you have experienced. My friend, every moment you have experienced is a gift you have offered yourself. Regardless of whether you perceived it as a lesson or not, all experiences have made you who you are today.

One thing I can guarantee is that you are headed in the right direction, because it is literally impossible to do otherwise. Bless every moment you have and are experiencing. Bless every positive and negative experience; bless every positive and negative moment.

Every Trip Helps Us Evolve

Everything we are currently experiencing in our lives comes about in order to assist us in evolving to a higher level of consciousness. Even what we now perceive as bad, sad, negative or upsetting is here to assist us in seeing life in a more peaceful, forgiving and loving way. Understand that a great part of the reason we experience things as bad, sad, negative or upsetting is because we have not yet learned to deal with these issues in a more peaceful, forgiving and loving way. Put another way, we are lost because we do not know the way, but once we find our way, the probability of getting lost again is reduced. And it is because we got lost once, we now know the way.

A passage from "The Experiment Hope" by Jurgen Moltmann illustrates that every part of our journey, regardless of its physical manifestation and our perception of that manifestation, can, if we so desire, be experienced with peace, and that gratitude need not wait to be experienced at the journey's conclusion. Moltmann writes:

> [32]*For more than three years, I was in a prisoner-of-war camp, and I understand something of the language of prisoners, the loneliness and the dreams of the "unhappy"*...

[32]See Notes, page xvii.

*Hope came to life as the prisoner accepted his imprison-
ment, affirmed the barbed wire, and in this situation,
discovered the real human being in himself and others. It
was not at his release, but even while in prison, that the
"resurrection from the dead" happened for him.*

Experiencing God During Difficult Situations

We can never come closer to God because God is already within us. God is in every moment, and we can come closer to experiencing Him by blessing and being thankful for every moment. God waits for us in every moment. God waits for us in every experience. He waits for us with everlasting patience and love.

In any difficult situation, ask God with all your heart to let you experience Him and He will. You will experience Him not because He is letting you do so, but because you are allowing yourself to experience Him. You do not need His permission to experience Him. You will experience God, because when you so desire, you are shifting your focus from an illusionary state (a difficult situation) to the truth (God). Allowing yourself to experience this in one difficult situation will open your mind to the possibility that you can experience God in all difficult situations. Experiencing God in a difficult situation will turn the challenging situation into an awakening opportunity and gift. During the difficult situation, try to focus on God and His absolute love for you. Allow yourself to feel this absolute love. Let it flow through your body. Let it touch your heart. Realize that God is not there because it is a difficult situation, but because He has always been there. You see it as a difficult situation, but God sees only your growth. In the moment, focus on fear, or focus on God's love for you. You have free will and it is your choice to make. In the moment, you can focus on one or the other but not both. The choice is yours. Choosing fear will offer you anxiety, stress, confusion, pain and regret. Choosing love will offer you peace of mind and joy. Choose as you will.

God knows that you reach for Him in every moment, every situation, regardless of whether you are conscious of it or not. God knows that every moment, every situation, regardless of how you choose to perceive it, brings you closer to experiencing and remembering your Godself. God blesses all your efforts. Every situation is a gift God offers you to remember your trueself. Bless these situations for what they truly are and you will come closer to the realization of who you truly are. My friend, you are a child of God. The child of God can only experience a difficult situation if he or she chooses to. The child of God will experience a difficult situation only if he or she values illusions. The child of God will experience a difficult situation only if he or she misperceives reality.

Imagine, if only for a moment, how much more peace you could experience in your daily existence if you would only allow yourself to see all experiences, both positive and negative, as gifts, regardless of lessons learned. Imagine that instead of constantly analyzing and judging your experiences, you smile and are thankful for having them. My friend, listen carefully, for the beginning of knowledge lies in this simple shift in perception. Imagine a life where, instead of asking "why" or "why me," you simply trust and say "thank you." How much more peace and joy would this simple shift in perception bring to your life and to those around you? My dear friend, heaven is indeed available on Earth - now.

Guideposts

Be open to new experiences, for they are often signs and guideposts that the universe offers us as guidance. Most of us move throughout the day on autopilot, not paying attention to signposts, considering them every day data that we process on one level or another. For example, a few days before a business trip to New Orleans, I was driving on I-95 headed north to West Palm Beach, Florida. Off to my right, I saw a billboard advertising renewing driver's licenses via the Internet. I thought to myself, "this sounds like a great idea, a real time saver." In my mind, I gave the state of Florida points for using the Internet in such a productive manner. I usually don't pay any attention to billboards, but this one stuck in my mind. I promised myself that next time I had to renew my license I would do it via the "Net."

A few days later, I flew to New Orleans. I had to drive to Baton Rouge, Louisiana, so I headed to the car rental place where I had a reservation. I handed over my driver's license, but the lady behind the counter told me that she was sorry but my driver's license had expired and she could not rent a car to me. After my initial shock and embarrassment, I laughed to myself as I remembered the billboard. I told myself that I should have known better. I took it in stride and thanked God for the advanced warning. I promised Him and myself that I would pay more attention to the signs He sends me in the future. The lady behind the counter was very nice to me and told me that she could get me a cab for a good rate. I thanked her and asked her to please do so. Ten minutes later, a nice older gentleman arrived in a cab to pick me up. As I got inside his cab, I noticed the name of his cab company: Saint's Cab Company. Again, I began to laugh. Again I thanked God for His sense of humor. The older gentleman turned out to be a real character. We enjoyed each other's company during the one hour drive to Baton Rouge. He was so nice, and gave me such a great deal, that I asked him to pick me up the next night to drive me back to the New Orleans airport. He was happy to do so because he had a good time with me and the fare was a lucrative one. Now every time I go on business trips to Baton Rouge, instead of renting a car, I call my new friend at the Saint's Cab Company.

Progress in our development and life does not always come in the form that our egos expect. Trust that your soul is moving you in the right direction, but learn to analyze and take a look at what is happening in your life. There are many things that bother us that we simply let go of without analyzing why it bothered us in the first place. These types of things build up until one day we have a breakdown. The breakdown itself would never have occurred if we listened to the hints, watched for the signs, analyzed and moved toward resolution.

Much of our progress forward, new ideas and lessons will not come in exactly the form the mind expects. Some people simply give up because they cannot see any correlation between what is happening in their lives and their wishes, hopes and dreams. Even the opposite of what we think we want might be happening, and the ego has taught us to judge, curse and hate the opposite of what we think we want. To the ego, the opposite of what we want is bad and unwelcome. To the Godself, every moment, regardless of its physical manifestation, is a gift and a step in the right direction.

People themselves are great guideposts and often show us where we are. They act as mirrors to show us something about ourselves. The degree to which people love, support, and acknowledge us is in direct relation to the degree to which we have learned to love, support and acknowledge ourselves. For when we acknowledge that we are worthy of love, we open the door to it, and it is by opening the door that we let others in.

Be Open to Changing Directions

There exists a mass thoughtform, a mass illusion that the future will be worse than the present. Many spiritual people even share in this view and see the future as grim. This is, in part, the reason why change is difficult for most people. Because of this, many people sometimes feel safer and more comfortable with the way things are. Those who participate in this thoughtform usually prefer to leave things as they are and to hang on to the old ways. People who are not open to change constrict their boundaries, and their world becomes more and more narrow and limited. They nitpick and focus on petty things. We have all met people who make mountains out of molehills. These people's concerns seem so minor that we almost stop taking them seriously. They behave this way because they have stopped taking chances, stopped expanding their lives and stopped growing. If someone has a very narrow view of the world, their ideas that support this view will be more furiously defended because it is all they believe they have. As they begin to expand their lives, so too will their ideas expand, and what once affected them will affect them less.

Many people who resist change need a helping hand in expanding their perceptions of reality. Gently assist those who are closing themselves off to change and growth to expand. As you help them expand, you will see that their judgments of your life and the way you have chosen to live it will also lessen. As you gently help them expand, they in turn will give you more freedom, but not because you are doing anything different in your life, but because they are simply more open to change, to growth and acceptance of others. Change and acceptance of others is a natural expression of personal growth. As you free your brother, you free yourself, for you and your brother are one and the same. And this will be as great a lesson for you as it will be for him.

Thank the Road for Its Bumps

There will be bumps in almost every road down here. The key to living a more balanced life is not to judge, curse or avoid the bumps but to see them as blessings. The ego-self will want us to see bumps as bumps because it has already taught us how to react to them. The ego has already taught us that we have every right to judge, curse or try to avoid the bumps. It has already taught us that such a reaction is normal and correct. But has reacting in such a manner ever brought any of us true peace of mind and joy? Has reacting in such a way ever brought more clarity and balance to our lives? Thus, is it such a stretch to say that the ego's normal and correct way of reacting to bumps has little or nothing to do with us achieving peace of mind, joy, clarity, and a balanced life? If we deal with bumps by judging, cursing or by trying to avoid them, we have bought into the ego's thought system as being real. If we have bought into the ego's thought system as being real, then is it any wonder why achieving peace of mind, joy, clarity and a balanced life appears difficult to do?

Wipe the Windshields Clean: Getting Clear

One night of focusing and obtaining clarity will save you weeks, months or even years of confusion. When you start feeling dissatisfied with your life or current situation, take a night for yourself, quiet the mind and ask your soul how you can make these feelings clearer. Fine-tune the picture in your mind. Take time to clarify the issues. Put these thoughts on paper. Be precise. The more precise you can be, the quicker you can gain clarity. Such clarity will assist you in making better decisions and save you time.

Spiritually, the clearer you are in understanding that everything that happens is assisting you in one way or another, the more peace you will have on your journey toward achieving this goal. Mentally, the clearer you are in setting up guidelines and steps toward attaining your goal, the faster you will obtain it. The small physical steps taken toward your goal and the small successes allow the mind the peace of knowing that it is getting closer to achieving its goal. The clearer your purpose, the clearer your goals; and the less energy you waste, the quicker you accomplish what you desire.

There are No Limits on This Road

> [33]*If it falls your lot to be a street sweeper, sweep streets like Michelangelo painted pictures, like Shakespeare wrote poetry, like Beethoven composed music...*
>
> Martin Luther King Jr.

Your purpose in life - your life's mission - will be something you love and take great joy in. Joy is a natural expression of one who is fulfilling his or her purpose. What offers you peace? What gives you joy? What do you love to do? All these are clues to the destiny that you're trying to reach, your life's mission. Believe in yourself and trust that the universe is in your corner. Reach within, listen to the whispers of your heart, and bring what is within you out into the world. This is how you will begin to manifest and live your wishes and dreams.

There are mass thoughtforms that set up certain limits, boundaries, rules and regulations that the ego says you must follow. Respect what people see as real, but if it does not fit with what your heart and soul wish to bring forth, experience and express,

[33]See Notes, page xvii.

then follow your heart. Be sure to ask yourself why you are doing what you are doing. The question of why you choose to participate in an activity is actually more important to answer and understand than the question of what activity you want to participate in. Ask your soul if what you are currently engaging in is something that you are doing for yourself and your highest good, because it brings you peace of mind and joy, or if it is something that you are doing because your family expects you to fulfill their dreams. Are you doing this to please them, to live up to an image of your peers, or to receive recognition from society?

Imagine, just for a moment, that you had no images to fulfill, no pressure from your family, friends, peers or society; what would you do with your life? What would bring you peace of mind and joy? How could you best serve this world? My brother and sister, the only limits that exist in this world are those we choose to see and allow to be real within our minds.

Other Passengers in the Car: Relationships

34*"You have many lovers, and yet I alone love you. Other men love themselves in your nearness. I love you in yourself. Other men see a beauty in you that shall fade away sooner than their own years. But I see in you a beauty that shall not fade away, and in the autumn of your days that beauty shall not be afraid to gaze at itself in the mirror, and it shall not be offended. I alone love the unseen in you."*

(Jesus talking to Mary Magdalene) Kahlil Gibran

My brother and sister, the ego would have us search for some-one who is our opposite, murmuring that this mysterious person will make us happy, complete and whole. The ego provides us with the main rule of its game, that we must play the game with one partner to truly experience victory, success and happiness. Notice how the ego subtlety hints and whispers that we must search out-

34See Notes, page xvii.

side ourselves to find and experience happiness, completion, victory and success. For if we must search outside ourselves, then by the process of elimination, happiness, completion, victory and success cannot be within us now. Notice how the ego suggests that the opposite of who we are will make us happy. What is the ego implying with such a statement?

Like prisoners, we play the ego's game because we believe that this is the only game in town, that this is the only game that will, in the end, satisfy our needs. So again, we play the game and end up losing and alone. We become upset, but soon other egos come to our own ego's defense letting us know that this is just how the game is played. Other egos tell us not to worry, that we might lose again but some magical day we will win and find "the one." They talk to us about their pain and how this pain is absolutely normal and felt by everyone. And so, in the end, we relent to their constant assurance and once again, when we are ready, we start the game again.

Other egos tell us to remember our pain. They tell us that this will help us succeed in our next game. So we carry this pain, like a virus, from the previous game into our current game and this colors and affects everything we see. We believe that this pain will protect us in our next game, but instead of victory we infect everyone we meet. Soon we and our partners experience pain, become sick and again we lose the game. We blame ourselves, our partners, everyone and anyone who might have participated in the game. Our pain and sickness grows, but again other egos tell us that this is normal. They tell us to take some time off, to get well before we return to the game. They tell us that we're getting better and better at this game and that some magical day, when we least expect it, we will find our "complete opposite," and that partner will make us happy and whole. We have trouble believing that, but again we accept that this is really the only game available, the only game that will some day offer us the victory of finding that mysterious person who will make us happy and whole. We believe this because we see and experience everyone else playing this same game. They seem to suffer and complain just like we do, thus it must be real; it just must be the way it is.

Every game we lose makes us feel more like a failure, for the ego tells us that the only way we can win is if we play the game with one partner for the rest of our lives. Thus, every game that ends before the end of our lives or that of our partners' is defined and seen by us and everyone else as a failure. And without thinking much about it, we believe this definition and we begin to see ourselves as a failure. With an emotional knife, we inscribe this belief in our hearts and we carry the scars and pain to the next game. And so we begin each new game with this painful virus, with this perception and belief that we are a failure, and that we are incomplete. We somehow still believe that this conviction will help us win and find completion and happiness. My dear brothers and sisters, we have not failed; it is this whole game and its rules that are a fraud, a scam, a deception and a lie.

If we truly saw ourselves as whole, we would have no opposite. We call our brother or sister an opposite because we perceive him or her as having something we don't. We believe that we will find in someone else what is lacking in ourselves. We believe that such an individual will make us complete. We desire completeness, but no one can give us what we already have. Completion is not acquired but realized. If we bring someone into a relationship because we believe he or she will offer us something that we lack, then we will find the relationship lacking. We will find it lacking because no one can fill the empty holes we believe ourselves to have. If we see ourselves as incomplete, as lacking, then we will keep creating areas of lack in our lives that this individual sooner or later will be unable to fill. As he or she becomes unable to fill these areas, we begin to look for someone else who might be more able to fill these new needs. This becomes a downward spiral that can only end when we realize that no one can make us happy and whole other than ourselves.

As we recognize our wholeness, we look for an individual who is himself or herself whole. This relationship will not be lacking because we can now understand that there is nothing we lack. The relationship shifts from trying to get what we lack into one of sharing our wholeness.

My brother and sister, because we are already whole, we are also already successful. The truth is the truth, and our only decision is to recognize it or to veil it. Every moment with our brother or sister is a success; for in such a moment, we are either experiencing our truth or making an effort to recall it. My brother and sister, there is not one relationship we have ever had, be it for 50 seconds or for 50 years, that has been a failure. Every moment and every brother and sister with whom we have had contact allows us the opportunity to recall our wholeness. Just as the ego-self has us take failure and pain from a past relationship, the Godself would have us take knowledge, love and forgiveness. In the end, what we decide to take from a relationship is a decision we choose to make. In the moment, we have our choice of teachers. Each teacher has lesson plans available for us to follow.

Be still for a moment and review the lessons you've taken from past relationships. Once you understand the lessons you have experienced, you will know whose teachings you have been following.

Buckle Your Child's Safety Belt, but Don't Leave Him in the Car

We have not inherited the earth from our fathers but are borrowing it from our children.

Native American proverb

Carl Sandburg once wrote, "A baby is God's opinion that the world should go on." Bringing a child into the world is one of the greatest gifts that God can offer us and one of the greatest gifts we can offer humanity.

I have not lived long, but I have lived long enough to understand that raising a child with love is the most important job in the world. I have walked the streets of my country long enough to know that this is so. I have talked to children who are loved, children who are lost, children who are happy and healthy, children who are sad and sick, children with beautiful homes and those who are homeless.

I can, with an honest heart, tell you that the soul who you now call your son or daughter has chosen you as his or her dad or mom. Out of about six billion men and women, he or she, with God's assistance, chose you. At times, you might think that you're not ready for the responsibility, but let me remind you that there is someone much wiser than all of us, who knows you are. So whenever fear or doubt come knocking at your door, remember who has chosen you, and laugh the fear and doubt away.

My friend, if you have not yet found the clarity to live a life that brings you joy, then so be it. But at least allow your children and those around you to follow their hearts. Do not, under any circumstance, allow your ego-self to imprison them. Share your experiences. When the child is young, set boundaries, offer him advice. When he is older, offer him advice, but do not be attached to its outcome. Each of us has a purpose to fulfill, so do not judge others by what you think they should or should not be doing.

If you offer your brother freedom, you will silently be teaching yourself how to be free. For the same key that frees your brother is the one you will someday use to free yourself. If you choose to imprison him, then you will be his jailer, and you will find yourself behind the same walls you use to incarcerate him. Many times, children take on the goals and thoughtforms of their families. Offer your children the freedom to choose their own way. If you do nothing else but this, you have had a successful life.

The following is a poem about children by philosopher Kahlil Gibran that beautifully illustrates what I'm trying to say:

[35]*Your children are not your children*

They are the sons and daughters of life's longing for itself.

They come through you but not from you,

And though they are with you, yet they belong not to you.

You may give them your love but not your thoughts,

For they have their own thoughts.

[35]See Notes, page xviii.

You may house their bodies but not their souls,

For their souls dwell in the house of tomorrow,

which you cannot visit, not even in your dreams.

You may strive to be like them, but seek not to

make them like you,

For life goes not backward nor tarries with yesterday.

You are the bows from which your children as

living arrows are sent forth.

The archer sees the mark upon the path of the infinite,
and He bends you with His might that His arrows
might go swift and far.

Let your bending in the archer's hand be for gladness;

For even as He loves the arrow that flies,

So He loves also the bow that is stable.

We are Now on the Road of our Choosing

When you were born, you cried and the world rejoiced.
Live your life in such a manner that when you die, the
world cries and you rejoice.

Indian Proverb

My friend, regardless of the physical manifestation, you currently have what you want in your life. You are experiencing what
you want to experience. And you are reacting to your experience
the way you want to react. To some, this is a difficult concept to
accept. My friend, take responsibility for your destiny. You have a
great deal more control over your life than your ego will allow you

to acknowledge.

The greatest gift you can offer yourself and others is having your own life work. Do not concern yourself with comparing yourself to your brother or sister, for that is one of the ego's traps. Instead, go inward and compare your life to that of your highest will. It is this one and only comparison that will make the greatest difference in your life. Compare the life you have with the life you want. Compare the life you have with the life that will bring you the most love, peace of mind and joy. My brother and sister, stop, be still, and in the moment, in the now, review your current life and compare it to the life you truly desire. Do this and you will start taking responsibility for your destiny. For it is in the now where your destiny is created, and it is in the now that you offer yourself the clarity you need to fulfill your dreams.

11

DREAMS, PRAYER, OUT-OF-BODY EXPERIENCES, AND MEDITATION

Imagine flying in spirit form - over faraway lands you have only seen in books or on television. This is possible. Imagine going to heaven and experiencing the place you call home in between incarnations. This is possible. Imagine meeting your spirit guides and having the most wonderful conversations; receiving knowledge about your life and the issues you are now dealing with. This is possible. Imagine seeing and conversing with any relative or friend who has passed on, and laughing as you share old memories. This is possible. Imagine the most beautiful sceneries painted in the most brilliant and dynamic colors you have ever seen. This is possible. Imagine listening to angels sing. This, and so much more, is possible if you decide to be conscious for a small part of the eight hours during sleep at night.

God has given us the precious gift of free will and freedom, but we must choose what we want to experience. Free will does not suddenly stop once we fall asleep. Most people live their lives in different levels of the dream state, and sleep is just one of them.

The world that is ours to explore during the dream state will surpass any conception that we may now have of it. Four subjects that I will touch on to assist you on your journey are lucid dreams, out-of-body experiences (OBEs), prayer and meditation. I will discuss these topics briefly, for there are many books available on these subjects.

Before we go any further, I would like to remind you that the main use for these tools is to assist you in remembering who you are. Like all tools, they can be used, with or without discernment. How you use them is your choice. If you choose to use them with discernment, they will assist you in remembering your Godself, and bringing this Godself into your daily experience. This will offer you greater peace of mind and joy in each moment. If you use them without discernment, you will simply add to your confusion. It is again your choice to make.

Dreams

There is much knowledge that can be extracted from dreams. Some people tell me that they have trouble remembering dreams.

Allow me to offer a little advice on this issue. By following the steps below, you will be better able to recall your dreams.

- Buy a dream journal; keep it on your nightstand.

- Meditate for at least five minutes before going to bed, and tell yourself that you will remember your dreams. Use it as a mantra. Say to yourself over and over: "I will remember my dreams." This allows you to set the intention.

- During the night, if you awaken after a dream, write it down in your journal. (I keep a tape recorder next to my bed, so that I don't need to turn on the light. In the morning, I simply transcribe the tape into my journal.)

- Learn to recognize that moment before waking, when you haven't moved physically but you know that you are about to wake up. Do not move physically, and do not open your eyes.

- During this brief period of time, teach yourself to review all the dreams you can recall that night.

- After recalling all you can, your first physical movements should be to open your eyes, pick up your pen and begin journaling your dreams.

- If possible, repeat the procedure every night. You will get better with practice.

- Start sharing your dreams with someone with whom you feel comfortable and see if this person has a different take on what the dream symbolized.

- Keep practicing. Just as consistent exercise makes your muscles stronger, so too will practicing these steps make you more conscious of your nightly journeys.

Another technique you can follow that will assist you in having more lucid dreams is to set your alarm clock for a few hours before waking. When the alarm sounds, turn it off and go to the bathroom or walk around for a couple of minutes, then reset your alarm clock for your usual wake up time (I keep two alarm clocks). Meditate for five minutes and go back to sleep. This might seem like a pain in the neck to do, but if you're having trouble achieving the lucid dream state, this will put you in a lighter dream state, and help you to achieve your goal of remembering your dreams and having lucid dreams.

Lucid Dreaming

Lucid dreaming differs from ordinary dreaming in that with lucid dreaming, you consciously control your reactions, your actions and the direction of your dream. In your non-lucid dreams you have no conscious control over your reactions, actions or the direction of your dream. In a non-lucid dream you are simply in a reactive state. Take for example, a dream most of us have had, that of being chased. In the dream state, most often you don't realize what you are really running from. In this state, you become afraid, you keep running until you wake up or simply move to another dream. In the lucid dream state, you recognize that you are dreaming, and you are then able to take control of your reactions and what is occurring in the dream. Here's what happens during a lucid dream: First, you realize you're dreaming. Second, you lose all fear, and I mean absolutely all fear that you had in the non-lucid state. Third, you then turn around and ask what is chasing you to tell you what it represents. Fourth, you can continue the dream or move to another subject that you would like to deal with.

Let me continue by giving you a personal example of a non-lucid dream that became a lucid dream. During a non-lucid dream, I was running away from something. I don't recall exactly what it was, but I do recall being afraid and running from it in a very cowardly manner. Suddenly, I realized that I was dreaming and that I was in a dream. When this realization occurred, it was like night and day. One second I was running from something I believed to be monster-like, and the next second I lost all fear. I became conscious that it was a dream I was experiencing, and once I "got it," I simply lost all fear because I knew that there was nothing to fear from a dream. Regardless of how scary the dream might have been, all fear was gone; not because the scenario in the dream changed, but because I knew it to be a dream. When you move from a non-lucid state to a lucid state, the once frightful setting now literally becomes your playground.

So I went from running away from a monster to losing all fear in about a second. The switch is literally that dramatic. I lost all fear, stopped running and turned around to face what was coming my way. Suddenly, I understood that whatever was coming toward me was still coming at about the same speed, but I had no fear. I now felt that it was going to pass me on my right and so I stuck my right arm out in an effort to stop it. I was going to stop it, and ask it what it represented. I was going to see if it had anything to say to me. But, as soon as I had that thought, whatever was chasing me passed through my arm. I felt the breeze on my arm, but saw nothing. I was really running away from nothing!

In order to expand on my point about losing all fear, let me quickly share another lucid dream. I was in a non-lucid dream and suddenly I realized that I was dreaming. I became lucid in the dream and found myself standing on a railroad track. I have no conscious recollection of what happened to get me on the tracks, but there I was, on railroad tracks, and as luck would have it, a train was coming toward me at full speed. I was not immediately concerned because the train seemed to be about 15 seconds away from crushing me. Although I was in a dream state and could only react to the dream, I felt that I had more than enough time to step out of the way. At that moment, it felt like a very logical and healthy way to react to this scenario.

All of a sudden at about TC -10 (or Train Crash minus 10 seconds), I had the realization that I was simply dreaming. In a one to two second span, I lost all concern about the train crushing me. In two seconds, I went from the prudent belief that I should step away from the tracks, to losing all fear, saying to myself, "hmmm, this could be a very cool experience. I've never been hit by a train before."

So there I was, now at TC -7, watching a train (with many

passenger cars, I might add) coming full speed toward me, and yet I felt not one ounce of fear or trepidation. That is literally what it's like when you have knowledge that all you are currently experiencing is a dream (mental experience) or an out-of-body experience (spiritual experience). It is not always perfectly clear if you are experiencing a dream or an OBE. However, as long as you understand that you are experiencing one of these two states, you are in full control and you do not experience fear. Now I find myself at TC -3, and I begin relishing the moments before impact. I have no idea what it will be like. I only know that because what I am experiencing is only in my mind (dream) or because I am in my spirit (OBE), I will not be hurt. There is a small sense of pride that I have no fear. At TC -1, I have no fear of the impending impact and I am fully caught up in what is about to happen. Then, the impact occurs and I am very surprised by what happens. I'm surprised, because even though I believe myself to be in spirit form, I literally feel the train impacting my soul. There is no pain involved with the impact or throughout the experience. All I "physically" feel is a sudden gust of wind hitting my body. The train's impact on my spirit is like that of a sudden gust of wind. I feel like I've been lifted a little above the tracks but not above the train. The train going through me feels like the continuation of that first gust of wind. After the train passes through me, the gust of wind ends. All I can now say to myself is, "Wow, that was cool!"

After the experience was over, I told myself to wake up so that I could journal my experience. I definitely did not want to forget it. Since then, I've tried being hit by cars, buses and airplanes, and I'm glad to report that I don't have one single scratch from those experiences (kids, please don't try this in your physical bodies). Now, if you were in a situation like this in a dream or OBE, and you were not lucid, all that would happen is that before the train hit you, you would step aside if you had the time. If you did not have the time, you would save yourself by abruptly waking up, just as when you have dreams of falling and you are not lucid or in control, you usually wake up before you hit the ground. By the way, even though the odds say that you will wake up before hitting the ground, even if you hit the ground you will not die - at least I have not died the few times that I've hit the pavement. In the same situation, if you were to become lucid or have control, you would simply stop yourself from falling, land peacefully or begin to fly. A lot of times when you have that sensation that you are falling, all it is, is your soul coming back into your physical body. When this is the case, your body might slightly jolt as the soul re-enters it. You might even hear a thump-like noise. All this is just the soul re-entering the body at a time when you are coming back into the conscious state.

The steps to learning to lucid dream are basically the same as learning to remember your dreams. Simply replace the meditative intention of remembering your dreams with an intention of becoming lucid or aware in your dream. Tell yourself that the next time you dream, you will ask to see your hand. Use "I want to see my hand" as a mantra before going to bed. Repeat this mantra for five minutes. What this does is switch the control from your unconscious mind, where you are simply reacting to what is occurring in the dream, to your conscious mind where you are giving the instructions to your dream. Sometimes when you become lucid, you find your surroundings either foggy or dark. In such a case, simply ask for clarity. Say to yourself "clarity now" until the environment around you becomes clearer. Keep demanding clarity until your field of vision is as clear as you wish it to be. The shift from the non-lucid state to the lucid state is usually noticeable if not dramatic.

I remember being in a dream where I was walking through my childhood home in Venezuela (my physical body was dreaming this in Miami). Suddenly, I became aware that I was dreaming. As soon as this happened, I felt my soul literally being sucked into my old home. The trip seemed to take about three seconds, traveling at about five hundred miles per second. And no, I was not in a frequent flyer program at that time. You might ask, "How do you know that one second you are dreaming about your childhood home, and the next you believe yourself to be inside it?" Well, all I can say to you is that the only way you are ever really going to "get it" or "believe it" is to "experience it." And you will if it's truly your desire to do so.

Sleep Paralysis

Sleep paralysis occurs when the mind awakens, as the body still sleeps. Sleep paralysis offers you a great opportunity to have many productive adventures. Again, fear is usually your first response, so most often the opportunity is experienced negatively. A large number of people have experienced this condition. People in this state believe themselves to be awake, but for some reason their entire bodies are paralyzed. Not only are they unable to move, but they cannot even scream for help. Some people say that they have tried to scream, but nothing comes out. Most people in this state panic, and have a very difficult and frightful experience. Again, the solution is very simple. You need not panic or have a frightful experience. All you need to do is to stay composed, understand the situation and relax. After you have done this, simply think of your big toe (left or right, it does not matter), and try to slowly get some movement out of it. Put all your concentration on your big toe, and once you get some movement, start trying to move the other toes on the same foot. Little by little, you will recover all movement. If you are experienced with sleep paralysis, this is an excellent time to begin a meditation or even leave the body. If you experience this state, but are not in the mood to meditate or leave your body, simply go back to sleep, and the odds are good that the next time you awaken or are in a dream state, you will not be paralyzed. If not, just think "big toe" and relax.

Precognitive Dreams

Some people are concerned that certain dreams are premonitions of future events. A lot of these dreams have to do with airplane or car crashes, or relatives or people themselves dying. One difference between the average dream and a precognitive dream is the point or stage in the sleep cycle in which the dream occurs. A dream has a greater chance of being precognitive if it occurs right before you wake up. Such a dream is sometimes offered as a premonition, a warning of impending danger, or just something you should be on the lookout for. It is given to you right before you wake up, so that you have the best chance of recalling it. If this type of dream is offered to you in the start or middle of your sleep cycle, you will probably not remember it by the time morning arrives. If it does occur at the start or middle of your sleep cycle and you remember it, simply write it down in your journal. If you remember this type of dream, it is probably of some use to write it down, but don't be overly concerned. Yet, please note that paying attention to your gut feelings takes precedent over any specific instruction or information offered in this book.

Let me offer a real life example of a precognitive dream that occurred when I was living in Boulder, Colorado. It was a Friday, and a friend and I had decided to party in Denver that night. I got home around 6:00 p.m. and because a long night was ahead of us and I would be driving, I decided that it would be prudent to take a nap. I set the alarm clock for 8:00 p.m., meditated for about 10 minutes and went to bed. While asleep, I experienced a dream. In the dream, I was in my car with my friend Alex in the passenger seat. We were on our way home, driving on a four-lane road with two lanes going east and two lanes heading west. The east/west lanes were divided in the middle by a double line. Alex and I were in the slower or right lane headed west. The road heading west was on a small decline. Suddenly and without warning, a car in the left lane next to us cut in front of us. After my immediate shock, I became angry and decided to try and pass it. Just as I changed lanes to pass it, I saw, almost in front of us, a car coming toward us at a high rate of speed on our side of the road. There was very little time to do anything but prepare for impact. All I remember thinking was an expletive (very spiritual last words, I later thought). Just before impact, the car going east on the wrong side of the road threw itself back into the eastbound lanes, lost control and crashed. This jolted me out of the dream. I looked at the clock and it read 7:59 p.m. A second later, the alarm sounded.

Because I know to pay very close attention to dreams I receive right before waking, I decided that before Alex and I left for Denver, I would share it with him. As we rode in the car right before getting on the highway east to Denver, I stopped and told Alex about the dream. Alex had been my friend for a few years, so he was used to my eccentricities. Right after I finished telling him about the dream, he became extremely nervous, put his seat belt on, and wondered out loud if we shouldn't stay in Boulder and walk to the nearest bar. We had a serious discussion, and again went over the situation. In the end, we decided that since nothing really happened to us in the dream, we would be extremely careful, and continued with our plan to spend the night clubbing in Denver.

We got on the highway heading east to Denver. The highway from Boulder to Denver had four lanes: two lanes headed east from Boulder to Denver and two lanes headed west from Denver to Boulder. The highway was separated by a continuous cement divider that prevented drivers from making U-turns. The trip to Denver took roughly forty minutes. Probably for the first time in my life on any prolonged journey, I obeyed all posted signs and speed limits. The trip was uneventful, and we were both relieved once we finally made it to Denver. Alex and I enjoyed our time in Denver, and around 2:00 a.m., when the bars began to close, we decided it was time to head back home to Boulder. As the minutes ticked past 2:30 a.m., I completely forgot about the dream. We were on our way back to Boulder on the same highway. Again I was driving and Alex sat in the passenger seat. Both of us felt relaxed as we discussed the people we met at the bars. As we drove on the two lane road back home to Boulder, Alex and I were in the slower or right lane heading west. The road going west was on a small decline just as it was in the dream. In one second we were both relaxed and laughing; suddenly, and without warning, the car next to us in the left lane cut right in front of us. After my immediate shock, I became angry and thought about passing it. The car came so close to hitting us that I could literally see the other driver's eyes in her rear view mirror as she drove in front of us. In the split second that I saw her eyes, I also saw an expression in them that I had never seen before. It was an expression of total fear, but also of concern for me. It was an expression that, still to this day, is strongly imprinted in my memory. In the second that followed, that expression jolted the dream back into my conscious mind, and one second after that, a car speeding on the wrong side of the highway passed us on our left side going east on a west bound highway!

If I had passed the lady, we would have crashed head-on into the car driving on the wrong side of the highway, a highway that was divided by a continuous cement divider. The combined speed of the crash would probably have been between 130 to 160 miles per hour. Simply put, no one would have lived. I never saw the other car coming, and I didn't, not even for one second, imagine that such an event was possible. In those few seconds when I saw her expression, and the dream sprang into my conscious mind, I made the decision to relax. Less than a second after making that decision, the car went past me, going the wrong way. If I had reacted instead of being relaxed, Alex and I would have died or maybe, as in the dream, the car traveling on the wrong side would have lost control and crashed without affecting us. About a second after the car passed us, I again looked at the eyes of the lady driving in front of us through her rear view mirror. Again, I saw in her eyes an expression that I had never seen before. It was an expression of total shock, but also of total relief. After a few moments of catching our breath and articulating some very unholy adjectives, Alex and I looked at each other in astonishment. Both of us were grateful to be alive, and for the second time in my life, on any prolonged journey, I obeyed all posted signs and speed limits.

The next morning, I looked through the newspaper for accidents on the Denver to Boulder highway, but I did not find any, and the newscast was also free of accident news. I figured that, thanks to the grace of God, the individual driving at that high rate of speed on the wrong side of the highway made it home alive.

Prayer

Prayer is powerful. Pray as you will. Pray to whomever you wish. But if I may offer a little advice, it is to pray from your heart and learn to listen. Most people offer words or prayers that they were taught as children, then get up and go to wherever they think they need to go to. Again, pray as you will, but in my own personal life, it has been the prayers that came directly from my heart that produced the most notable results. Also, instead of getting up and leaving after you have had your say, try to sit still for a little while and listen. As any friend would appreciate your listening to him or her, so too would God. Yes, God speaks to you more than you know. In fact, God is always communicating with you in some way or another. Yet the reason that you do not always hear Him is because you are not always listening. My friend, God speaks to all of us, yet few among us choose to listen. If you would sit still for even five minutes a day and just listen to God and feel His presence within you, this simple act would forever change your life.

The following excerpt from Soren Kierkegaard's Journals illustrates the importance of listening to God:

> [36]*The immediate person thinks and imagines that when he prays, the important thing, the thing he must concentrate upon, is that God should hear what he is praying for. And yet, in the true, eternal sense, it is just the reverse: the true relation in prayer is not when God hears what is prayed for, but when the person praying continues to pray until he is the one who hears, who hears what God wills. The immediate person, therefore, uses many words and, therefore, makes demands in his prayer; the true man of prayer only attends.*

My First Experience with Prayer

> [37]*I have been driven many times to my knees by the overwhelming conviction that I have nowhere else to go.*
>
> Abraham Lincoln

My father figure was my grandmother, a very old-fashioned, tough Latina woman from Venezuela. To illustrate how tough she was, she was read her last rights in April 2001 and passed away on March 20, 2002. She was the type of woman who believed in spanking - hard spanking, I might add. Well, maybe it was a little more than spanking. My grandmother was well versed in her ability

[36]See Notes, page xviii.
[37]See Notes, page xviii.

to use any available tool, belt or shoe to make her point. People in this country call it child abuse, but back then we were told that it was discipline.

When I was young, I remember praying many nights to God to make me big, so that the hitting and spanking wouldn't hurt so much. Well, I got what I prayed for; by the time I was in fifth grade I was almost six feet tall, and about 220 pounds. To say the least, I was very grateful to God for making me physically large. But I then began to notice the sizeable difference in height and weight between myself and my classmates. I began to worry that I might not have set very clear parameters. Maybe God misunderstood; maybe He was making me too big. So I started praying again, but this time using clearer parameters. I reminded God that my intent was never to be ten feet tall and one thousand pounds which was, at the time, where I truly believed I was headed. I started praying for my growth to stop. Since then, I have grown only four inches and I have remained around 220 pounds. For a young man, that first experience with prayer was pretty dramatic, and it demonstrated to me that someone was indeed listening and assisting. The next story that I will share also reinforces my belief that God really answers prayers.

God Answers Prayers

In the mid nineties, I began preparing myself for a Master of Business Administration Program (MBA). I applied to four schools, and after submitting the application packages I began planning my interview schedule. I had four trips to make to programs all over the United States. Anyone who has ever gone through this process can tell you that there's a lot of work to be completed for each school. It can be a confusing time because you don't know where you'll end up or even if you will be accepted to where you wish to go.

One day I had had enough of worrying and wondering which school would accept me and I decided to lie down, meditate and pray about the situation. I lay on my bed, meditated for a few minutes, prayed for clarity and fell asleep. About an hour later, I woke up in the sleep paralysis state. I had been through this before and understood what it was. Understanding the situation, I decided that this was a good time to meditate and ask for guidance. Soon enough, I felt the vibration in my body changing. At that time, I was aware of the vibrational shift that usually precedes my leaving my body. I had read about out-of-body experiences (OBE) and had even had a few semi-conscious experiences, but I had only had one totally conscious OBE.

In my first totally conscious OBE, I answered for myself two of the deepest questions a human being can ask himself: "Can I really exist without my body and can my soul actually curse?" During the experience, I remembered the vibrations quickening in speed and raising in volume. Fear had stopped me so many times before, but this time, I was ready. The vibrations quickened to the point where it felt more natural to leave my body than to stay in it. I gave the okay to go and I was gone. Immediately, I found myself shooting out of my body and ended up five feet over it. I must say that the first phrase that I ever uttered while out of my body was not "this is one small step for me and one giant leap for mankind." I just looked around in total awe, and when I realized what was really happening, I yelled, "What the [expletive] am I doing up here?" After that now infamous first phrase, I shot myself right back and, with one big thump, re-entered my body and the experience was over.

So, overcoming fear was still very much a major part of the out-of-body experience for me. Now, once again, I found myself in the meditative state that allows for conscious OBEs and once again I had to fight the fears which I now know are not real, but I had made them real because of my belief in them. I again felt the vibrations in my body quickening. I had read about this, but it was definitely very different to read about it than to actually experience it physically. Not only was I feeling a very real vibrational quickening inside my body, but there were also a lot of strange and loud noises that accompanied this shift. I had read that this was totally safe and I believed it, or so I thought. I kept telling myself to keep it together, to stay strong, that it was all right. I kept telling myself that all the fear I was experiencing was simply an illusion I was creating. So I stayed on course, yet the vibrations seemed to quicken and the noises got louder. It was literally like an earthquake occurring inside my body, yet I somehow understood that there was no physical movement occurring. I knew that my physical body was completely still, and yet I felt I was traveling at 200 miles per hour in a '72 Land Cruiser, on a bumpy dirt road, during an earthquake measuring 9.0 on the Richter scale.

I then felt like my spirit wanted to shoot out of my body. I kept telling myself to keep it together, that I was creating all the fear I was experiencing. I literally felt myself wanting to leave my body, and that all I had to do was give the okay. The feeling was similar to traveling in your car at a high rate of speed, sticking your hand out the window, and creating a cupping shape with your hand. You would feel intense wind pressure against your hand, making you use the strength in your arm to keep your hand upright. At some point, there would be too much pressure against your hand. That was how I felt - like I was literally keeping myself inside my body. All I had to do was to let go, and I would have been released. At that point, it felt more natural to leave my body than to stay in it.

Just as I finally got up the courage to let go to see what would happen, I remembered that my mother was in the house. My first thought after that was, what if the books that I read were wrong? What if I somehow leave my body, and can't find my way back? What if I die and my mother is the first one to find my lifeless body in my room? Death was really not as big of a deal as my mother being the first to find my dead body. Although I felt I had the courage to leave, I did not want my mother's pain on my conscience. At least that's the excuse I used at that time. So there I was, ready to physically leave, but not emotionally secure enough to let go and too worried about coming back. I remember telling myself, "Okay, if someone can guarantee me a ticket back, I will be more than ready to leave." I then asked my spirit guides to give me a sign that I would be okay, that it would be safe for me to leave. Suddenly, at what seemed to be 50 yards above me, there appeared a white bird, and behind the white bird there appeared to be the sun. For a moment, I became mesmerized by the beauty and realism of this scene. The white bird flew in a figure eight pattern, yet it stayed in front of what I thought was the sun. It had the brightness of the sun but it did not at all hurt my eyes. Then again, I was not using my physical eyes to see this, but I could still "see" it. Although the bird flew in a figure eight, the sun was always its background. I say background, because I could always see the entire bird, and it always seemed to fly in front of this bright light.

Again, my ego struck, and I told my guides, "Gee guys, this is great. It is a very beautiful sign, but what I really need is a simple yes or no answer to the question 'will I be able to come back alive?'" I know my guides are very spiritual beings, but I often wonder if they ever think, "Man, this guy is a real pain in the ass!" Here I am, being offered one of the most awe-inspiring experiences I have ever had, and I keep asking for more assurances.

My friend, I'm sure some of you have wondered if your guides can actually be patient enough to handle the way you choose to grow. Well, let me tell you that if my guides have been generous and patient enough to handle me, then I'm sure your guides are generous and patient enough to handle you.

So after a few moments of waiting to hear a yes or no answer, I simply let fear take control and decided to abruptly end the session. The white bird made me feel that it would have been okay to leave the body, but for whatever reason, my ego needed to hear a yes or no answer. When I did not get a clear yes or no, I simply ended the session. Later, I felt bad about not leaving my body and joining the white bird, but in the end I chose to chalk it up as a learning experience. Although I knew I did not have to, I apologized to my guides for letting such a wonderful opportunity pass me by. I promised that I would not forget the experience, and that next time, I would be more physically and emotionally prepared.

With mixed emotions, I opened my eyes. On one hand, I felt bad for allowing such a wonderful experience to end so abruptly. Yet on the other hand, I was proud of getting to the point I had, past all those fearful thoughts. And so the experience ended, and I still had no clue why I experienced what I experienced. I had asked for clarity regarding which MBA program would be best for me, and what I got in response was a white bird in front of a sun. I did not think anything else of the experience. I thought to myself, "Well, this time I did not get an answer, maybe I'll try asking some other day." So I simply put it away in my memory. I was very grateful for the experience, yet I felt that the whole experience did not bring any more clarity to my concerns. Or so I thought!

My number one choice for the MBA program was the University of Notre Dame, a well known Catholic institution. Although I was raised as a Catholic, I had gone to church only a small number of times. The topic of religion was never really discussed in our house, and I did not begin thinking about religion until late in my college years. I slowly began to respect what I had thought Jesus tried to teach the world, and yet I also felt extremely uncomfortable with the constant judgment from the Catholic Church and its leaders. At the same time that I judged the judges for judging, I began to respect Catholic institutions such as Notre Dame for their dedication to ethics and community service programs. After college, I told myself that if I ever got a post-graduate degree, I would seriously consider going to Notre Dame. So, when the time came to apply to MBA programs, Notre Dame became my first choice because I liked the idea of balancing business and ethics courses along with the opportunity to be of service to the community. No other program offered that kind of balance.

Three months after my white bird experience, I took a trip to interview at Notre Dame. I landed in Chicago and drove two and a half hours east to South Bend, Indiana. It was early February and it was windy and cold. If you had lived near the equator for most of your life as I had, "windy and cold" would be considered a very kind description. As uninviting as the weather was, once on campus, I felt like I was on sacred ground. I had not yet interviewed at any other school, and I felt apprehensive and a little uncomfortable. Although I did not have the proper coat or the proper shoes to be walking around in the snow, I decided to take a walk around campus to try and calm my nerves. As I was walking around campus, a large basilica drew my interest. Although my knowledge of churches was limited, I believed this had to be one of the most beautiful Catholic cathedrals in the country. I walked inside and was awed by the magnificent glass murals. Each one depicted a story from the Bible. As I neared the pulpit at the center of the church, I turned to my right and was shocked by what I saw. I simply could not believe what I was seeing.

There it was on a glass mural - the white bird in front of the sun. Below the bird stood a woman surrounded by a group of men. Like a child, I ran around inside the church trying to find the nearest church supervisor. I found an old man in his seventies who looked like he had worked in the basilica forever. Excitedly, I grabbed his arm, and asked him to come with me. I remember him staring at me like I was crazy. But I was also twice his size and a third of his age, so he must have found it prudent not to resist. When I finished dragging the man from one side of the church to the other, he sighed with relief that the journey was over. I pointed upward, hoping to get a wise biblical answer to what was being depicted in the mural. The old man looked me and said, "Yeah...what?" I responded with "the bird and the sun, the bird and the sun." He backed up a little trying to get a better picture of what was going on with me (or he might have been trying to get a head start on his escape). I didn't think he understood the importance of the occasion for me, so I started telling him the whole story.

"Listen man," I said. "You have to hear this. I had this incredible vision where this white bird was flying in front of a sun, just waiting for me to leave my body and join it!"

Well let's just say that this statement did not seem to ease his concerns about my sanity! Later on, I laughed about it, but at the time I thought I was being perfectly clear. In my mind, this guy was seventy and a believer, thus he must have also experienced this same kind of vision sometime during his life. Yet, as I told the story of what happened to me, the old man seemed to be getting more and more nervous. Maybe he thought I was going to turn into Satan, create a hole in the middle of the church, and take him down with me! Obviously, he was uncomfortable with my story, so I stopped, took a deep breath and asked him one more time, "Could you please explain to me what is being depicted in this mural?" Finally, he told me the story. The mural depicted the story of the Holy Spirit descending on the Virgin Mary and the disciples. This scene had taken place after the death of Christ.

So there I stood, in total awe that the Holy Spirit, the spirit of God, would consider me important enough to even know who I was. All I knew back then was that to even believe myself to be in the same company as the Virgin Mary and the disciples was probably considered blasphemy at best. Now I know that those "higher beings" would never see another being as "lower." We are all equally loved by God. In His eyes, we are all His children. Only in our confusion could we have made a God that could create any one being more beautiful and deserving of His love than another.

After this experience, I became calm about my upcoming interview. I simply knew that everything would be okay. When the time came to walk into the admissions office, I felt calm, collected, confident and cool. The office receptionist told me that the individual who was supposed to interview me had called in sick. At that second I thought, "I traveled three thousand miles to be turned away, and asked to come back another day?" She must have seen the disappointment on my face, because she told me, with what appeared to be a mischievous smile, "Don't worry, the Dean of Admission herself wants to interview you!" Well, you might agree with me that this statement might make the average person a little nervous, but I actually felt at peace. I simply felt that the cards were being stacked in my favor. Before meeting her, I knew that this was the perfect person to interview me. And so I walked into the Dean of Admission's office calm, collected, confident and cool. We talked for nearly an hour about everything from my work experience in Venezuela to meditation (excluding the little white bird story). The interview went as well as I could have hoped. The director and I seemed to get along very nicely, and the interview flowed. After the interview ended, I thanked her for her time and she thanked me for traveling three thousand miles (yes, you bet I used that fact). I got back into my car, very happy to have had such a positive experience, and started on my way back to Venezuela.

Over the next four weeks, I interviewed at three other schools. It was now mid-April, and it was getting close to decision time. I had received two positive responses, and one waiting list response, but I had received no response from Notre Dame. I was again getting a little tense waiting for their answer. So, on a Wednesday night, I headed to my "Course in Miracles" group. When it was my time to share, I went on and on about my concerns. The facilitator patiently waited for me to finish, and then asked me if I trust God. In shock, I replied, "What do you mean - of course I trust God!" Then she said, "Yes, but do you really trust Him?" Right then and there, I understood what she was saying: if I truly trusted God, I would not worry about where I was headed; for wherever I was headed would be the perfect place for me. Right then and there, I understood that worrying was the complete opposite to trust, and when I choose to trust I never need to worry. The facilitator asked if I was ready to release my worry to God and replace it with trust. With my whole heart, I said, "yes!" And when I did, I felt a weight lifting off my right shoulder and back. It literally and physically felt as though a weight had been lifted, yet not only had it been lifted off my back, but I could also feel the weight moving above me, and somehow I felt the weight moving through the roof. I felt like I had released it, and that it was somehow moving toward God's light, where it would be dissolved.

I felt very blessed by the whole experience. I had so shifted my perception that, for a while, I felt like I was walking on air. From that moment on, I never worried about where I was headed, or where I was going to spend the next two years of my life. Regardless of how much longer I would have to wait for a decision from Notre Dame, I knew that I would not spend another restless second. Yet as God would have it, I would not have to wait long at all.

The following afternoon, I was headed out the door when the phone rang. Although I am someone who is not too concerned about answering phone calls, I figured I would just pick it up, say "hi" to the person and then politely excuse myself by saying that I was on my way out. I picked up the phone, and the lady on the line asked for James Blanchard. I told her that I was James Blanchard, and she asked me to please hold for the Dean of the Admissions Department of Notre Dame! I decided it was prudent to find the nearest chair so I could immediately sit down and catch my breath. Notre Dame's

Dean of Admissions came on the line, congratulated me for being admitted and welcomed me to the University. I believe my brilliant response was "Huh...what?" Thankfully she did not judge my brilliance and, after composing myself, I thanked her about seven times for the opportunity. Let's just say that the next day I woke up with a sore face from having a permanent 18-hour smile.

And so the circle closed, from asking for guidance with regard to my MBA, to receiving what I thought to be a beautiful yet unrelated vision, to being awed by its message, to being nervous and apprehensive about the upcoming interview, to the absolute and immediate release of fear. Thankfully, I gained the knowledge that there was someone in the universe who knew that things would be okay. I went from being very concerned about a specific issue, to learning that if I choose to trust, I need never again worry. All this resulted from a simple but sincere prayer.

Do Pets Go to Heaven?

Now let me offer a couple of small but very personal examples of how putting prayer, dreams, OBEs and meditation together can turn judgment into understanding, sadness into gratitude and pain into peace of mind and joy.

Texas was born in 1985. He was a greyhound in a basset hound's body. As with all baby bassets, his ears were as long as his body; they dragged on the floor making it unnecessary for us to mop it. Many times during his first year of life he tried to show us his athleticism by trying to chase us, only to step on his ears and drop to the ground. He would see us laugh then give us a look, the look that seemed to say, "Dude, it's not me, it's these damn ears." Nonetheless, a few seconds after the look he would again begin the chase.

Texas didn't turn out to be the athlete his heart told him he could be, but he did turn out to be a very smart dog. When we played fetch with other dogs in the park he would almost never get to the ball first. But if the ball seemed to be lost, he could always beat other dogs and was the first one to find it. In Miami, we had a two-story garden. I would throw the ball down toward the first level and the other dogs would run to that first level and search all around the garden for the ball. But Texas seemed to analyze the throwing motion, and he seemed to know by the movement of the arm the specific area he should search. His dog friends would get to the lower level first but Texas was the first to find the ball. Even in those instances where his dog friends would find the ball first, he would make sure to take it from them just before he turned the corner to meet me. I would always congratulate Texas on his victory, and he would smile and ask for another throw. He could be on the verge of a heart attack, with what appeared to be no oxygen left in his lungs; but no matter, he would smile and ask for another throw. On occasion, the ball would go into the neighbor's yard. When this happened, he would immediately find either a broom or the swimming pool stick and take it to the spot where the ball went over the fence. Then he would bark continuously, and I mean continuously, until I came down to retrieve it.

He saw and learned how we slept, and he too would get up on the bed (sometimes with a little assistance), take the covers off, snuggle in, put the covers back on himself (up to his neck) and of course use the pillow for his head. He was one of those dogs you could talk to and feel that he truly understood what you were saying.

When Texas was two years old, I went off to college, and did not see him that much for the next five years. After college when Texas was a mature seven-year-old, we rekindled our relationship and I took him with me to Venezuela. I worked three years in Caracas, the capital of Venezuela. He enjoyed his time in Caracas as we lived in a home with a large garden in the mountains overlooking the city. In the daytime, he would hang with his neighborhood friends but he was always there for me when I came home. After dinner, we would hang together on the big patio couch that overlooked the city. He liked getting on the patio couch (with a little assistance) and on top of my stomach or right next to me as I lay there. We would sit and talk a little, but mostly we looked down toward the million city lights. A cool breeze usually filled the air. Sometimes we would both be in awe as the fog rolled through the house making it seem like we were all alone in our own little cloud.

Three more years went by. Texas was now a little more than middle aged, at 10 years old. I was headed back to the United States to get my MBA. Sadly, we separated once again, and another three years passed us by with very little interaction. During my time away he developed a close relationship with Norma (the lady who took care of the house), and I went on to finish my studies.

After receiving my MBA, I returned to Caracas. Texas was now an aging 13-year-old basset hound. Before my departure, Texas would come to the patio couch, put his two front legs on the couch, and I would lift him up. Now, after dinner he would still come to the patio couch to check out the city lights but he would just look at me. With his basset hound stare, he would inform me that two paws on the couch was simply no longer possible. Thus I would bend to the floor and lift his now overweight body onto the couch.

Another year passed, and Texas was now a tired 14-year-old basset. After dinner, I would go to his couch in the corridor and sit with him. Sometimes he would look at me as if to say he wanted me to carry him to the outside patio couch, and so I did. I understood that his eyes did not work too well and that now the city lights must have looked like one big blur. But he could probably still feel the fog rolling in, and that memory seemed to bring him peace. It would be our last year together.

By the time Texas turned 15, he was almost blind and could not walk very well. I wanted to put him to sleep, but over the seven years Norma had developed a very close and loving relationship with Texas. She would stop me and cry every time I wanted to take him to the vet, because she knew that I thought it was time for Texas to go home, back to heaven. Texas had been an excellent companion and a very good and patient friend. I talked to Texas about going back home, and I felt, as I always did, that he truly understood and agreed with what I was saying. I knew in my heart that it was time for him to move on, and I can honestly say he felt the same way. But it was very difficult for Norma to agree to put him down and I was not going to do it until she said it was okay to do so.

Finally, after crying her eyes out, Norma gave the okay. So Texas and I went off to the veterinarian. I promised Texas that I would be the last thing he saw on Earth. I promised him that he would be all right where he was going and that we would never forget him. In the vet's office, we talked a little more and I told him that he had been a very good friend, that he had made a lot of people happy and that he should be proud of the way he lived his life.

I lifted Texas one more time up onto the vet's table. He seemed to understand that his mission was now over and he gave me a very peaceful basset stare. The vet injected Texas, and I made sure that my face was right in front of his as he slowly closed his eyes. I tried to keep my cool in front of him, but later broke down in the car. I also knew that Norma would be devastated.

I got back home and went to my room. Norma was in her room crying. I sat in my meditation chair to breathe for a while. I prayed for Texas, prayed that he would have a smooth transition and thanked him for being my friend. After an hour in meditation and prayer, I went to my bed and passed out.

Just before waking, I felt a weight on my stomach. I knew exactly who it was; I had felt that weight on my stomach many times before. It was Texas! We then began a "human" conversation, which went like this:

"Texas?"

"Yes."

"What are you doing here?"

"I just wanted to stop by and say thank you."

"Thank you?"

"Yes, thank you for everything." (In that acknowledge-ment I also understood that he was thankful I had the strength to put him to sleep.)

"You know, Norma is in a lot of pain about your passing."

"Yes, I know."

"What should I do?"

"Tell her to come and visit me."

"How do I do that?"

"You'll know."

"I love you, Texas."

"I love you too, James."

With those last words, I felt his weight lifting from my stomach, and he was gone. I woke up and wrote my experience down in my journal. I then got up from the bed and went to work. When I got home from work, Norma was not at the door to meet me. I understood this to mean that she was probably still having a very difficult time with Texas' passing. I found her in the kitchen and I could tell she had been crying. I sat her down and told her my experience. She seemed both relieved and excited. She asked if she too could have such an experience. I told her that I absolutely believed it was possible for her to reconnect with Texas. She asked how, and I offered her the following exercise, or, as I now call it, invitation.

Invitation #10 - Reconnecting with a Loved One

- Before going to bed, sit on a chair next to or near your bed.

- Take 10 deep, slow breaths. With each intake, feel light coming in and filling your body. With each release, feel the stresses of the day also being released.

- Breathe normally. Concentrate on the top of your head. Fill it with light and feel it getting heavier and more relaxed. Then do the same with your forehead, eyebrows, cheeks and chin. Feel those parts of your body getting heavier and more relaxed.

- Next, do the same and spend a little time with your neck,

shoulders, chest, back, stomach, thighs, calves and feet. Fill them with light and feel them getting heavier and more relaxed.

- Say a few prayers. Any prayers are fine, especially ones that come directly from your heart.

- Invite in your guides (you need not know who they are) or any self-actualized being with whom you feel comfortable.

- Bring forward whatever problem it is you are worried about. Speak from your heart. Ask for guidance in regard to the issue you are dealing with. Be open to receiving guidance, be it through dreams, thoughts or other means. (In this instance, I told Norma to ask to receive peace with regard to Texas' passing, and to be open to whatever she believed she needed to ask, however she needed to ask for it.)

- Have faith that you have been heard and that you will receive an experience or response with regard to your question.

- Be silent for a while. Feel the light that surrounds you. Feel the peace and gratitude that surrounds you.

- Offer gratitude for the time you have spent in this peaceful place with your guides and friends. Offer thanks for their assistance with this issue.

- Slowly begin to move your hands and feet. Begin to move the rest of your body. Open your eyes. Go to bed. Sleep.

This invitation will work. This invitation will bring you more peace with regard to whatever issue you bring to light. Trust, speak from the heart, listen and be open - nothing more is asked of you. You may do this invitation as many nights as you wish. The more you do it, the more connected you will feel. The more you bring problems and issues to light, the easier they will be for you to see, work on and resolve. The more you bring problems and issues to light, the less you will worry about them during the day and the more peace you will experience. The more you bring problems and issues to light, the more you'll feel connected to this light, the more gratitude will be offered and the more grateful you will feel.

After Norma performed the exercise, she felt much more at peace. The next morning, she excitedly told me about an experience she had while asleep. She told me that she knew she had an experience while asleep, and she could not refer to it as a dream because it just seemed too real. In the middle of the night, she felt herself being lifted. Soon she found herself in a never-ending green field. She mentioned that it was the most beautiful green she ever remembered seeing. In the distance, she saw something running toward her. In a few moments, she realized that it was Texas! Not the old Texas, that could barely walk, but a much younger and vibrant Texas. This Texas was running like he did back in his fetching days. Norma was so happy to see him that tears of joy started running down her cheeks. Then, as Texas came closer, he jumped into Norma's arms. Norma was still standing up, thus this jump must have been about three feet off the ground. As I mentioned before, Texas had never been much of an athlete, and this three-foot jump probably beat his best Earth jump by about three feet! It was obvious that Texas was doing very well. Texas and Norma rolled around the grass and played for a while. Then a very happy Norma and a very happy Texas both said goodbye. Norma told me the story with tears in her eyes, but they were no longer tears of sadness and pain but tears of gratitude and joy.

Pluto

I will briefly touch on one more case where this invitation was helpful. It involved my brother Roberto and his dog Pluto. Pluto was a Rhodesian Ridgeback, a beautiful, caramel-colored, 80-pound dog with a powerful bark. But his powerful bark was no contest to the kindness and gentleness of his heart. He was a pure-bred dog, from a very well-known and respected breeder. Pluto's life span should easily have reached 10 years. But as life would have it, at a year and a half of age, we found out that he had bone cancer. The last six months of his life, Pluto slowly deteriorated. Both my mother and Roberto were having a difficult time with this experience.

Three months after the diagnosis, my brother asked me to

see if spiritually I could do something for Pluto. At the time, my brother lived with my mother in Miami, Florida and I was living in Caracas, Venezuela. I meditated as in the previous invitation, and soon left my body. I found myself in the kitchen, in Miami where Pluto would sleep. I saw how his right front leg had been bandaged. I came closer to him and began doing Reiki (energy healing) with my hands. But whenever I began, he would walk away. I tried three times, but each time he walked away. This told me that he didn't want the treatment done, which indicated that he was ready to go back home. I left and returned to my body. The next day, I told Roberto about my experience, that I believed that Pluto was ready to go home, and that the most humane thing would be to put him to sleep. This was very difficult for my brother to hear and impossible for my mom.

Another month passed with Pluto suffering, barely able to walk. My brother and mother again took him to the vet, and the vet advised them that the most humane thing they could do was to put him to sleep. Again, this was very difficult for them to hear, as they were not yet ready to let him go. Two more weeks passed, and I knew that things must have been really rough because now my mother was calling to see if I could do something "spiritual" to help Pluto. I told her that it was just time to let him go back home, but she would have none of that. In the end, I promised her that I would see what I could do. So, once again, I meditated and used the invitation. I soon found myself on a dock. As I sat down to understand what was going on, I saw Pluto heading toward me. But Pluto was not alone, he was with another dog that I got the distinct impression was Pluto's guide dog. He was a smaller, black, hairier dog. He looked a lot like a big poodle. I found the combination very strange, but was made to understand that this was the dog that would help him with his transition. I sat on the dock as Pluto and the other dog came to me. They stopped, looked at me, made me understand something, then got on a boat. As they boarded the boat, they turned back to me and mentally asked me to release them from the dock. I got up from where I was sitting, and untied the ropes on the bow and stern of the boat. I threw the ropes onto the boat and the boat departed. I understood that Pluto was ready to leave and that it was only a matter of my mother and brother letting him go. They seemed to be asking for my assistance in this effort. The next day, I expressed my experience to my brother and mother and told them that I believed that they should allow Pluto to go. They seemed to understand, but they still could not put him to sleep.

In the last month of Pluto's life he could not walk. My brother and mother spent a lot of time with him but it was of no physical use. This last month did allow them the mental and spiritual peace of mind that there was no other way, but they still suffered.

Finally, they were ready to let him go. My brother took Pluto to the vet. He stayed with Pluto throughout the injection process, and he was with Pluto as he closed his eyes and slept. The whole experience was very difficult and draining. I offered them both a way they might better deal with the pain. My brother took my advice but my mother didn't. I offered my brother the invitation, and he took it to heart and tried it.

He did it in the middle of the afternoon and then went to take a nap. Before waking from the nap he found himself again in the vet's office, right before the final injection. He mentioned that the clarity of the experience made it almost seem real. The vet's office was just like it was in those last moments. But this time he could really see everything that went on. This time when the vet injected Pluto, my brother again saw Pluto close his eyes. But this time, he watched as Pluto's soul slowly raised itself above the physical body. Then the soul, still in dog form began to walk away on an upward 45 degree angle from the body. My brother saw in the distance a small, light-filled circle. Pluto was now walking toward this circle. The circle seemed to be at the end of a tunnel. In between the circle and Pluto, there appeared a smaller, black-haired dog. As soon as Pluto reached this dog, he turned around and looked at Roberto. They connected eye to eye one more time. Roberto said Pluto kind of smiled at him. Then Pluto and the dog began running toward the light and Roberto mentioned that they seemed to jump up through it. After they went into the light, Roberto woke up. He immediately called me and told me about his experience. Roberto received a great amount of inner peace, thanks to the experience and the knowledge that Pluto would not only be okay, but that he would not be alone.

A year and a half later, Roberto, being a big dog lover, researched and looked for another dog. After much thought, he finally settled on a Portuguese water dog, a dog he could put on his kayak, and swim with. The Portuguese use these dogs for fishing. They go with the Portuguese fishermen on their boats to help retrieve fish that fall through the nets. The Portuguese also use these dogs to send messages between boats. These dogs look like big black poodles, something you probably should never mention to Roberto or any Portuguese water dog owner! Roberto gave his dog the name "Costeau," after Jacques Costeau, the late, great French oceanographer. I'm glad to report Costeau is now five years old, and very healthy and happy.

My friend, prayer, dreams, out-of-body experiences and meditation are simply tools. They may or may not be useful in your journey toward remembering your Godself. You may choose to work with one, two or more, or none at all. Either way is fine. Offer a little willingness to remember, and let your heart be your guide. Yet, please do not be disheartened if you use one of these tools and do not obtain visible results immediately. Understand that the answer may not come in the manner you anticipate. Trust that a shift will take place. Trust that the answer will come, and allow it to emerge in the way it is offered. Know that every effort to remember your Godself is sincerely appreciated and celebrated by many more than you could ever know.

12

At Peace with the Afterlife

⸢ We might feel that we have a relatively good idea of the afterlife and where loved ones go after they have passed on. Yet with all this understanding, faith and trust, it is perfectly okay to grieve. Grieving has nothing to do with our understanding or lack of it. Grieving simply has to do with feeling whatever it is we need to feel for however long we believe we need to feel it. People should be allowed to grieve in whatever way they believe they need to grieve. Allow them the space they need. Listen to them. Pray for their peace, and pray for the departed one.

At no time in this chapter do I try to advise anyone on how they should feel or react to a loved one's passing. There is no one correct way of acting or reacting to such an event. And no one, regardless of how knowledgeable he or she believes himself or herself to be, should ever judge another brother or sister for how he or she chooses to react, or how long he or she chooses to grieve. There might well come a time when a brother or sister might appreciate some clarity with regard to the afterlife. When that time comes we will know it, but before then, our ear, compassion and prayers will be very much appreciated.

The following excerpt was written by Joseph Bayly in his book, "Acts of Love," after he laid three of his sons to rest. It may give you some insight on how to comfort loved ones as they grieve.

> [38]*I was sitting, torn by grief. Someone came and talked to me of God's dealings, of why it happened, of hope beyond the grave. He talked constantly; he said things I knew were true. I was unmoved except to wish he'd go away. He finally did.*
>
> *Another came and sat beside me. He just sat beside me for an hour and more, listened when I said something, answered briefly, prayed simply, left. I was moved. I was comforted. I hated to see him go.*

[38]See Notes, page xviii.

This section, as well as this entire book, is written with absolute respect for whatever you personally believe you need to go through to reach a more peaceful place. However, I believe this chapter will bring you to a more peaceful place within your heart and mind when it comes to the subject of the afterlife. I have reached a peaceful place with regard to this subject and, as I've said before, you and I have a lot more in common than your ego might currently allow you to perceive. Thus, if I can find a more peaceful place, so can you. I, as well as many people before me, have crossed the spiritual and mental barriers that the ego has told us exist between ourselves, our departed brothers and sisters and the afterlife.

So What Happens When We Die?

Our birth is not our beginning and neither will our death be our end. As birth is a continuation of our soul's journey, so too is death a continuation.

Depending on the circumstances surrounding our passing, we might choose to remain on the physical plain for a while. The more sudden the death and the less consciously prepared we are for it, the longer we will probably stick around. Once out of our bodies, we will experience a pulling sensation away from our physical body. We'll feel more relaxed than afraid. The pulling sensation will give us the sensation of passing through a tunnel.

Some of us have heard how in the moment before an accident, people have reported that they saw their lives pass in front of them, and that moment became so slow that it seemed to take forever. Mountain climbers who have fallen but survived have reported that they don't remember experiencing the fall because while falling they had this "life review," and felt peace. Most of those who have fallen never experienced the terror of falling. It would be safe to say that even those who fall and die probably do not experience the terror of falling and their last few seconds of life are actually very peaceful. Individuals who were victims of attempted murder, who technically die and were later revived, have reported this same effect. They talked about how, during the experience of being murdered, they saw a light and sensed peace and love surrounding them. In this light, they often saw and felt other individuals or spirits, and they felt supported by these souls. Except for the very beginning of the experience, they recalled no anxiety, suffering or pain. They, in fact, died and left the planet with extreme peace, love and with a sense of being supported. I have no problem saying that individuals who are murdered and pass on do not die alone. They do not die in pain, but in an atmosphere of great love and support around them. I also see no reason why this would not be the same for individuals who die in car or plane accidents. From all that I've seen, heard, read and experienced, no brother or sister ever dies alone. Many of their brothers and sisters welcome them home, and their return is celebrated with great joy.

During the process of dying, the soul feels a pulling sensation toward the light. Some people choose to stay near their bodies until the funeral. However, souls really have little or no interest in their bodies once they are released. It feels as if they are looking at an old empty suitcase, they simply have no attachment to it. The main reason a soul chooses to hang around is to assist those left behind through the transition. A soul understands that it will see all those left behind soon enough. The soul will try to reach out to those in pain in order to comfort them. But this is where a problem occurs: those left behind are usually in grief, due in part to the false belief that they will never see their loved ones again. Because of this grief, it is much harder for the soul to get through to these people. Sometimes, because of how these people are feeling, the only time the soul can comfort them is during sleep. In dreams, the soul will come to the individual and tell him or her that they are fine. If an individual is able to be calm, meditate or sit quietly, the soul will have a greater chance of consciously letting him or her know that they are fine and at peace.

I would like to add another writer's view on the subject of death and dying. I have chosen some passages from Pat Rodegast's "Emmanuel." Pat channeled a spirit that referred to itself by the name of Emmanuel. I have met with Pat and Emmanuel and find them to be honest, wise and believable.

On Dying Young

[39]*An individual dies young because he has completed his task. The being that has passed will be reminded of his task and that it was indeed his time. He will be offered a glance of the future of all those left behind, and he will find comfort and peace in this.*

You are an eternal being. Your brother is an eternal being. Once you leave this earth, this so-called young soul becomes a very old soul.

On Preparing for the Loss of Loved Ones

[40]*There are two answers. Loved ones are never lost. You must experience it in your own way. Of course, you will miss the physical being but when you learn to go beyond that, there will be no missing at all. Even as you sit in your human form, once you allow yourself - notice the word "allow" to believe that you exist beyond the physical, you will touch hands with those who have left. And it will be real. It will be more real than the physicality that you had touched before.*

Are you aware that the physical body is a shield or a shell? It does not reveal but rather hinders revelation. If you did not have need of illusion you would not need a physical body at all.

What should you do immediately following the death of a loved one? That is an excellent question. First, the willingness to let that person go to the next step in their evolution is extremely helpful, not only to you but to them. A "farewell," a "bon voyage," a "Godspeed." Then the rest of you look at each other and give comfort and assurance, and provide all the hugs and tis-

---

[39]See Notes, page xviii.
[40]See Notes, page xviii.

*sue that are necessary. Next, take yourself to a place of
great luxury and enjoy an incredible feast. Salute the
soul that has completed its task. Give a toast to the time
you will meet again and go about the business of your
own lives.*

Death is not only a time of mourning. It is a time of truth.

*Karmic ties can be formed by an unwillingness to
express any negativity thus holding resentments that go
into the soul consciousness to return in another life. By
your dealing with the negative emotion, by cleansing
the relationship, you are helping both of you. The saying "Don't speak ill of the dead," is nonsense. There is
no such thing.*

Suicide

There is no punishment for someone who commits suicide. The
soul is not judged for having ended its life. The soul is never judged
by anyone other than itself. The soul that commits suicide usually
experiences a sense of embarrassment that it has lost or squandered
away an incredible opportunity. It soon understands that next time
it comes to Earth it will need to deal with these issues. It welcomes
this "second chance" to learn to deal with issues and circumstances
in a more productive manner.

The only ones who truly suffer are those people who are left on
Earth. Then again, the amount of grieving done by those left on
Earth is, in the end, equal to their misperceptions of the situation.
That being said, we should never judge how an individual reacts to
such an incident. Behind every veil of illusion lies the gift of truth.
The veil has the density and weight we give it. The gift will be
revealed once we have chosen to lift the veil. The amount of hurt
and pain we experience is equal to our belief in the reality and final-
ity of suicide. The more strength we give to the illusion of suicide,
the more we will hurt. The more strength we give to the illusion that
we will never see that person again, the more sadness we will feel.

The more strength we give to the illusion that the individual does not exist any longer, the more alone we will feel. The more strength we give to the illusion that the individual who committed suicide is now suffering, the more we will suffer. The more strength we give to the belief that this individual is being judged by God, the more we will judge ourselves for what happened. The more strength we give to the illusion that we cannot live without that individual in our physical proximity, the less we will want to live our lives. The more we choose to live in the past and in the illusions of "what ifs," the more weight we will carry with us into the present. Never judge a brother for how much strength he gives to illusions. He will give strength to illusions as long as he finds them valuable.

The best thing we can do for ourselves and someone who has chosen to take his or her life is to simply pray for them, to send them our love, strength and support and to ask God for love, strength, and support for ourselves. If we choose to suffer, our suffering will come to the attention of the soul that has committed suicide. The soul will need to see what it has helped cause. In absolute terms, it would expedite the process for the departed soul if we simply let it move forward. The more we suffer from its action, the more it is "held back" to experience the full extent of its action. For example, if we go to that person's grave and sulk in pain over its action, it will "come down" to see what its action caused. It is of extreme importance to note that this is not done as a punishment to the departed soul but as a continuation of its lesson plan, the complete comprehension of the full effect of its action. Equally so, there will be significant lessons for those left behind, but how and when they choose to learn them will be up to them.

My friends, we may choose to learn through joy or through pain. I will respectfully offer this one fact: we will eventually come to terms and obtain peace with regard to our brother or sister's action. The time it takes us to allow this peace to be experienced is up to us. Yet know that this much is true: our brother or sister will see and experience the full result of his or her action. Again, the soul does this not because it is being punished, but because this is the best way for it to truly learn and understand what it has helped cause. We have the choice to let it see us by its gravesite in pain, or praying for peace in our rooms. We need to react the way we need to react, and there is no judgment in that. But understand that our brother or sister will be greatly strengthened by our prayers, and will find wonderful relief in our peace.

Again, I offer Pat Rodegast's view on suicide from "Emmanuel:"

[41]*Your brother took his life and brought it home. Although the inadvisability of suicide is spoken of, it is all right. It is clear that when one chooses to quit school, it is necessary to come back again and learn what could not be learned at the time. I speak to you from eternity, and there is no limit to the number of lives one can have.*

Your brother is learning many valuable things. He is home. He is well. He is working, and will design a curriculum next time that will be more compatible with his willingness and his needs.

It is to yourself that you must direct your attention. What does it mean to you to have a brother who killed himself? You need to hear the voice of God within you that knows it's all right, that he is eternal. Hear the message he gave you. No one acts alone. No one acts in a vacuum. No one kills himself without leaving a legacy of growth behind.

There is no punishment in God. There is only eternal love and understanding. Suicide is merely a foolish act, and as such, it reaps its own reward and there you are.

Your prayers and blessing will be much appreciated, but more than that, your gentle and sweet understanding of the futility of the act (of suicide) will be most welcome.

[41]See Notes, page xviii.

Entering the Spirit World

Most of us have already read or seen television accounts of people who said they died and went through a tunnel, and toward "the light." The most eloquent way that I have read this light being described was in the book "A Course in Miracles." The description is as follows:

> [42]*Beyond the body, beyond the sun and stars, past everything you see and yet somehow familiar, is an arc of golden light that stretches as you look into a great and shining circle. And all the circle fills with light before your eyes. The edges of the circle disappear, and what is in it is no longer contained at all. The light expands and covers everything, extending to infinity, forever shining and with no break or limit anywhere. Within it, everything is joined in perfect continuity. Nor is it possible to imagine that anything could be outside, for there is nowhere that this light is not.*

How does being in this light feel? It is a lot to ask someone to describe such a feeling, for no words I write could ever closely clarify this feeling. This is something we need to experience to truly understand. And, my friend, we don't need to have a near death experience to feel this light. All we need do is simply ask to experience it, and if it serves our higher purpose, it will be offered. The following is the closest I can come to offering a physical experience that will give a partial sensation of being in this light.

Invitation #11 -
A Physical Experience of How "The Light" Feels

Imagine yourself in Tucson, Arizona in August. The temperature is in the 100's, a dry heat with not a cloud in the sky. Indoors, you have just completed an incredible workout; you lifted weights, did cardiovascular exercise and stretched your muscles. You go outside and head for the pool. You lie outside the pool for 20 minutes on your stomach and 20 minutes on your back. You let the sun beat

[42]See Notes, page xviii.

down on your skin as the sweat begins to flow from your pores. After 40 minutes, you get up and head for the pool.

The pool is heated to a very comfortable 90 degrees. You walk very slowly and deliberately into the pool and you feel your body leisurely merging with the water. Close your eyes. As you do this, you slowly feel the change in every inch of your body. You head deeper into the pool and as you do, the pool begins to refresh every inch of your once hot, sweaty and tired body. Your skin merges with the water and it becomes more difficult for you to tell where your skin ends and the water begins. You move toward the shaded area of the pool. You stretch out your arms as you go deeper and deeper into the pool. You tilt your head back, letting the water cover your ears. All becomes quiet. Only your eyes, nose and mouth are now above the surface. You are now in another world. You start taking slow, deep breaths; you begin to quiet the body and the mind. Your skin and the water completely end their separateness and begin to merge. Your skin is no longer your boundary, for now you simply extend into the water. You now become the water, and at the same time you know that you are still you. It's as if every one of your skin's cells have grown roots, and these roots have grown and expanded into the water until you are no longer able to see or feel them. But you know they are now connected to all and that they, in turn, connect you to all. And as you are now connected to all, you become part of that whole and that whole is somehow you. You are now boundless and yet at the same time, the individual who is you still very much exists.

Keep your eyes closed and offer a prayer of gratitude for your life. Imagine a ball of light and love growing from your center as you continue to thank God and the universe. As you continue to be grateful, this ball of light and love begins to expand until it fills your entire being. Let these feelings and emotions overflow and extend themselves through every cell of your body. Like waves, let them continue to flow from within you out to God, to the universe, to everyone and all. Do this for around five minutes. Then allow the same love that you expressed and expanded to the universe to be returned. Feel the waves of light and love being sent to you. Allow yourself to absorb them. Feel God, the universe and all light, love and support being offered. Feel yourself allowing it to be received. Receive for the next five minutes or so. Continue until the giving and receiving become one. Now that you've dismantled your personal barriers between giving and receiving, you can understand that as you give - you receive, and that they are indeed one. Continue to send gratitude and love, and allow yourself to continue to receive this wonderful energy as long as you wish.

My friend, this is the closest I can come to offering you what "the light" feels like. Again, if you wish, drop all thoughts of fear, and before going to bed ask to experience this light sometime during the night. Ask my friend, the universe waits for you to ask.

The Tunnel

Many of us have the idea that once our spirit leaves our body, it enters a tunnel and simply moves in the direction of the light. In fact, it doesn't so much as move toward the light as much as it's pulled toward it. Even though it is being pulled, as always, it has a choice of either allowing itself to be pulled in, which is the natural sensation, or stopping the pulling and staying between dimensions. The pulling sensation can be similar to that of being on the surface of a smooth flowing river and being pulled downstream toward the ocean. As the spirit is being pulled toward the light, it gets brighter and wider. But this light does not hurt it's eyes, simply because it does not use physical eyes.

Some souls, especially those that left without warning, might become a little upset that they left their families behind. If this is the case, their guides will show them their families' future in order to calm them down and allow them to move forward. People who die suddenly can arrive with the frustration of being taken before having resolved certain issues. In such cases, their guides will also meet them in order to help them remember not only why they chose such an exit but to also show them that their families will be okay. The bottom line is that there are no accidents. A soul with its guide's assistance chooses when, where and how it will exit Earth. This is what's best for the development of the transitioning soul, and will allow for the most growth possible for those left behind. Therefore, in actuality, the soul's transitioning is literally a gift, not only to itself, but also to all those left behind. Once in the light, the first person the soul meets is its guide. There is also the possibility that it will be a soul mate, best friend or close family member. It will be someone with whom the soul is very familiar, someone who will be best able to assist it in this part of the transition. The closest person to the soul spiritually will usually meet it first, then the second closest, and so on. Something interesting to note here is that even if its "soul mate" of many lifetimes is its closest peer on the spiritual side and if this soul mate is still alive on Earth, he or she could still be the first to meet the soul. This is possible because it is extremely rare that a soul brings one hundred percent of its soul or energy to a specific incarnation. Thus, a certain percentage of its soul mate's energy will be "left behind." Regardless of how much it is, that energy will be more than capable of greeting the soul as it returns home.

Although this may seem like a trip into the unknown, there is really no fear involved. The transitioning soul might be a little confused, especially if it left quickly, but fear is not an issue at all. Soon after, it begins encountering a lot of other souls that were close to it. It will usually meet them in order of closeness. The soul it has cared and shared with most throughout its lives will meet it first, and so on in descending order. This "welcoming party" is arranged in order to make the transition more comfortable.

Once a soul is more developed, and has gone through the transition enough times, the soul needs less and less hand-holding or comforting. It simply becomes an unnecessary part of the journey. The advanced soul will simply bypass this stage, leave the hellos, kisses and hugs for later, and go on to its destination.

My Spiritual Home

The soul ultimately goes to its spiritual home. The place where I go literally looks like the city where I live today, but about 250 years in the past. The city is Caracas, Venezuela. Today it is a very populated South American city with millions of inhabitants, lots of buildings, smog and narrow streets. A dirty river passes through it, bordered by concrete walls. The river is a naturally flowing river turned into a canal, and there is lots and lots of traffic. On the other hand, it is surrounded by a beautiful mountain range. It has a beautiful, wide river coursing naturally through the valley, and there are around two hundred homes in the valley. There is not a cloud in the sky, but interestingly enough there are three suns. In front of those three suns are three houses, and in those three houses live thousands of doves. I have seen thousands of doves leaving the houses, and one usually comes to me, and sits a couple of inches above my left hand. It is a place of great peace and joy for me, which I, on rare occasions, at least lucidly speaking, visit during my out of body experiences.

Destination - Heaven or Hell

Is there such a thing as a literal heaven or a literal hell? I don't know. But I can share a couple of stories with you that will assist you in drawing your own conclusions. The first one will be about heaven, and my visit there. The second story will be about hell, and a very interesting story I heard about, which to me goes to the heart of what hell probably is.

One night I was dreaming that I was in a sword fight, and my brother Roberto and I were dueling against three strangers. I killed one (yes, I said kill; on rare occasions, I still kill people in my dreams). The second one ran away and my brother was fighting the third one. As the second one ran away, I went to assist my brother. As I swung at my brother's attacker, he ducked, and I slit my brother's throat. It was definitely a deadly blow and I was devastated that I had just ended my brother's life. As our third enemy ran away, I fell to my knees in sorrow, and my brother, lying in a pool of blood, could only look up at me. On my knees, I could tell that he wanted to communicate something to me, but his wound and lack of strength did not allow him to speak. Finally, gathering the last of his strength, he somehow found the energy to speak. He looked up at me and said, "I forgive you." I cried in terrible anguish as my brother lay dying from his wound.

Suddenly, I became lucid enough to remember one of my favorite lessons from "A Course in Miracles," "There is No Order of Difficulties in Miracles." As I remembered the lesson and my training in Reiki (energy healing), I put my hands over the wound. I told myself, and believed with all my heart, that there was no order of difficulty in miracles. So I asked God for the power to heal the wound. Right after my request, I felt a surge of energy that felt as if two bowling balls of light passed through my arms and out of my hands onto my brother's neck. After an instant, I looked down and my brother was completely healed.

I became so grateful that God allowed my brother to live that I started to praise and thank Him. I was so ecstatic to have my brother back that I simply could not stop praising God. I praised God like I've never praised him before. As the praising continued, I heard a voice in the distance. As I continued to thank God, the voice became more pronounced. It was saying, "Hallelujah." But it was not just saying "Hallelujah," it was singing "Hallelujah," and in the most beautiful voice imaginable. Try to recall the most beautiful individual performance you have ever heard and multiply it a thousand times. I continued to thank God for my brother's life, and as I did, the voice singing "Hallelujah" became more pronounced and more beautiful. Yet by now, it was not one angel singing but ten, and that chorus was better than any church choir I had ever heard. My thanking God merged with the chorus of angels praising God but now it sounded not like a ten-angel chorus, but one hundred angels singing Hallelujah, in praise to God. They kept singing that one simple word over and over, in praise to God. I began to join with them in my praise to God and I began to sing with them. I then realized that it was not hundreds or thousands of angels singing "Hallelujah," but millions of angels singing "Hallelujah, Hallelujah, Hallelujah!" And I knew that these angels sang in eternity, and I had joined them, for a moment in time. The joy in praising God was so great that I felt extreme gratitude for just being able to be thankful. After a while, there came a point when my ego began to wonder if I would ever come back. As a result of that fear, in a moment's time, that thought brought me back to Earth and back into my body. As I look back, I wish I had stayed longer praising God, but I understand that I had work to do regarding fear-based thoughts. Nevertheless, I was and am very grateful for the experience.

I later read that some believe that God is surrounded by a group of angels who praise Him constantly. That belief sounded a little foreign to me until that night. I mean, how could an angel praise God for eternity and not get tired or bored? Today, I truly believe that there is such a place, and that for a moment in time I had the honor and pleasure of being part of that place. Now, is this the place they call Heaven? I don't know, but I do know that I was somewhere very special, somewhere very close to the source.

Will I Get Bored in Heaven?

I will not go any deeper into what happens while in heaven, for there are better and more complete books on this subject. Two excellent books on what is sometimes referred to as our "in-between lives" or our lives in-between physical incarnations are "Journey of Souls," and "Destiny of Souls," by Michael Newton, Ph.D. A question that is sometimes asked of me is: could we ever get bored in heaven? I will answer this question with a beautiful and yet simple quote from Larry Libby's "Someday Heaven."

> [43]*If you are thinking you might get bored or tired after being in heaven for a while...don't worry! Try to imagine something with me. Imagine you are a little bird who lives in a tiny cage made of rusty metal. And inside your cage you have a food dish, and a little mirror, and a tiny perch to swing on.*
>
> *Then one day, some kind person takes your cage to a big, beautiful forest. The forest is splashed with sunlight. Proud, towering trees cover the hills and valleys as far as you can see. There are gushing waterfalls, and bushes drooping with purple berries, and fruit trees, and carpets of wild flowers, and a wide blue sky*

[43]See Notes, page xviii.

*to fly in. And besides all these things, there are mil-
lions of other little birds, hopping from one green limb
to another and eating their fill, and raising their little
families, and singing their hearts out all through the
day. Now, little bird, can you imagine wanting to stay
in your cage? Can you imagine saying, "Oh please
don't let me go. I will miss my cage, I will miss my little
food dish with seeds in it. I will miss my plastic mirror
and my tiny little perch. I might get bored in that big
forest."*

Is This Hell?

I personally do not believe that there is such a place. But let me
tell you the story of someone who did believe that there was such
a place called hell. There was a man in his mid-fifties who, according to him, had lived "a very bad life," and had been "a very bad
person." He was someone who had lied, cheated, stolen and even
murdered. This man "knew" that he was going to hell when he
died. Although he did not know too much about his Catholic faith,
he knew that the good go to heaven and the bad go to hell. He
would tell everyone who would listen that he knew he was going
to hell. This man was a self-described "bad ass," "scumbag" and a
"crook." He knew he was going to hell and he was proud of it; he
believed he was tough enough to take it.

So, as life would have it, he had a heart attack one day and he
stopped breathing for a few minutes. He was clinically dead. While
dead, he said that he found himself in a very dark place and as he
looked around, he saw that there were fires all around, and around
those fires were little deformed devils with pitchforks. It was an awful
place and the only sounds heard were screams of pain. He could see
people being tortured by these devils. It was just the way he had
always imagined. As he became more aware of his situation, he began
to see these devils coming closer to him. The pride of knowing he
was going to hell now turned to fear. He was in a panic as these devils
started to torture and burn him. Like a pack of wild dogs they tore at

his flesh and chewed into his bones. After what felt like an eternity, he couldn't take it anymore. The pain and torture he saw others and himself enduring became too much for him to handle.

After enduring all he could, he began to cry out to Jesus. He began asking Jesus to forgive him and to give him another chance. After crying out loud from deep in his soul for Jesus to forgive him and to come and save him, he saw in the distance a beam of light, and as he kept asking for Jesus to come and save him and forgive him, he saw that indeed it was Jesus who was coming. When Jesus appeared in front of him, Jesus smiled and simply said to the man, "Can't you see, this is your illusion?" As Jesus said these words, the man himself began to see hell melting away. From top to bottom, hell slowly melted away and what this man saw was that he had been in heaven the whole time.

He realized that he had created the hell around him and that he had always been surrounded by heaven. The love of heaven had never left him. The love of heaven had always surrounded him. It was simply that he had chosen not to see it. Hell, very simply put, was and is an illusion that he had chosen to believe in, that and nothing else. It was hell he believed he was going to and it was his hell where he found himself after death. By choosing to believe in the illusion, he made it real.

We can choose heaven or hell; that is our choice in every moment and step of life. Nevertheless, the truth is there waiting for us to acknowledge it. It will wait for us as long as it takes, for it has everlasting patience. It is there for us in every situation, every moment, and in every person. In every situation, moment and person, we can choose to see and experience heaven or hell. We have been given free will, yet regardless of what we choose, God always loves us. Our path to heaven is lit with forgiveness, acceptance and love. We need only choose it and we will find heaven even here on Earth. Heaven is here, and heaven is now. It is our choice that allows us to feel and experience this. All souls go to "heaven" or the "spirit world" both good and bad, young souls and old souls. But after physical death, some may take longer than others to realize where they truly are.

Judgment: An Eye for an Eye

As I said before, a soul is never judged by anyone other than itself. It reviews its life; it sees how it treated people, and how it made them feel. The interesting part is that, the soul can now actually feel what the other person felt as it dealt with him or her. If it made a person laugh, it will feel this person's joy; if it made a person angry or sad, it will feel the person's frustration and pain. This is what the Bible refers to as "an eye for an eye." It is this and nothing else. The soul will experience how it made others feel. It will experience what it was like to be in the other person's shoes at that moment when the interaction occurred. If it caused someone pain, it will experience pain. Equally so, if it was kind to someone, it will experience gratitude. If it said a kind word, it will feel the appreciation. Even if it felt that person offered no appreciation, it will become aware of exactly how the soul made the person feel. This exercise will allow the soul to more fully understand how its actions and reactions affect those with whom it interacted. Later on, the soul will get together with its peers to review its actions and get their perspectives. It will also meet later on with higher-level guides to review its experiences. It is important to note that none of these reviews occur in order to judge the soul. Judgment is never reported as an emotion someone felt during this process. These reviews are done in order to visit all possible perspectives, angles and reasons for the soul's actions and reactions.

An eye for an eye is in no way an excuse for revenge. It is in no way a call to strike back at a brother or sister. It in no way is offering permission to attack a brother or sister for what we believe they did to us. An eye for an eye simply states that our brother or sister will experience how he or she made us feel. This is not done as revenge or as a punishment, but as a learning device to assist developing souls in more fully understanding the consequences of their actions. Thus in the end, we will experience the full extent of any actions we took in order to punish or take revenge on our brothers and sisters. Once we do so, we will clearly see and experience the futility of such actions. And in the end, we will not curse God, or our guide, or our brother or sister for experiencing this review, but we will thank all involved for our new understanding and their participation in the lesson plan.

Lost Souls

If a person, for whatever reason, chooses not to go into the light, he or she remains "behind." When the soul remains behind in the physical world in spiritual form it is sometimes referred to as a "lost soul" or a ghost. Most of the time, a lost soul does not realize that it has passed on, or it refuses to believe that it is dead. There are people or channels who help these lost souls understand that they are dead, and that it's time to move on. My first experience with this was quite dramatic, and something I will definitely never forget.

I have a friend (let's call him Pete) who, in a past life, sold people. He was a slave trader, if you will. Yes, I know, these are the type of people my Mama told me to stay away from. Anyway, part of his mission in this life is to bring "lost souls" into the light. Pete is a psychotherapist in this life. One day in early 1997, a client, let's call him John, came in for a counseling session. During this session, John said he had been feeling guilty about a friend's death. This death had occurred more than 30 years ago in Vietnam. He had been driving a jeep with three other soldiers. His friend was in the back seat. The jeep went over a land mine and exploded. All were thrown from the vehicle and his friend was the only one who sustained deadly injuries. His friend's wound was in the chest area and there was nothing anyone could do. He had trouble breathing and very soon after the blast, he died.

John was having trouble with the fact that he was psychic, and had had a very strong feeling that this was going to happen. He mentioned it to his friend; and not knowing that John had these powers, his friend laughed it off, and John chose to not let it bother him. He also chose not to force his friend to believe him. John had been feeling very guilty that he should have done more. He felt that his friend's death should never have happened.

A couple of days after the psychotherapy session, I was meditating with Pete and his wife (let's call her Ann). Pete went into a trance and John's friend came into his body. Pete started breathing very erratically, in very short, forced breaths. Although Pete and Ann had helped a lot of lost souls find their way to the light, I could tell that Ann, who facilitated the sessions, was very concerned about Pete's breathing pattern. The concern on her face and in her voice scared me, and I felt that maybe I would be more comfortable outside the room. Then, a couple of thoughts entered my mind. One was that although I was half Pete's age, he was in much better shape than I was. This meant to me, mathematically speaking, we had an equal chance of having a heart attack, but Ann did not seem concerned about me. Two, I thought the lost soul that entered Pete's body would go crazy and kill us all (remember, this was my first experience with this kind of phenomenon, and this lost soul was a Vietnam vet). I was afraid, to say the least. But I decided to get a hold of myself, calm my own breathing and see what would happen.

Ann, still nervous, began to give instructions to the soul to calm down. The soul explained that he couldn't breathe because an explosion had torn his lungs apart. Ann insisted that his lungs were fine, and that he should try to breathe normally. Finally, Ann's efforts to calm him down seemed to be working. The soul was still breathing forcefully through my friend's body, but was slowly able to communicate with Ann. Ann asked the soul what had happened. He said that there had been an explosion, that he was on the ground bleeding and unable to breathe, and that he thought that he was dying. He also said in a very angry voice that his friend, who was driving, knew that this was going to happen, and that it was his friend's fault.

Apparently this soul did not know that he had indeed died; he believed that he was still at the accident scene suffering, unable to breathe and dying from the blast. Remember, this happened 30 years ago. Ann tried to explain to the soul that his friend really wasn't sure of his abilities at the time, that he did have psychic powers, and that he was very sorry that this had happened. The soul had a difficult time buying it; he was still very angry. Little by little,

Ann convinced the soul to calm down. She started working with the soul, trying to convince him that he had died.

What had happened when the soul died was that one of the last things he saw was the blast from the explosion. The blast was like a bright white light. So when the soul died and was pulled toward the white light, he began to think about the light from the explosion. Thus, he refused to be pulled into the light and stayed in this dimension, suffering and believing he was still dying. Now, I must mention that time "here" and time "there" are not the same. Exactly how they are mathematically related, I do not know, but I do believe the soul did not know that he had been suffering for thirty years; he probably believed that only a few minutes had passed.

Finally, Ann was able to calm the soul down. She asked him to look at the light. She asked him to think about his family. After about ten seconds, the soul became emotional and said to Ann that he couldn't believe it but in the light he could see his mother. She asked him to converse with her, and he said that she was reaching down and asking him to go with her. Ann asked him to reach up to her. A few moments later, you could see and feel this soul leaving my friend's body. The soul left and went with his mother into the light. And so the session ended.

Apparently, those in the spirit world could not reach him because he did not believe that he was dead. Once Ann was able to physically calm him down and talk him away from the pain that he was concentrating and focusing on, the soul could now understand what was truly going on. Being calm allowed him to understand that the accident was over and that he had indeed passed away. By being calm, he was able to look at the light without fear. Once he allowed himself to look into the light, and to be open to focusing on something other than the pain, his mother appeared in order to assist him through the process. When he saw that his mother was in the light, and that it was safe, he allowed the light to pull him in toward his mom.

It was a very emotional moment for me and I was very grateful to have been a part of it. Ann later told me that she was the most worried she had ever been. In previous sessions, my friend's guides were always there making sure that nothing bad or dangerous happened. Although during the difficult part of the session, Ann asked her husband's guides to intervene and get the soul out, they did not. Obviously, they weren't as concerned as Ann, or as scared as I was.

Making Peace with a Loved One Who has Passed On

My grandmother, as I mentioned before, had always been more of a father figure than a mother figure to me. She had a very strong personality. Her personal relationship with me, my brother and mother was that of Dr. Jekyll and Mr. Hyde. Her tongue was sharper than any knife and she had an absolute inability to ever say that she was wrong. I never, in my 33 years of life with her, heard her say she was sorry. I grew up with my grandmother, mother and brother. Although she seemed to care for us, it was a very physically, verbally and emotionally abusive environment to grow up in. I don't think she ever realized how much she mentally crushed us every time she verbally, emotionally and physically attacked us.

My grandmother, before she passed away, had been very sick for about a year and a half. Although we had nurses providing 24-hour care, our family also took turns sleeping in her bedroom. My night was Wednesdays, and as soon as I was given Wednesday night, I felt that was the night she would choose to go. So for a year and a half, we took turns sleeping over. On the night of March 20, 2001, we all felt the time of her passing was near. Then again, with my grandmother, you never knew.

Most of the family visited that day, and by 11 p.m., most of them had gone home. The nurses and I were in her bedroom and my Aunt Cari was in the kitchen. At 11:30 p.m. I decided to go to sleep so I put the recliner chair next to my grandmother's bed. My body faced her body. I had left a couple of feet between the recliner and her bed so that the nurses could get next to her if they needed to do so.

I began to meditate. I prayed, three "Our Fathers" and three

"Hail Mary's." I then mentally invited my guides into the room, and then invited, one by one, Mother Mary, Jesus and the Holy Spirit. Next, I invited my grandmother's guides and family members she knew who were on the other side. I asked them all to join me in filling the room with love and light. The feeling in the room was great. I literally felt as if I wore a one-foot-thick coat of peace and love from my waist up. I then asked them to help end my grandmother's suffering and take her home. A few moments after my request, the nurse tapped me on the shoulder and told me that my grandmother had opened her eyes once, closed them, and had finally passed on. It was 12:12 a.m.

As soon as I got up from the recliner to see my grandmother, my Aunt Cari ran into the room. She was very upset, and a little panicked. Although now completely out of the meditative state, I could still feel that one-foot-thick layer of peace coating my upper body and head. I immediately calmed my aunt down and told her that my grandmother, her mother, was finally at peace. She calmed down pretty quickly and began to make phone calls. I later asked her how she knew that Mamina, my grandmother, had passed away if no one had told her. She said that Mamina had come to the kitchen in spirit form seconds before she passed away to tell her that she was now leaving. By the time she ran into the room, my grandmother had passed on. Once the family began arriving at the house, I openly shared with them my experience and it seemed to bring them peace, especially to my uncle, my grandmother's only son, who had always been extremely close to her.

Three days after her death, I went into meditation and quickly found myself out of my body, being taken to a room. I say taken because many times when you're out of your body, you are taken by the hand or hips by a guide to different places. In this room, there was a simple wooden table and two chairs. In one of the chairs, there sat my grandmother. I saw her, and sat down on the opposite chair. I was not in shock that I was there with her, for I knew that this would happen sooner or later. But I was amazed at how she started our conversation. She looked at me and began to talk. "I'm sorry" were her first words to me. These two simple words carried so much weight that just hearing them from her helped me release a lot of feelings I had suppressed. I considered myself to be a spiritual being, and I had made myself believe that these two words were really not necessary for me to hear from her. I absolutely felt that I was above needing to hear those two words. But I now know that I was completely wrong. For those two little words allowed me to free myself from a lot of the hidden pain and anger that I thought I was above feeling, but I now know I still retained toward her. In the spirit world, a small phrase like I'm sorry is not so much two words that express regret. In that space, those words can carry with them a massive thoughtform - many of the reasons why you are sorry, and it was this that I felt. With those two words, the past was truly forgiven, and with true forgiveness came an absolute release, a total letting go of thoughts and emotions I had once thought I had already dealt with but had simply hidden away from my awareness. I'm sorry - no other two words could have offered me so much freedom when it came to my relationship with my grandmother. There was an immediate acceptance on my part, and we were then free to continue our relationship on a much deeper and meaningful level.

Relationships Continue

A relationship does not need to end with the physical departure of a loved one. The relationship can consciously continue even after death. The relationship will continue and peace can be found. The relationship is as eternal as your soul; it is simply your free will to decide how conscious you choose to be during its development. If you truly desire peace with a loved one who has passed away, then you will achieve peace. Only the barriers you believe exist can stop you from achieving a peaceful state in any relationship, with any person, dead or alive. My friend, if you hold pain, anger, regret or sadness in any form toward someone who has passed on, will you allow yourself to be open to the possibility that you can also achieve the opposite? Love is eternal and it is eternally available. Forgiveness is eternal and it is eternally available. If your pain, anger, regret or sadness has survived even your brother or sister's death, will you not allow yourself the possibility of believing that love and forgiveness can also survive? The ego might have convinced you that in this world such a deed would be impossible to accomplish. I will remind your heart, and your heart will remember, that there is nothing easier or more rewarding. There is nothing more fulfilling, and there is nothing more beautiful and liberating.

At the end of this section, I suggest an invitation that will offer you the possibility of peace. It will be as easy to attain as your honest intention to attain it. My friend, angels and guides are at your beck and call, and you simply need to invite them to assist you. They will, with honor and pleasure, heed your call. You might have previously believed that obtaining peace with a brother or sister who has passed on is impossible. I will offer you the opposite of what has brought you pain, anger, regret and sadness. You have allowed pain, anger, regret and sadness to exist even after death. Will you not, for a moment, open your mind and allow the possibility that love and forgiveness can replace such emotions even after death? Offer your brother one honest moment of forgiveness and in return you will obtain an eternity of freedom, peace of mind and joy.

Invitation #12 - Obtaining Peace with a Loved One Who has Passed On

My friend, the ego would have you believe that obtaining peace with a loved one who has passed on is difficult or even impossible to accomplish. But the only barriers that exist between accomplishing or not accomplishing this are the ones that you yourself have chosen to believe and perceive as real. To experience such an event, all you need is your honest and deep desire to do so, and your faith in the possibility.

In Chapter 11, I offered you an invitation after the story about Texas. The same meditation used for that invitation may be used here. Simply set the intention by speaking through your heart and expressing what you desire to achieve. It is that simple. If, for whatever reason, you do not have an experience that first night, do not judge or criticize yourself. Simply keep trying until you achieve or receive peace in regard to what you are trying to accomplish. Be open, for peace may arrive in many forms. Do not concern yourself with form, with achieving or receiving a specific type of experience, but simply invite and be open to receiving peace. Peace will be offered, and soon you will experience a shift.

Have We Met Before?

There is a spiritual place that you visit before incarnations that is sometimes referred to, among other names, as "the recognition chamber." It is here that you will first encounter certain individuals with whom you will work in your next incarnation. You have known many of these souls before, but it is here that certain keys to their physical appearance will be previewed for your memory. It can be the way they look, their laugh, the way they look at you, a first kiss, the way you dance together, the way you hold each other, a simple touch. Any of these or many others might be keys, hints or triggers for you to realize that you have work to do together. It could be a professional relationship, a love relationship, a friendship; there is work to be done together, something that will help both of you grow into more complete beings. It is because of the importance of such a relationship that a hint or memory is offered, so that once this hint is stroked, something from within turns a light on and tells you that this is someone you should get to know better. You might experience physical feelings and ask that person if you have ever met before, or equally possible, you might hit it off and want to continue the relationship, regardless of form.

When you're with an individual and something clicks, or something calls to you, it probably is a trigger, a reawakening memory that there is something more to be done with this person. It could be one of a hundred different triggers, but only your specific trigger will reawaken your memory. You might later ask friends if there was something special about that person that struck them, and they might say, "no, nothing," but it is not them he or she came to teach and learn from, but you. My friend, in such cases, it is wise not to let the opportunity pass you by. If you do, then so be it. But as you continue to grow, you will also continue to get these types of feelings. Become aware my friend, for great gifts and learning opportunities are in store for you. Do not underestimate the power of your gut feelings. Do not underestimate yourself.

Re-entry

Ah, to begin anew! And so you come to the point in your in-between life, where it is now time to head back to Earth in another body. On average, I would say that there is little, if any, hesitation to come back. You have had enough time to reflect, to work on yourself, to assist others and to play. It is time to move into the next incarnation, and you are ready. From what I have experienced, people on average are happy, excited and ready to come back.

There are, on occasions, those who are not so ready, who need a little more encouragement to realize that this is what is best for them. If the soul needs encouragement to come back, it will be offered by its guides and also by other souls that will be working with it in the life to come. Ultimately, the soul has the choice of when to come back, yet the wisdom of the timing is always quite clear. Sometimes, especially after a previously difficult life or with a challenging life ahead, it needs a little support to come back. But once it realizes the wisdom of it, the soul drops most of its apprehension. When the undecided soul decides to take the plunge, it is shown appreciation by all others that are and will be affected by its decision.

The question of when a soul actually enters the body is an interesting one. A woman, if she is very aware of her body, and if she keeps a journal of her feelings throughout the pregnancy, could most probably tell you the exact day the final connection occurred. Something changes - a deeper love and a more solid oneness with the child are experienced.

To Be or Not To Be

The soul is wise; it knows whether it is going to be born or not. If it is not going to come to term and does not need to experience the abortion or miscarriage and all the emotions that go with it, it will not occupy the body of the fetus. If, for whatever reason, it is useful for the soul to experience the whole physical and emotional process of the abortion or miscarriage, then it will do so, and use it as a learning experience.

If the soul wants to be born, and it is in its best interest to be born, it will be born. If a woman has a miscarriage, then the soul will simply wait for its next opportunity. The miscarriage is a gift the woman offers herself and the soul. Although this might be very hard or even impossible for expecting parents to believe, it is so. It is, in absolute terms, a gift the woman and soul offer to all involved. The soul most often does not need to experience the miscarriage or abortion, and thus is not in the fetus when this event occurs. But there are also many times that the complete physical, emotional and spiritual connection needs to be made between the mother and soul before a miscarriage or abortion occurs. The soul will stick around as long as possible and leave before any physical pain is felt by the soul.

The soul will usually merge with the fetus between the fourth and eighth month of pregnancy. If the soul is inexperienced, it will need more time and will arrive earlier in the pregnancy (fourth to sixth month), to give it time to merge with the fetus. Souls do not usually merge with the body in the first trimester because there is simply not enough brain matter to work with. If the soul is more experienced, it will wait until later in the pregnancy (sixth to eighth month) to complete its connection to the fetus.

The soul will comfort the mother through pregnancy, through miscarriages or abortions. The soul holds no ill will toward the mother or father for terminating the pregnancy. In such cases, there is a very high probability that the same soul will re-enter the mother, if she decides to get pregnant again. If the mother, for whatever reason, can have no more children, then this soul will look to be reincarnated and be born to a close family member.

Adoption

In the case of adoption, the soul understands that it will be born into an environment where it will most probably be put up for adoption. In most of these cases, the soul already knows which family or families it will grow up in. It understands the reasons and the opportunities that it will be offered by the adopting parents. The soul has chosen such an experience because it was the best way to learn the lessons it came to learn. It is because of this that being born and raised by adopted parents is, in and of itself, as great a gift as being born and raised by genetically similar parents. The soul has a memory that reminds it that this is true. The conflict occurs when the mind will not join with the soul, or higher self, in acknowledging this. They are equally great gifts, because this is what the soul has chosen to experience in order to give itself the best possible chance to learn the lessons it came here to learn. Great peace is found once this memory is recalled.

If the soul is going to be adopted or born to gay parents, it already knows this, and it is this situation that the soul chooses to experience. In the case of adoption by gay parents or being born to gay parents, the soul chooses such an experience because it is the best way to learn the lessons it came to learn. It is because of this that being born and raised by gay parents is, in and of itself, as great a gift as being born and raised by heterosexual parents. The soul has a memory that reminds it that this is true. The conflict occurs when the mind will not join with the soul, or higher self, in acknowledging this. They are equally great gifts, because this is what the soul has chosen to experience in order to learn the lessons it came here to learn. Great peace is found once this memory is recalled.

Gay, straight, adopted, genetically similar parents, are all gifts, but love is by far the most beautiful environment for the soul to be born into. Yet, if the soul is to experience something other than love, then that too has been its choice, and the sooner it remembers this, the sooner it will find peace. The soul has the ultimate choice of physical environment, be it wealthy, middle class or poor, in urban or rural settings. It has the choice of physical body type, be it healthy, deformed or unhealthy. It has the choice of color and nationality. What it chooses, in the end, is the greatest gift it can offer itself, for it allows the soul to set itself up for what it came to do and learn. The world would say otherwise, but it is as much a gift to be born poor as to be born rich. It is equally a gift to be born healthy or unhealthy, with one arm or two. It is equally a gift to be born black or white, brown or yellow. It is equally a gift to be born in the USA, or in Africa, China, Afghanistan or France. They are all gifts, because this is what the soul has chosen to experience in order to accomplish the lessons it came here to learn. Great peace is found once this memory is recalled.

Are People Born Gay or Is It a Choice?

I have heard discussions on whether or not people who are gay are born gay or whether or not they made a choice to be gay. Some people from religious backgrounds insist that being gay is a choice, while most gays take the position that it is not a choice - they are simply born this way. I will offer you another explanation that, if viewed from a place of love, makes both parties right.

A soul is wise. It is well aware of itself; it understands where it comes from (God) and it understands the energy that created it (God's Love). It comes to Earth in order to express this truth into and throughout the physical plane. It chooses the environment and circumstances that will best assist it in awakening the memory of this truth, not only to itself but also to all around it, especially those in its soul group. Its soul group can be anyone it comes into contact with, from family members, to friends, to peers.

A soul is not some empty energy source that is desperately waiting to incarnate in order to fill itself up with whatever scraps its human experience provides. A soul is already naturally filled and fulfilled by its truth; the love it represents. Before coming into the physical world, it along with its guides develops a scenario that will best assist it in bringing this memory into its physical existence. If being gay is what will best serve it and those around it to reawaken the memory of love, then that is what the soul will choose as a manifestation of its physical self. If being gay is what will best serve this purpose, then the soul will be sure to choose a body that will genetically assist it in moving in this direction. Being gay provides many challenges as well as many opportunities for all those involved to look past the fairy tale that the ego's world tries to sell us about gays, and into the love that they, in truth, embody.

Remember our discussion regarding bringing blocks up to the awareness of love's presence so that they can be looked at, understood and dismantled? Remember the gratitude I mentioned you would experience once these blocks were dismantled? Remember how gratitude could be your only sane response to any and every individual who assisted you in dismantling your personal blocks to the awareness of love's presence? If you see a gay brother or sister with anything other than love, then understand that you are blocking yourself from experiencing love in the present moment. When it comes to your perception of gays, if you are choosing separation, judgment, fear or any other "negative" emotion and expression instead of love, then understand that you are choosing such blocks, and you are ultimately responsible for dismantling them. But do not despair for you are not alone, your gay brother or sister is here for you, to assist you in the dismantling process.

So is being born gay a choice? Let's take a quick walk through the process. First, a soul chooses to be gay because this specific manifestation will bring forth whatever blocks it, along with its soul group, have to the presence of love. Second, the soul chooses the physical body that has the genetic capacity of carrying out such a choice. Third, the soul is born into this body, thus the belief that gays are born gay, is a true statement. Finally the soul either chooses to express its natural self, that of being gay, or that of staying in the closet, so to speak. There is no judgment if a soul chooses to come out or not. The soul's natural state is the state of peace, thus the soul is free to do whatever it believes offers it peace. If it believes that staying in the closet is what will offer it peace, then it is free to do so. If it believes that coming out is what will bring it peace, then it is free to do so as well. Thus both parties who believe gays are born this way and those who believe being gay is a choice are correct in their assumptions. So, as a good man once said, "Can't we all just get along?"

My brother and sister, God does not make mistakes. Being gay is as much a gift to this planet and the people on it as being straight. Let go of all the judgments and fearful behaviors that the ego insists that you use to separate yourself from your brother and sister, for what has such behavior truly offered? Express yourself in the way that offers you peace; nothing more is asked of you in order to experience peace in every moment. Offer love to your brother and sister and you will feel this love flowing through you and throughout your day.

My friend, when your children leave your house for school, do you not make sure that they have everything they need? Do you not think that God is as wise? Do you not think that God makes sure you have everything you need before you leave His house? My brother and sister, you have chosen to leave your true home for a while. Trust that you have everything you need, and remember, play nice with the other kids in school.

Epilogue

My friend, this is not the end but a beginning, for every moment allows you to begin anew. The moment is no longer some perception you must defend against, but has now become your playground, a place you now know you create by what you choose to believe and focus on. Now you understand that what you believe is within your mind, and because it is within your mind, you have the power to decide how you will experience the manifestation of the moment.

You need no longer look toward the sky to find God. For you now know that the possibility of experiencing God is available to you in every moment, in everything and in everyone. You now know that it is not what your brother or sister says or does that defines his or her being, but rather the love that he or she represents. It is this knowledge that will close the gap between you and the people in your life. It is this knowledge that will close the gap between who you think you are and who you truly are, have always been and will always be – your godself.

I am most deeply honored that you have taken some time during your journey to stroll on this beach with me. We did not know each other, but we have met, will now depart, and will someday unite again. My friend, know that although our physical proximity is no longer essential, our connection to each other is eternal. For as you allowed me to strengthen my belief by the creation of this book, so too have I hopefully reawakened some memories within your heart and mind. By reawakening these memories, I am simply reminding you of who you truly are. My friend, there is nothing easier than being who you truly are. Being who you truly are takes no effort at all, it is an effortless accomplishment.

Rejoice, for there is nothing more for you to learn. There is nothing more for you to learn because all wisdom already resides within you. My friend, you and your brothers and sisters are perfect love. Simply extend what and who you are into the world, and you will find this world a more loving place. You might have temporarily forgotten this, but you have now chosen to remember. I would like to conclude this section with a quote from a speech given by Jesse Jackson during the July 17, 1984 Democratic National Convention. I have chosen this quote because it, in very simple terms, summarizes my feelings at this point in the book.

> [44]*If in my high moments, I have done some good, offered some service, shed some light, healed some wounds, rekindled some hope, or stirred someone from apathy and indifference, or in any way along the way helped somebody, then this campaign has not been in vain... If in my low moments, in word, deed or attitude, through some error of temper, taste or tone, I have caused anyone discomfort, created pain or revived someone's fears, that was not my truest self... I am not a perfect servant. I am a public servant doing my best against the odds. As I develop and serve, be patient. God is not finished with me yet.*

[44]See Notes, page xix.

A beginning...

Acknowledgments

Every effort has been made to provide accurate source attribution. Should any attribution be found to be incorrect, the author welcomes written documentation supporting correction for subsequent printings. For material not in the public domain, selection was made according to generally accepted fair-use standards and practices.

Notes

Chapter Two

1. Roger Von Oech, *A Whack on the Side of the Head,* Copyright 1998 (Warner Books).

Chapter Three

2. Erich Fromm, *The Art of Loving,* Copyright 2000 (Perennial Publishing).

3. Sanaya Roman, *Spiritual Growth: Being Your Higher Self,* Copyright 2000 (H.J. Kramer).

4. Kathleen W. Fitzgerald, *Jellinek's Disease: The New Face of Alcoholism,* Copyright June 2003, (Wales Tale Press).

5. Kahlil Gibran, *My Soul Counseled Me,* (Copyright and publisher unknown).

6. Dr. Helen Schucman, Dr. William Thetford, *A Course in Miracles,* Copyright, 1975 (Foundation for Inner Peace).

Chapter Four

7. Henry David Thoreau, *Life Without Principle,* Copyright 1997 (Folcroft Library Edition).

8. Norman Cousins, *Human Options,* Copyright 1981 (W.W. Norton & Company).

9. Dr. Martin Luther King Jr., "The Drum Major Instinct," Sermon delivered at Ebenezer Baptist Church, Atlanta, Georgia, February 4, 1968. Copyright The Estate of Martin Luther King, Jr.

10. Leo Buscaglia, *Born for Love: Reflections on Loving,* Copyright 1992 (Random House).

11. Jack Canfield, Mark Victor Hansen, *Chicken Soup for the Soul,* Copyright 1993 (Health Communications).

Chapter Five

12. Author Unknown, *Inscription on Crypt in Westminster Abbey.*

13. President Theodore Roosevelt, "Citizenship in a Republic," Speech at the Sorbonne, Paris, April 23, 1910.

14. Dan Millman, *No Ordinary Moments,* Copyright 1992, (H.J. Kramer/New World Library).

Chapter Six

15. Hannah Whitehall Smith, *The Christian's Secrets of a Happy Life,* Copyright 1999 (Baker Book House).

16. Author Unknown, *An Unknown Confederate Soldier.*

17. Dan Millman, *Way of the Peaceful Warrior,* Copyright 2000 (H.J. Kramer).

18. Emmanuel, Pat Rodegast, Judith Stanton, *Emmanuel Book 1,* Copyright 1985 (Bantam Books).

19. Michael Newton, *Journey of Souls: Case Studies of Life Between Lives,* Copyright 1994 (Llewelyn Publications).

20. Hannah Whitehall Smith, *The Christian's Secrets of a Happy Life,* Copyright 1999 (Baker Book House).

21. Betty Eadie, *Embraced by the Light,* Copyright 1994 (Bantam Books).

Chapter Seven

22. Max Lucado, *No Wonder They Call Him Savior,* Copyright 1998 (Thomas Nelson, Inc.)

23. Corrie ten Boon, *The Hiding Place,* Copyright 1984 (Bantam Books).

24. Dr. Helen Schucman, Dr. William Thetford, *A Course in Miracles,* Copyright 1976 (Foundation for Inner Peace).

25. Anne Frank, *Diary of a Young Girl,* Copyright 1993 (Prentice Hall).

Chapter Eight

26. Kahlil Gibran, *Jesus the Son of Man: His Words and His Deeds as Told and Recorded By Those Who Knew Him,* Copyright 1995 (Knopf).

27. Lilly Walters, (www.motivational-keynote-speakers.com) *One Hand Typing and Keyboarding Manual: With Personal Motivational Messages From Others Who Have Overcome,* Copyright 2003 (ABC Schermerhorn Walters, Co.).

Chapter Nine

28. Victor E. Frankl, *Man's Search for Meaning,* Copyright 1997 (Beacon Press).

29. Gregory M. Lousignont, Ph.D., *The Best Day of My Life,* Copyright 1993 Gregory M. Lousignont, Ph.D. All rights reserved. Reproduced with permission of author.

30. Bob Benson, *Something's Going On Here,* Copyright 1977 (Impact Books).

31. Charles R. Swindoll, *Strengthening Your Grip,* Word Books, Waco, TX, Copyright 1982, p. 207.

Chapter Ten

32. Jurgen Moltmann, *The Experiment Hope*, Copyright 1975 (Augsburg Fortress).

33. Dr. Martin Luther King Jr., *"Facing the Challenge of a New Age,"* Sermon delivered at Holt Street Baptist Church, Montgomery, Alabama, December 3, 1956, Copyright The Estate of Martin Luther King, Jr.

34. Kahlil Gibran, *Jesus the Son of Man: His Words and His Deeds as Told and Recorded By Those Who Knew Him*, Copyright 1995 (Knopf).

35. Kahlil Gibran, *The Prophet*, Copyright 1923 (Knopf), p. 17.

Chapter Eleven

36. Soren Kierkegaard, (Copyright and publisher unknown).

37. *Abraham Lincoln. Abraham Lincoln Observed: The Civil War Dispatches of Noah Brooks* edited by Michael Burlingame (Baltimore, Johns Hopkins University Press, 1998), p. 210.

Chapter Twelve

38. Joseph Bayly, *A View from the Hearse*, Copyright 1985 (Life-Journey Books).

39. Emmanuel, Pat Rodegast, Judith Stanton, *Emmanuel*, Copyright 1985 (Bantam Books).

40. Emmanuel, Pat Rodegast, Judith Stanton, *Emmanuel*, Copyright 1985 (Bantam Books).

41. Emmanuel, Pat Rodegast, Judith Stanton, *Emmanuel*, Copyright 1985 (Bantam Books).

42. Dr. Helen Schucman, Dr. William Thetford, *A Course in Miracles*, Copyright 1976 (Foundation for Inner Peace).

43. Larry Libby, *Someday Heaven*, Copyright 2001, (Zonderkids).

Epilogue

StandUp For Kids

StandUp For Kids is a 501(c)(3) not-for-profit organization founded in 1990 to help rescue homeless and at-risk youth. With national headquarters in San Diego, California, StandUp For Kids is run almost entirely by volunteers, and has established more than thirty outreach programs in fifteen states.

The mission of StandUp For Kids is to help homeless and street kids. This mission is carried out by a national volunteer force whose on-the-streets outreach efforts will find, stabilize and assist homeless and street kids in their efforts to improve their lives. The organization's mission shall also be furthered through deterrence and resource programs provided in schools and via the Internet.

The purpose of StandUp for Kids is to empower homeless and at-risk youth toward life-long personal growth through an on-the-streets outreach program, to create in these youth a sincere caring and belief in themselves through open, straightforward counseling and educational programs, thereby helping them acquire the life skills necessary to become effective members of their community.

In addition to helping homeless and at-risk youth with immediate necessities such as food, clothing, shelter and personal hygiene, StandUp for Kids offers a wide array of services, including: assistance in finding housing, education assistance, vocational development, counseling, health services, transportation to self-help meetings, and legal assistance. Volunteers also conduct life-skills training, covering such areas as budgeting, banking, apartment cleanliness and safety, shopping and cooking, nutrition, and hygiene. Laundry services and lunch and snack facilities are made available, as well as mail and message services.

StandUp For Kids
83 Walton Street, Suite 100
Atlanta, Georgia 30303

Phone: 1.800.365.4KID

Fax: 888.453.1647

www.standupforkids.org

Tax ID# 33-0414855

About the Author

James Blanchard Cisneros was born in Geneva, Switzerland and grew up in Caracas, Venezuela. James' writings and beliefs are universal in nature. He believes that "everyone has the right to find his or her own way, and whatever tools an individual chooses to use, or whatever roads he or she chooses to travel on to find peace of mind and joy should be respected."

An entrepreneur and art aficionado, James is President of Cisneros Capital Group and owner of La Boheme Fine Art Gallery in Coral Gables, Florida. He is also a Board Member of Cisneros Children's Foundation, an organization that provides financial assistance to children's organizations in the United States and Latin America. James is also Director of Outreach for Miami's StandUp For Kids, a nationally acclaimed volunteer organization committed to the rescue of homeless and street kids. James has a Bachelor of Arts degree from Regis University and a Master of Business Administration degree from the University of Notre Dame.

Notes

Notes

Notes

Notes

Notes

Notes

Notes

Notes

Notes